ARTHUR O'SHAUGHNESSY, A PRE-RAPHAELITE POET IN THE BRITISH MUSEUM

Arthur O'Shaughnessy's career as a natural historian in the British Museum, and his consequent preoccupation with the role of work in his life, provides the context with which to reexamine his contributions to Victorian poetry. O'Shaughnessy's engagement with aestheticism, socialism, and Darwinian theory can be traced to his career as a Junior Assistant at the British Museum, and his perception of the burden of having to earn a living outside of art. Making use of extensive archival research, Jordan Kistler demonstrates that far from being merely a minor poet, O'Shaughnessy was at the forefront of later Victorian avant-garde poetry. Her analyses of published and unpublished writings, including correspondence, poetic manuscripts, and scientific notebooks, demonstrate O'Shaughnessy's importance to the cultural milieu of the 1870s, particularly his contributions to English aestheticism, his role in the importation of decadence from France, and his unique position within contemporary debates on science and literature.

Jordan Kistler is a Teaching Fellow in Victorian Literature at the University of Birmingham, UK. Her work focuses on the often-overlooked Pre-Raphaelite poets of the 1870s.

Among the Victorians and Modernists

Series Editor:
Dennis Denisoff, Professor of English, Ryerson University, Toronto

This series publishes monographs and essay collections on literature, art, and culture in the context of the diverse aesthetic, political, social, technological, and scientific innovations that arose among the Victorians and Modernists. Viable topics include, but are not limited to, artistic and cultural debates and movements; influential figures and communities; and agitations and developments regarding subjects such as animals, commodification, decadence, degeneracy, democracy, desire, ecology, gender, nationalism, the paranormal, performance, public art, sex, socialism, spiritualities, transnationalism, and the urban. Studies that address continuities between the Victorians and Modernists are welcome. Work on recent responses to the periods such as Neo-Victorian novels, graphic novels, and film will also be considered.

Arthur O'Shaughnessy, A Pre-Raphaelite Poet in the British Museum

JORDAN KISTLER
University of Birmingham, UK

LONDON AND NEW YORK

First published 2016
by Routledge
2 Park Square, Milton Park, Abingdon, Oxon OX14 4RN

and by Routledge
711 Third Avenue, New York, NY 10017

Routledge is an imprint of the Taylor & Francis Group, an informa business

© 2016 Jordan Kistler

The right of Jordan Kistler to be identified as author of this work has been asserted by her in accordance with sections 77 and 78 of the Copyright, Designs and Patents Act 1988.

All rights reserved. No part of this book may be reprinted or reproduced or utilised in any form or by any electronic, mechanical, or other means, now known or hereafter invented, including photocopying and recording, or in any information storage or retrieval system, without permission in writing from the publishers.

Trademark notice: Product or corporate names may be trademarks or registered trademarks, and are used only for identification and explanation without intent to infringe.

British Library Cataloguing in Publication Data
A catalogue record for this book is available from the British Library

Library of Congress Cataloging-in-Publication Data
Kistler, Jordan.
  Arthur O'Shaughnessy, a Pre-Raphaelite poet in the British Museum / by Jordan Kistler.
    pages cm — (Among the Victorians and Modernists)
  Includes bibliographical references.
  ISBN 978-1-4724-6735-5 (hardcover) — ISBN 978-1-315-56801-0 (ebook) — ISBN 978-1-4724-6737-9 (epub)
  1. O'Shaughnessy, Arthur William Edgar, 1844–1881—Criticism and interpretation. I. Title.
  PR5115.O4Z75 2016
  821'.8—dc23
  2015031555

ISBN: 978-1-4724-6735-5 (hbk)
ISBN: 978-1-315-56801-0 (ebk)

Typeset in Times New Roman
by Apex CoVantage, LLC

 Printed in the United Kingdom by Henry Ling Limited, at the Dorset Press, Dorchester, DT1 1HD

Contents

Acknowledgements		*vii*
List of Abbreviations		*ix*
Introduction		1
1	'Dreary Creeds' and 'Sham Wits': O'Shaughnessy's Poetic Representations of Nature and Science	23
2	'I Carve the Marble of Pure Thought': Work and Art in the Poetry of Arthur O'Shaughnessy	61
3	'The Purest Parian': The Formalism of Arthur O'Shaughnessy	87
4	'Those too sanguine singers': Arthur O'Shaughnessy's French Influences	115
5	'Love's Splendid Lures': Arthur O'Shaughnessy's Medievalism	141
Conclusion		177
Bibliography		*181*
Index		*195*

Acknowledgements

Many thanks to Professor Josephine McDonagh, Professor Mark Turner, Professor Catherine Maxwell, and Dr David Latham for their invaluable insights, comments, and suggestions. Special thanks to Dr John Holmes for his continued advice, guidance, and friendship. Further thanks to my colleagues at King's College London – Dr Alison Wood, Dr Mary Henes, Dr Mary Shannon, and Dr Maria Damkjaer – for their support. Special thanks to Dr Sarah Crofton and Dr Will Tattersdill, for everything.

A number of archives and libraries have been of immeasurable help to this work. I would particularly like to thank Diarmuid Kennedy at the McClay Library, Queen's University, Belfast; Liane MacIver at the Central Archive of the British Museum; Daisy Cunynghame at the General Library of the Natural History Museum; the staff of the Rare Book and Manuscript Library, Columbia University; and all the staff of the David M. Rubenstein Rare Books and Manuscript Library at Duke University.

List of Abbreviations

BMOP	British Museum Original Papers
BMSCM	British Museum Standing Committee Minutes
KJV	King James Version
OED	Oxford English Dictionary

Introduction

I.

> I do not forget the somewhat sceptical thrill I received, late in 1869, on being told that our official ichthyologist was "writing poetry". Would it be about fishes?[1]

So Edmund Gosse quipped in his 1925 *Silhouettes*, reflecting on the life and career of his friend Arthur O'Shaughnessy, poet and naturalist at the British Museum.[2] Though Gosse's remark was meant to be humorous, it reveals the tension that is at the heart of O'Shaughnessy's poetry: the apparent incongruity of zoology and poetry. Gosse's joke suggests that an ichthyologist could only have one possible interest in life – his fish. And, he insinuates, the dullness of that career would naturally lead to dull poetry. Biographical accounts of Arthur O'Shaughnessy, whether written by friends or critics, nearly always discuss his career at the British Museum in this vein, suggesting the absurdity of a poet working as a zoologist, represented as a distinctly unpoetic career – even 'prosaic', in the words of W.D. Paden.[3] O'Shaughnessy himself was acutely aware of the perceived dullness of his working life, and thus throughout his body of work the Museum is portrayed as anathema to poetry. For O'Shaughnessy, his job at the Museum was purely a way to earn a living, a means to support his poetry.[4] He writes, 'Without [this job] I should not have had leisure to seek out and & develope [sic] any individual strength that was in me, – what I have written & begun would have been *in me* but *I should have been nothing.*'[5] Yet, at other times he portrays his two careers as being in competition, with his work at the museum seen as potentially detrimental to his 'poetic spirit' and certainly his critical and commercial success as a poet.

---

[1]   Edmund Gosse, *Silhouettes*, Essay Index Reprint Series (Freeport, NY: Books for Libraries Press, 1971), p. 173.

[2]   Like O'Shaughnessy, Edmund Gosse was a poet and British Museum employee, although he is best known for his literary criticism and the fact that his father was the famous amateur naturalist and author Philip Henry Gosse. Edmund Gosse's best-known work is *Father and Son* (1907), an autobiographical account of his strained relationship with his religious father. Gosse is also remembered for several biographies of literary men, including Algernon Charles Swinburne (1917).

[3]   W.D. Paden, 'Arthur O'Shaughnessy in the British Museum: or, the case of the misplaced fusees and the reluctant zoologist', *Victorian Studies* 8, no. 1 (September 1964): 7–30 (p. 7).

[4]   O'Shaughnessy applied for the position in the Natural History Departments because of the pay increase it granted him. Previous to this promotion, he had been employed as a transcriber in the Department of Printed Books.

[5]   Writing to Lord Lytton, 4 November 1870, quoted in Paden, p. 17 (the original letter is housed in the Knebworth Archives).

Thus, both O'Shaughnessy and his critics portray dullness as potentially infectious, spreading from his zoological work to his poetry. 'Would it be about fishes?' Gosse wondered. Could he *help* it being about fishes?

O'Shaughnessy's career as a naturalist was treated as an absurdity by many of his contemporaries and critics. Thus Thomas Wright writes, 'few more delightful instances could be given of the square man in the round hole.'[6] Edmund Stedman focused on the apparent chasm between science and literature, writing, 'Seeing him there, surrounded like an Egyptian neophyte, by groups of stuffed reptiles and fishes, I wondered whether he found it more difficult to keep up his heart for song than other stray minstrels have.'[7] And L.C. Moulton notes: 'He was full of interest even in his "specimens" at the museum – his butterflies, his lizards, his serpents. He had come, before his death, really to be recognized as an authority on reptilia.'[8] It is the 'even' and the 'really' in these lines that draw our attention; it is a compliment to the poet, she suggests, that he could find interest *even* in his work, and he should be congratulated for having gone so far as to become an authority in the subject. That she herself could not understand the interest in butterflies, lizards and serpents is readily apparent.

In a similar vein, Dr Richard Garnett, another friend and sometime biographer of the poet, characterized O'Shaughnessy's career, saying, 'before his death [he] had come to be recognised as an authority on the class Reptilia, especially lizards and serpents, creatures always fascinating to persons of poetic temperament'.[9] What an amusing link to try and draw between O'Shaughnessy's poetic and scientific careers! Although snakes do feature in some decadent poetry, they rarely appear in O'Shaughnessy's verse, and what's more, the poet didn't work on serpents at the Museum, except tangentially in the catalogue of the collection.

In fact, few of O'Shaughnessy's friends seemed to know exactly *what* he did at the museum, among his jars and specimen. This is evinced clearly by the continued perpetuation of the notion that O'Shaughnessy was primarily an ichthyologist – a scientist of fish. While he did assist Albert Günther in his catalogue of the fish in the British Museum collection, O'Shaughnessy's own published papers are exclusively on tropical lizards – no fish, serpents, or butterflies among them.[10] The fact that even his close friends were unable to accurately report what

---

[6]   Thomas Wright, *The Life of John Payne* (London: T. Fisher Unwin, 1919), p. 21.

[7]   Edmund C. Stedman, 'Some London Poets', *Harper's New Monthly Magazine*, 64, no. 384 (May 1882), p. 883.

[8]   Moulton, p. 19.

[9]   Richard Garnett, 'Arthur O'Shaughnessy', *The Poets and the Poetry of the Century*, ed. Alfred H. Miles (London: Routledge, 1906), vol. 8, p. 189.

[10]   O'Shaughnessy notes that in 1864, upon being transferred from the Geological Department back to Zoology, he was employed in the Spirit Room under Dr Albert Günther, working on the first volume of Günther's catalogue of fish. This work continued until 1867, but primarily involved indexing and proofing, rather than true study of the fish of the collection. In 1867 his attention was transferred to lizards, which is where his focus lay for the remaining 14 years of his career as a naturalist (BMOP, C.11996).

Introduction 3

O'Shaughnessy spent 17 years of his life doing is highly suggestive. It is also revealing that O'Shaughnessy's preserved correspondence rarely even mentions the Museum, let alone the work he performed there.[11] Apparently he was no more interested in discussing his work with his artistic friends than they were interested to learn about it.

In order to be seen as a poet first and foremost, O'Shaughnessy attempted to create a divide between natural history and poetry in his work and life, denigrating the former while glamorizing the latter. With no training as a naturalist, O'Shaughnessy was inexperienced and uninformed when he began his career in the Natural History Departments of the British Museum at the age of 19. However, because he did not wish to be defined as a 'naturalist' rather than a poet (and suffer the kind of remarks that Gosse would later make), O'Shaughnessy refused to put the requisite amount of effort into learning his profession, a patented attempt to distance himself from the Museum. He spent his working-day breaks in the British Museum library, reading French novels, poetry, and the histories of such diverse subjects as Kabala, Ancient Greece, and medieval art, rather than attempting to learn the Linnaean system of classification or anything else that might aid him in his position at the Museum.[12] This effort to distance himself from his work meant that O'Shaughnessy was woefully unsuccessful in his career at the museum and often faced censure from his superiors for his lack of knowledge and lack of effort. The more O'Shaughnessy was criticized for his work, the less enthusiasm he had for it and the less effort he put into it – thus, the more he was criticized. From this negative environment O'Shaughnessy tried to escape to the idealized life of a poet, putting all his energy into being successful in this second career. However, as we can see from Gosse's recollection of his friend, O'Shaughnessy never escaped the labels of 'naturalist' and 'ichthyologist' among his literary friends and future critics. A poet holding an ordinary 'day job' was still an oddity at this time, and accounts of O'Shaughnessy rarely fail to mention this fact.[13]

The tension between O'Shaughnessy's career at the Museum and his poetry underlies both O'Shaughnessy's poetry and its critical reception.[14] Although Gosse continues on from the quotation above to assert that O'Shaughnessy's poetry was

---

[11] The Museum is mentioned only in passing in his correspondence, and then only with his closest friends and family – J.T. Nettleship, Helen Snee, and Bulwer-Lytton. See the letter from Lytton dated 27 May 1870, an undated letter from Nettleship ascertained to be from the autumn of 1870, and a letter of 13 December 1871 from Helen Snee. Duke University Manuscript Collection, 6th 11:A Box 1, c.1.

[12] Queen's University, Belfast, O'Shaughnessy Manuscript Collection, MS 8/8.

[13] As W.D. Paden asserted in 1964, 'Today we are accustomed to the fact that a minor British poet may return after each of his imaginative flights to some secure and sheltered niche in the ramifications of the British Civil Service. One of the first to do so was A.W.E. O'Shaughnessy' (Paden, p. 7).

[14] Thus in 1976, S.C.A. Holmes asserted that O'Shaughnessy 'lived in the days of the dullest "alcohol bottle zoology"'. 'Arthur O'Shaughnessy: a poet among the Lacertidae', *Journal of the Society for the Bibliography of Natural History* 8 (1976): 28–30 (p. 28).

4   *Arthur O'Shaughnessy, A Pre-Raphaelite Poet in the British Museum*

not about fishes, the possibility that it might have been lingers in readers' minds. Gosse suggests, 'No odder haunt for a poet can be conceived than the queer little subterranean cell, strongly scented with methylated spirits of wine, in which he worked for fifteen years with grim creatures pickled round him in rows on rows of gallipots.'[15] On the surface of this quotation, Gosse merely tells us that O'Shaughnessy was out of place in the Museum; however, the use of 'a poet' rather than 'the poet' can be seen to imply that O'Shaughnessy was not a poet, could not be a poet, because he worked in that 'queer little cell', that the presence of 'grim creatures' negated any poetry that was in him. In fact, in the critical afterlife of O'Shaughnessy, his biography, and more specifically his 'day job', takes the focus, often to the exclusion of his verse.[16]

The perceived mundanity of having to 'earn a living' resonates throughout O'Shaughnessy's poetry; this present work will trace the impact of this 'prosaic' labour upon O'Shaughnessy's poetic life, considering O'Shaughnessy's poetry in the light of, and as a reaction to, the perceived burden of the necessity of earning a living at the Museum. Henri Lefebvre's Marxist notions of the atomization and alienation of the petty bourgeois in capitalist societies, as outlined in his three-volume *Critique of Everyday Life*, will form the theoretical backbone of my analysis. Louis A. Renza has suggested that Marxism is a uniquely appropriate way to approach minor literature:

> It would appear, then, that a decisively nonbourgeois mode of criticism like Marxism, one fully aware of the ideological investment in canonical distinctions made by bourgeois criticism like Bloom's, is better suited to discuss minor literature's "becoming minor." The very category of minor literature exemplifies bourgeois culture's refusal to consider artwork *as* "work," specifically, minor literature as *alienated* literary labor.[17]

Renza's focus on the contested notion of art as work underpins my argument regarding O'Shaughnessy's formulation of his own poetry as inherently removed from all ideas of production or labour. I suggest that O'Shaughnessy approached his employment at the museum, and in contrast his poetry, in the terms of Marx's notion of alienated labour:

> What constitutes the alienation of labour? Firstly, the fact that labour is *external* to the worker, i.e. does not belong to his essential being; that he therefore does

---

[15]   Edmund Gosse, 'Obituary: Arthur O'Shaughnessy', *The Academy* 457 (5 February 1881): 98–9 (p. 98).

[16]   For instance, some of the most recent critical work on O'Shaughnessy was produced in the 1960s by W.D. Paden, who wrote two articles about the poet, neither of which addressed his poetry at all. In addition to Paden's article on O'Shaughnessy's career at the British Museum, see 'Arthur O'Shaughnessy: the Ancestry of a Victorian Poet', *Bulletin of the John Rylands Library* 46 (1964): 429–47.

[17]   Louis A. Renza, *'A White Heron' and the Question of Minor Literature* (Madison, WI: University of Wisconsin Press, 1984), p. 18.

Introduction 5

not confirm himself in his work, but denies himself, feels miserable and not happy ... Hence the worker feels himself only when he is not working; when he is working he does not feel himself.[18]

Lefebvre usefully extends Marx's notion of alienation specifically to the petty bourgeois, demonstrating that the bourgeois insistence on individualization during the nineteenth century in fact exacerbated feelings of alienation, not just from labour but from the entirety of everyday life:

At the same time the individual, more and more involved in complex social relations, became isolated and inward-looking. Individual consciousness split into two (into the private consciousness and the social or public consciousness); it also became atomized (individualism, specialization, separation between differing spheres of activity, etc.). Thus at the same time a distinction was made between man "as man" on the one hand and the working man on the other (more clearly among the bourgeoisie, of course, than among the proletariat). Family life became separate from productive activity. And so did leisure.[19]

Lefebvre's notion of the 'divided life' in capitalist society, between 'man at work' and 'man at leisure', is a particularly helpful framework within which to read O'Shaughnessy's verse. In O'Shaughnessy's poetry there is a pervasive rejection both of his life as a 'worker', by which he means museum naturalist, and the everyday details of that life – cities, crowds, and bureaucracy. This rejection leads to a glorification of 'leisure time' (as opposed to 'work time'), which for O'Shaughnessy takes the form of an escapist world of art, completely disconnected from the realities of his life. This in turn led him to embrace the Romantic posture of the withdrawn and isolated artist. O'Shaughnessy's early volumes, then, are dominated by a conception of art which exists solely in the negative space of his job at the British Museum.

As an artistic technique, the use of negative space highlights the composition of a work, focusing the viewer's attention on the form and technique as much as the 'subject' of the work.[20] When used to the fullest extent, negative space can, in fact, become the subject of the work, in which what is not being shown (or said) is just as important as the stated subject of the piece. Thus, O'Shaughnessy's poetry, as the negation of work, is as much 'about' that work as it is about the explicit subjects of the poems. As Michel de Certeau notes, the everyday is universal, and therefore inescapable. Addressing the attempt to study the everyday from within the everyday, he says:

---

[18] Karl Marx, 'Estranged Labour', *Economic and Philosophical Manuscripts of 1844*, http://www.marxists.org/archive/marx/works/1844/manuscripts/labour.htm.

[19] Henri Lefebvre, *Critique of Everyday Life*, trans. John Moore (London: Verso, 1991), vol. 1, p. 31.

[20] The OED defines negative space as 'an area of a painting, sculpture, etc., containing no contrasting shapes, figures, or colours, but framed by solid or positive forms, *esp.* one that constitutes a particularly powerful or significant part of the whole composition'.

6 *Arthur O'Shaughnessy, A Pre-Raphaelite Poet in the British Museum*

And since one does not "leave" this language, since one cannot find another place from which to interpret it, since there are therefore no separate groups of false interpretation and true interpretations, but only illusory interpretations, since in short there is no *way out*, the fact remains that we are *foreigners* on the inside – *but there is no outside*.[21]

One of the undertakings of this work, then, is to trace the seepage of the everyday, and more specifically O'Shaughnessy's work life at the British Museum, into O'Shaughnessy's imagined world of artificial art.

Lefebvre posits that the division of life into work and leisure leads to a pervasive sense of alienation from the self, particularly in the 'cultured man' of the nineteenth century – someone much like O'Shaughnessy:

For him "his" thought, "his" culture, are a part of his most intimate self. He carries them with him in the silence of his office, in the even-more barren silence of his "inner life". He tends to forget that thought is human and not "private" ... The "cultivated" man forgets the social foundations of "his" thought. When he looks for the secret of his behaviour and his situation in words and ideas that he has received from without, he imagines that he is looking "deep into himself". And at the very moment when he thinks the search for his own self is over, he is actually leaving himself, taking the path of alienation. Consequently his practical, everyday life, his *real* relations, he sees as external to him.[22]

Lefebvre's notion of 'inner life' that is conceived of as private but which is truly public and part of the everyday is especially pertinent to a consideration of poetry, which is often glorified as intimate and semi-private, but is also produced for public consumption.[23] Thus the relationship between poetry and the everyday becomes particularly charged when considered in the light of Lefebvre's theory of internal/external life. As I've demonstrated, apparent in O'Shaughnessy criticism is a perceived disconnect between the ordinary, quiet museum worker and the diseased and decadent poetry he produced. Lefebvre's theory of the divided man provides a useful foundation for discussing this perception of incongruity, as well as a theoretical rationale for O'Shaughnessy's insistence on his status as 'alien' in his own life.

Marx's assertion that in order to be happy a man must 'confirm himself in his work' is theorized by Lefebvre as the production of one's identity through work

---

[21]   Michel de Certeau, *The Practice of Everyday Life*, trans. Steven Rendell (Berkeley: University of California Press, 1984), p. 13.

[22]   Lefebvre, p. 238.

[23]   This is particularly true of the Pre-Raphaelite movement and its peripheral authors. Thus, W.H. Auden feels comfortable asserting: 'The earlier poets were, most of them, interested both in the political issues and the new ideas and discoveries of their time; the latter, for the most part, were not: they were primarily interested in their personal emotions and in poetry for its own sake.' *Nineteenth-Century Minor Poets* (London: Faber & Faber, 1966), p. 21. This later poet is exemplified for Auden in the figure of Dante Gabriel Rossetti.

Introduction 7

and labour: 'In his work man perceives and becomes conscious of his own self. If what he makes comes from him, he in turn comes from what he makes; it is made by him, but it is in these works and by these works that he has made himself.'[24] This making of oneself stands in clear contrast to alienated labour: 'And his labour, which ought to humanize him, becomes something done under duress instead of being a vital and human need, since it is itself nothing more than a means (of "earning a living") rather than a contribution to man's essence, freely imparted.'[25] In Marxian and Lefebvrian terms, alienated labour can stem either from the act of producing value for someone else rather than for oneself, as the free-market labourer does for the capitalist,[26] or from a lack of creative input into the act of production.[27] O'Shaughnessy's clerical work at the museum can be categorized as both. The solution to this alienation, offered by Lefebvre above, is labour that is humanizing and creative. Here we find the contrast between 'useless toil and 'useful work' posited by William Morris in 1884.[28] This study will suggest that O'Shaughnessy's poetry initially formulates him as an alienated worker and a divided man, in reaction to his job at the museum, but finally finds unity or 'totality', as defined by Lefebvre, in the work-pleasure that stems from accepting art work as useful work, culminating in his posthumous volume of poetry, *Songs of a Worker*, published in 1881.

II.

Arthur William Edgar O'Shaughnessy was born on 14 March 1844 in the borough of Kensington, the first child of Oscar O'Shaughnessy and Louisa Ann O'Shaughnessy, née Deacon. His younger brother, Oscar Frederick, was born two years later, in March of 1846. Little is known about O'Shaughnessy's father, except that, according to O'Shaughnessy's cousin Alfred W.N. Deacon, he was an artist who specialized in animal paintings, a humorous foreshadowing of O'Shaughnessy's own future career.[29]

Arthur's father died in 1848 at the age of 31, leaving Louisa to provide for her two small boys on her own. She turned for help to her sister, Caroline, 18 years her senior and unmarried, and the young family took up residence with her in 1848. The 1851 census records that Caroline Deacon, age 50, resided in Kensington

---

[24] Lefebvre, p. 163.

[25] Ibid., p. 166.

[26] Karl Marx, *Capital: A critical analysis of capitalist production*, translated from the 3rd German edition by Samuel Moore and Edward Aveling, and edited by Frederick Engels (London: Swan Sonnenschein, Lowrey, & Co., 1887), vol. 1, p. 147.

[27] Lefebvre, p. 166.

[28] William Morris, *Signs of Change* (Bristol, UK: Thoemmes Press, 1994).

[29] W.D. Paden, 'Arthur O'Shaughnessy: the Ancestry of a Victorian Poet', *Bulletin of the John Rylands Library* 46 (1964): 429–47 (p. 437).

8 *Arthur O'Shaughnessy, A Pre-Raphaelite Poet in the British Museum*

with her sister, Louisa, and two young nephews, aged five and seven.[30] The family continued to live with Caroline Deacon until her death in 1862.[31]

Although the family struggled financially during O'Shaughnessy's childhood, the children received a good education. By his teenage years Arthur was fluent in French, an accomplishment that would serve him well in later life. Both O'Shaughnessy children appear to have been well-schooled in music. Arthur was a talented pianist, and Oscar went on to become a music teacher and church organist in Chicago, Illinois. Music remained a great passion of O'Shaughnessy's throughout his life, and its rhythms and refrains – particularly those of Chopin – haunt his verse.

In 1861, at the age of 17, Arthur entered the professional world in order to help support his family, obtaining a position at the British Museum through the aid of Edward Bulwer-Lytton, the celebrated novelist and politician. O'Shaughnessy began his career at the British Museum as a transcriber in the Department of Printed Books, a position suited to his literary interests.[32] However, after serving there for three years, he began to hope for promotion to a position with the Departments of Natural History, a fast growing sector of the Museum thanks to the Victorian middle-class rage for collecting.[33] He obtained his certificate of examination in systematic zoology and undertook his career as a naturalist.

In 1869 O'Shaughnessy's first volume, *An Epic of Women*, was accepted for publication by John Camden Hotten, publisher of A.C. Swinburne's 1866 *Poems and Ballads*. *An Epic* was a critical, and somewhat a financial, success. The volume was favourably reviewed in all the top publications of the day, with the *Academy* praising: 'Of the formal art of poetry he is in many senses quite a master; his metres are not only good, they are his own, and often of an invention most felicitous as well as careful.'[34] As Gosse summed up a decade later, 'This book [*Epic*] had an immediate and very decided success, went into several editions, and gave its author at once a recognised place in English literature.'[35]

The publication of *An Epic* secured O'Shaughnessy's admittance to a prestigious literary circle. Before the volume, O'Shaughnessy, along with the poet John Payne and the artist J.T. Nettleship, had founded The Fetherstone Club, an essay club for men of literary tastes named for the hotel where it met. But after the publication of *An Epic* and Payne's own first volume, new and better doors were opened to them. Moulton reports: 'Soon after the appearance of these volumes, inscribed to each other, these two young poets began to be known in London

---

[30] 1851 Census of England, Kensington, District of St. Barnabas; Caroline Deacon household; digital images, findmypast.com.

[31] Paden, 'Ancestry', p. 439.

[32] O'Shaughnessy began his position as Transcriber 2 July 1861. BMSCM, C.9998.

[33] See Lynn Barber's *The Heyday of Natural History, 1820–1870* (London: Cape, 1980) for a popular account of the fads and fashions of specimen collecting prevalent among the middle and upper classes in Victorian society.

[34] 'Review', *The Academy* (15 November 1870): 32–3 (p. 33).

[35] Gosse, 'Obituary', p. 98.

Introduction 9

literary society, and were frequent guests at the far-famed evenings of Ford Madox Browne [sic], the artist, whose house was at that time a center of literary and artistic hospitality.'[36]

O'Shaughnessy sent copies of *An Epic* to Westland Marston, the playwright, Joseph Knight, the critic, A.C. Swinburne, and Dante Gabriel Rossetti, among others. This was a keen act of self-promotion that succeeded in gaining the young poet access to the literary society for which he had longed. The correspondence that followed from these gifts helped to draw the poet into the close-knit social circle of the Pre-Raphaelites and to further promote *An Epic*. Knight wrote a very favourable review of the volume and after exchanging a few letters with the young poet, Rossetti wrote to his other literary friends, recommending O'Shaughnessy to them and suggesting they mention him favourably in the press.[37]

Moulton describes the parties that O'Shaughnessy was invited to attend early in the 1870s at Ford Madox Brown's house at Fitzroy Square:

> And what men and women came there in those days! Some of them are ghosts now, and haunt, mayhap, the old rooms still. Rossetti was there, THE Rossetti, painter of poems, and poet of pictures; his sister, Christina, who is now so seldom seen outside her quiet home; their brother, William Michael, the critic, who afterward married a daughter of the Madox Brownes [sic]. William Morris came, too – he who divides his time, now, between writing poems that will live, and planning decorations for houses for other people to live in – and with him came his wife, whose beauty he sang and Rossetti painted, till she became part of the literary history of the Victorian epoch.[38]

O'Shaughnessy arrived on the literary scene early enough to catch Rossetti before his subsequent breakdown and withdrawal from society, and before the death of Oliver Madox Brown, which closed up the house on Fitzroy Square and ended the era of the parties described by Moulton above.[39]

O'Shaughnessy's friendships with Swinburne, Rossetti, and Morris, among others, have long characterized him as a 'Pre-Raphaelite poet'. However, he clearly fell into the category of the 'young men' of the movement, a generation behind its founders. This generation included Oliver Madox Brown and Philip Bourke Marston, son of Westland Marston. Despite the fact that O'Shaughnessy was a decade older than Madox Brown and six years older than Marston, the three young men became fast friends. We can see in these friendships, again, O'Shaughnessy's keen perception of how best to ingratiate himself within this literary circle. The older, more established Pre-Raphaelites tended to view the next

---

[36] Moulton, p. 15.

[37] *The Correspondence of Dante Gabriel Rossetti*, ed. William E. Fredeman (Cambridge and Rochester: D.S. Brewer, 2004), vol. 4, p. 545 and 553.

[38] Moulton, p. 16.

[39] William E. Fredeman refers to the years 1863 to 1872 as a 'prelude to crisis' for Rossetti, as 1872 marked the poet's withdrawal from society (*Correspondence*, vol. 4, title page).

10 *Arthur O'Shaughnessy, A Pre-Raphaelite Poet in the British Museum*

generation with fondness and a protective spirit, supporting and promoting their artistic efforts. Lionel Stevenson characterized this younger set of poets, saying, 'During a few years of the eighteen-seventies, a new generation of Rossettian disciples came into view, closely united by personal ties and poetic practices, until a strange fatality put a premature end to their careers. The group centred in the homes of two proud parents who were themselves distinguished personages.'[40] Although O'Shaughnessy was older than either P.B. Marston or Oliver Madox Brown, and was not a biological child of the movement, his subsequent marriage to P.B. Marston's eldest sister, Eleanor, reaffirmed his place within this diminutive movement.

Although the 'young men' of the movement received all the encouragement of children from their parents and were often protected in the popular press, they were clearly not viewed as equals within the artistic movement, and thus they remained somewhat on the 'periphery' – as Stevenson deems it – of Pre-Raphaelitism. Here, as with so many other aspects of O'Shaughnessy's life, we can see how a circumstance that benefited him during his lifetime – the fond protection of the older generation of Pre-Raphaelites – ultimately harmed his long-term reputation. Margaret Russett discusses how perceived 'secondariness', particularly in age, produces the language of minority in criticism of a poet, in *De Quincey's Romanticism*.[41] Despite this perceived 'late-coming' to the movement (which, after all, was founded only four years after O'Shaughnessy's birth), it is important to remember that Rossetti's first volume of poetry also appeared in 1870, only four years after Swinburne's *Poems and Ballads*. As Lionel Stevenson puts it, 1870 was 'the heyday of Pre-Raphaelite poetry'.[42]

During the printing of *An Epic* and the months following the publication of the volume, relations between Hotten and O'Shaughnessy broke down, and he chose to pursue publication of his second volume elsewhere.[43] He turned to the firm of Ellis & Green, then publishing William Morris and Dante Gabriel Rossetti, and *Lays of France (Founded on the Lays of Marie)* appeared in December of 1871. Although this was a mere 14 months after the publication of *An Epic,* O'Shaughnessy had been working on drafts of the *Lays* since at least 1867, before he began work on many of the poems that would later form *An Epic*.[44] *Lays* is comprised of five long poems, founded on five of the medieval *lais* of Marie de France, and a handful of short lyrics, relating to the themes of the longer narratives. It is a far more cohesive volume than *An Epic*, but was nevertheless not the popular success that

---

[40]   Lionel Stevenson, *The Pre-Raphaelite Poets* (Chapel Hill: University of North Carolina Press, 1972), p. 292.

[41]   Margaret Russett, *De Quincey's Romanticism: Canonical Minority and the Forms of Transmission* (Cambridge: Cambridge University Press, 1997), p. 7.

[42]   Stevenson, p. 293.

[43]   O'Shaughnessy found fault with Hotten's handling of bookseller's orders as well as his advertisement of the volume. See letters from John Camden Hotten to Arthur O'Shaughnessy, 27 October 1870 and 10 November 1870 (Duke).

[44]   Queen's University, MS 8/9.

An Epic had been. As Gosse sums up, the volume 'enjoyed a success of esteem, but did not very much attract the public'.[45] It was critically praised, with the *Athenaeum* saying it 'exhibits greater power than we were prepared for by his "Epic of Women"', but the volume did not sell.[46] Despite this, *Lays* contains what is nearly universally considered O'Shaughnessy's best poem: 'Chaitivel'. As the *Athenaeum* wrote in its obituary for O'Shaughnessy: '"Chaitivel", in "The Lays of France", shows, perhaps, the highest mark which he reached in the expression of imaginative passion.'[47]

The disappointing commercial reception of *Lays of France* did not deter O'Shaughnessy, and within two years his next volume was ready for publication. *Music and Moonlight* was published in March of 1874, to a lukewarm reception. The *Athenaeum* admitted, 'it would be incorrect to say that the new work is superior to either of its predecessors', and 'although distinguished by the same command of language and rhythmical flow as marks his former poems, there is less passion and exuberantly luxurious description in the work before us than in the ballads which first earned for Mr. O'Shaughnessy his place among poets. Even in finish and strength of diction experience and practice have not improved the author'.[48] Gosse's review for the *Academy* was much kinder, declaring the volume O'Shaughnessy's most original and insisting, 'the songs that are scattered here and there ... give firmer proof than ever of Mr. O'Shaughnessy's clear lyrical faculty, and of the certainty that he will enrich our literature with some of the very best songs written in our generation. Indeed it would be difficult to point to any one now writing who excels him in this class of work'.[49] Years later, however, Gosse said of the volume: 'Though containing some of his best productions, [it] must in fairness be called a failure, and one which, for a time, seriously injured his position.'[50]

O'Shaughnessy's first three volumes came out in quick succession – October 1870 to March 1874 – after which he did not publish a volume of poetry again in his lifetime. Gosse attributes this to the failure of *Music and Moonlight*; however, it would be fairer to note that a number of circumstances led to this creative lull. During these years O'Shaughnessy was focused on his personal and professional lives. In 1873 he married Eleanor Kyme Marston, eldest daughter of Westland Marston, and they soon began a family – this created the necessity of truly 'earning a living' and thus forced O'Shaughnessy to approach his zoological work at the Museum with renewed vigour.[51] As Lynn Barber notes, 'Professional

---

[45] Gosse, 'Obituary', p. 98.

[46] 'Review', *Athenaeum* 2306 (6 January 1872), p. 8.

[47] *Athenaeum* 2780 (5 February 1881), p. 196.

[48] 'Review', *Athenaeum* 2421 (21 March 1874): 382–3 (p. 382).

[49] Edmund Gosse, 'Review', *The Academy* (4 April 1874): 359–60 (p. 360).

[50] Gosse, 'Obituary', p. 98.

[51] Banns of Marriage, 26 June 1873, the Parish of St. Mark's, Regent's Park, in the County of Middlesex; digital images, findmypast.com.

12   *Arthur O'Shaughnessy, A Pre-Raphaelite Poet in the British Museum*

posts for naturalists were extremely rare, and such few as there were ludicrously badly paid ... salaries for scientific posts were calculated on the basis that anyone holding them must be a gentleman and therefore must have private means. Those scientists who did not have private means found it extremely difficult to earn a living.'[52] O'Shaughnessy did not have a private income, and thus had to find means of increasing his living within his position. Financial struggles plagued the O'Shaughnessys during these years, with Eleanor writing to Alfred Deacon: 'money [is] a commodity for which there are always such demands and so little where with to meet them.'[53]

The majority of O'Shaughnessy's scientific publications fall in the years of 1874 and 1875, as he strove to prove his worth within the Museum.[54] During these years the completion and opening of the new Natural History Museum in South Kensington loomed, helmed by Richard Owen, and O'Shaughnessy anticipated new opportunities that would come with the new location. As Paden notes, O'Shaughnessy 'was to look forward to the more suitable task of delivering lectures upon the zoological collections to the general public, gathered in a spacious auditorium at South Kensington'.[55]

O'Shaughnessy's courtship of Eleanor began as early as 1871, perhaps only shortly after his welcome into the literary circle in which her father circulated, and they were married on 26 June 1873, in the Parish of St. Mark's, Regent's Park, near the home of her father.[56] Eleanor was a very intelligent woman, from a literary family with literary aspirations of her own.[57] Moulton said of her: 'Mrs. O'Shaughnessy was a person of rare mental gifts. She was at once imaginative and witty.'[58] In 1875 Eleanor and O'Shaughnessy co-authored *Toyland*, a volume of stories for children. It is difficult to determine the proportionate contributions

---

[52]   Barber, p. 28.

[53]   Letter, Eleanor O'Shaughnessy to Alfred Newport Deacon, ca. 1875, Columbia University, Rare Book & Manuscript Library, MS #0956.

[54]   See 'Descriptions of a new species of Scincidae in the Collection of the British Museum', *Annals and Magazine of Natural History* 4, no. 13 (1874): 298–301; 'Descriptions of a new species of Skink', *Annals and Magazine of Natural History* 4, no. 14 (1874): 35; 'Description of a new species of lizard of the genus Celestus', *Annals and Magazine of Natural History* 4, no. 14 (1874): 257–8; 'Descriptions of new species of Gobiidae in the collection of the British Museum', *Annals and Magazine of Natural History* 4, no. 15 (1875): 144–8; 'List and Revision of the species of Anolidae in the British Museum Collection', *Annals and Magazine of Natural History* 4, no. 15 (1875): 270–81; 'Descriptions of new species of Gekkotidae in the British Museum Collection', *Annals and Magazine of Natural History* 4, no. 16 (October 1875): 262–6, among others.

[55]   Paden, 'British Museum', p. 28.

[56]   Edmund Gosse and Theophilus Marzial, another poet at the British Museum, served as groomsmen for O'Shaughnessy.

[57]   The letters of their courtship are full of discussions of poetry and music, another of O'Shaughnessy's interests (Columbia).

[58]   Moulton, p. 20.

Introduction   13

of each, but the prose is certainly very different from the sensuous or melancholy poetry for which O'Shaughnessy was known.[59]

In July of 1874 the O'Shaughnessys had a son, Westland Kyme Marston, but the child died less than two months later. The couple tried again, and friends record that the O'Shaughnessys had a second son. However, no record of the child's birth or death exists, leading W.D. Paden to posit that the infant was stillborn.[60] In any event, acquaintances record that the child did not survive. The first story of *Toyland*, entitled 'Old Gutty', is about the death of a child, and may reflect some of the grieving process of the O'Shaughnessys. They write: 'Was it not well, seeing how cold is the air of this world, often how scorching its sun, that these spring blossoms should be transplanted to the land where "everlasting spring abides"?'[61] Furthermore, they assert: 'Happy Mrs. Fraser, to have had such a child, and to feel that when, like that sorrowing mother of old, she asked of the angels if it was well with her child, like hers would be the answer – "It is well!"'[62]

Despite these platitudes, Eleanor was inconsolable following the loss of her children, and her grief was made worse by the deaths in close succession of her mother and younger sister, with whom she was very close. As the Marston's family friend Newton Crosland records, '[Eleanor's] digestion and health became disordered, and she resorted to whiskey as a remedy, with the results which might have been anticipated.'[63] It is difficult to say when, exactly, this problem began. As early as 1875 Eleanor was extolling the virtues of bitters and brandy to Alfred Deacon, suggesting, 'if you would take one on Sunday morning before going to church, you would feel the good effects of it all day.'[64] Her health deteriorated

---

[59] Colbeck reports: 'An examination of the copy O'Shaughnessy inscribed for Frederick Wedmore on 6 January 1875 reveals that O'Shaughnessy wrote the second and last tales, the first and third being the work of his wife.' Colbeck does not, however, reveal how this was determined. *A Bookman's Catalogue*, vol. 2, p. 624. This would mean that O'Shaughnessy wrote 'The Story of Noah's Ark' and 'Our Village', while Eleanor penned 'Old Gutty' and 'Our Theatre'.

[60] Although in 1964 Paden was confident that the birth had not been recorded ('Ancestry', 442), birth records from the relevant years record several infants who may have been the second O'Shaughnessy son. A Frederick O'Shaughnessy was born in the first quarter of 1876 in Kensington, the borough in which O'Shaughnessy was raised. Frederick was the middle name of O'Shaughnessy's brother, Oscar. A Francis Henry O'Shaughnessy was born in the third quarter of 1876 in Westminster. This name does not have any apparent family significance and is thus less likely than the previous child to be the second O'Shaughnessy son. Finally, a child merely denoted 'male' O'Shaughnessy was born in the second quarter of 1878 in Islington. This is the final O'Shaughnessy child born in London who could have been born to Eleanor, as she died in February of 1879.

[61] Arthur O'Shaughnessy with Eleanor O'Shaughnessy, *Toyland* (London: Daldy, Isbister, & Co., 56 Ludgate Hill, 1875), p. 62.

[62] Ibid., p. 64.

[63] Paden, 'Ancestry', p. 442, quoting Newton Crosland's *Rambles Round My Life* (1898).

[64] Letter from Eleanor Marston O'Shaughnessy to Alfred Deacon, ca. 1875 (Columbia).

14   *Arthur O'Shaughnessy, A Pre-Raphaelite Poet in the British Museum*

with her drinking, and one can only guess the strain it placed upon the marriage. Eleanor's letters to O'Shaughnessy record that he left her behind with her father, incapacitated by 'illness', while he took several trips abroad, enjoying the literary life of Paris unencumbered by his sick wife.[65] It was on these trips that O'Shaughnessy was introduced to Victor Hugo, and formed lasting friendships with the leading members of the Parnassian movement.

In February of 1879, at the age of 33, Eleanor died from cirrhosis of the liver. O'Shaughnessy had published a poem here and there over the years following *Music and Moonlight*, but after Eleanor's death his name once more began to appear regularly in print. He published several poems in memory of his wife, and began assembling his verse for a new volume. Unfortunately, he did not live to see the volume published; O'Shaughnessy died of pneumonia in January of 1881. His cousin and close friend, Alfred Deacon, was named his literary executor, and assembled O'Shaughnessy's remaining manuscripts into his final volume of poetry, *Songs of a Worker*, published in 1881.

The circumstances of O'Shaughnessy's death, and the way it was reported, further confirm the emphasis on everyday life and the burden of earning a living in discussions of his poetry. O'Shaughnessy had never been in good health and throughout his personal correspondence there are continuous references to illness.[66] In the archives of the Natural History Museum in Kensington, his only legacy is a series of sick notes to his superiors, excusing himself from work for weeks at a time.[67] His death by pneumonia could not have been surprising to anyone who knew him; the particular circumstances by which he contracted this specific illness should have been considered incidental and soon forgotten. And yet, friends and critics alike seemed to focus on those very circumstances. In 1925, Gosse wrote, 'In the mid-winter of 1881 he rode outside an omnibus without overcoat or umbrella, caught a cold on his lungs, and died – so it was reported – in the hands of a Mrs. Gamp.'[68] E.A. Sharpe and J. Matthay – also men who knew O'Shaughnessy personally – likewise draw attention to the 'bus, and add the detail of a night out at the theatre that led to O'Shaughnessy's death, writing, 'That evening he went to a theatre, came home on the top of an

---

[65]   Despite maintaining a fairly cheerful attitude in her letters to O'Shaughnessy, Eleanor seemed concerned about these periods of separations. She ends one letter saying, 'Write soon again my own dearest. I am longing to see you again. Don't let anybody pour little Nelly quite out of your heart' (letter from Eleanor Marston O'Shaughnessy to Arthur O'Shaughnessy, ca. 1875, Columbia).

[66]   His acquaintance William Sharp, in his biographical note on O'Shaughnessy in *Lyra Celtica: An Anthology of Representative Celtic Poetry*, rather oddly notes, 'always delicate, his death without any previous breakdown surprised none of his friends'. *Lyra Celtica: An Anthology of Representative Celtic Poetry*, ed. E.A. Sharpe and J. Matthay (Edinburgh: John Grant, 1924) p. 423.

[67]   See Correspondence 1868–1869 DF 100/11 and Zoological Department Letters 1877 DFZOO/12/21 at the Natural History Museum, South Kensington.

[68]   Gosse, *Silhouettes*, p. 176.

Introduction 15

omnibus, caught a chill, and died before any of his friends knew that he was seriously indisposed.'[69] Going to the theatre, riding a bus, catching a cold – these are ordinary, everyday occurrences, and yet they take the blame for ending O'Shaughnessy's life.

Characterizing his death in this way – as the consequence of living an ordinary life – speaks tellingly about the popular perception of O'Shaughnessy's relation to the everyday. Gosse manages to blame O'Shaughnessy's death on his working life, reporting that 'he had been suffering from a heavy cold, and I am informed that his zeal in going to the British Museum on Tuesday and Wednesday of last week greatly increased this'.[70] In later descriptions of O'Shaughnessy's death, the modern world in general is shouldered with the blame, symbolized by that mundane conveyance, the omnibus.

A fascinating – if skewed – portrait of O'Shaughnessy comes to us from the late Victorian writer Vernon Lee.[71] Her 1884 novel *Miss Brown* is a cutting criticism of the aesthetic movement of the 1870s and 1880s in London, centred on the characters Walter Hamlin and Anne Brown, modelled on D.G. Rossetti and Jane Morris. A secondary character, Cosmo Chough, has traditionally been assumed to be Swinburne – particularly as he is identified as a leader in the aesthetic movement with Hamlin.[72] However, as Leonee Ormond pointed out in 1970, the biographical elements of this character clearly identify Chough as O'Shaughnessy.[73] Unlike Swinburne, Chough occupies an 'inferior Government office' along with 'a whole band of other poets'.[74] He is depicted as having an infirm wife who is older than him, as well as being the subject of rumours about his parentage. In even the smaller details, O'Shaughnessy is the clear inspiration for this character: Chough is a talented pianist (a skill often remarked on by O'Shaughnessy's friends), he professes a native affinity for France, and he writes a poem entitled 'The Triumph of Womanhood', a series of portraits of the most wicked women of history – an obvious reference to O'Shaughnessy's 1870 'An Epic of Women'. Physically, as well, O'Shaughnessy is a close match for Chough, who is described as 'a little wiry man, with fiercely brushed coal-black hair and whiskers, dressed within an

---

[69]   *Lyra Celtica*, p. 423.

[70]   Gosse, 'Obituary', p. 98.

[71]   The pseudonym of Violet Paget (1856–1935).

[72]   Lee writes of 'The aesthetic school of poetry, of which Hamlin and Chough were the most brilliant exponents of the younger generation'. *Miss Brown* (Edinburgh and London: William Blackwood and Sons, 1884), vol. 2, p. 71. A portion of the character of Chough must be attributed to Swinburne, as there is a mention of 'Chough's new translation of "Villon"', a project of Swinburne's (vol. 3, p. 200).

[73]   Leonee Ormond, 'Vernon Lee as a Critic of Aestheticism in Miss Brown', *Colby Library Quarterly* 9, no. 3 (September 1970): 131–54. Despite her excellent work lining up the biographies of O'Shaughnessy and Cosmo Chough, Ormond misnames O'Shaughnessy as 'Alfred O'Shaughnessy' throughout the article.

[74]   Lee, vol. 1, p. 288.

16 *Arthur O'Shaughnessy, A Pre-Raphaelite Poet in the British Museum*

inch of his life, but in a style of fashionableness, booted and cravated, which was quite peculiar to himself'.[75]

The characterization of Chough is particularly interesting because rather than providing us with Lee's personal opinion of O'Shaughnessy, it gives a portrait of the impression he left upon his social circle as a whole. Lee didn't come to London until 1881, after O'Shaughnessy's death, and therefore never met the poet.[76] The character, then, is based solely on anecdotes she heard about O'Shaughnessy. In Chough we see reflected the general impression of incongruity between O'Shaughnessy as a person and the poetry he wrote. The novel calls Chough's poetry 'perfect indecent', yet it is asserted that 'Mr Chough was as modest as he was polite. His eyes shone, and he clasped his small hands in ecstasy at the idea of anything having pleased Miss Brown.'[77] He expounds on womanhood: '"That which you call disreputableness, my dear Miss Brown", cried Chough, "therein is their greatness".'[78] However, Miss Brown soon realizes that Chough leads a 'harmless' life, 'unacquainted with the beautiful, baleful ladies' he depicts in his poetry:[79]

> But the girls had got to understand Chough, and the fund of kindness and self-sacrificing gentleness which was hidden beneath the little man's poetical thin-skinnedness and the queer poetical veneer of mystic wickedness which he himself did not understand. He could not by any possibility be broken of his tendency to talk overmuch about Messelina, Lucretia Borgia, and La Belle Heaulmière; but by this time it was quite obvious that he had not the smallest experience of ladies of any such character, still less the faintest thought of giving offence by his allusions to them.

Lee's Cosmo Chough serves as an excellent summation of the impression of O'Shaughnessy with which we have been left: a man so ashamed of his humble background and civil service profession that he attempted to create himself anew in the vacuum of his working life, styling himself as a flamboyantly decadent poet.

In 1882 *Harper's New Monthly Magazine* published Edmund C. Stedman's 'Some London Poets', which included a brief sketch of O'Shaughnessy, the only deceased among the poets included. Stedman, an American himself, describes O'Shaughnessy as possessing 'an American earnestness of manner'.[80] By this Stedman appears to mean a kind of self-confidence – '[h]e seemed quite sure of his ground' – and enthusiasm for life.[81] Whether or not these are particularly

---

[75]   Ibid., p. 281.

[76]   Ormond writes: 'The latter [O'Shaughnessy] had died in January 1881, before Vernon Lee came to London, but she must have heard about him from Mary Robinson' (p. 142).

[77]   Lee, vol. 1, p. 277, p. 283.

[78]   Ibid., p. 289.

[79]   Ibid., vol. 2, p. 24.

[80]   Stedman, p. 884.

[81]   Ibid.

Introduction   17

'American' attributes, those who have done the most to preserve O'Shaughnessy's poetic legacy have all been Americans.

Stedman's article was followed 12 years later by Louise Chandler Moulton's *Arthur O'Shaughnessy: His Life and Work with Selections from His Poems.* Married to a prominent Boston publisher, Moulton was a poet and critic who wrote regularly for the *New York Tribune* and the *Boston Herald.* She summered in London, where she met O'Shaughnessy at one of Madox Brown's famed literary parties. Published 13 years after O'Shaughnessy's death, Moulton's selections helped to skew a later reception of O'Shaughnessy's work, shifting the focus to his shorter love lyrics. She deemed many of his other poems 'oversensuous', 'audacious', and, apparently worst of all, 'Swinburnean', and chose to exclude them from her volume.[82] Thus, from *An Epic of Women* she rejects 'An Epic of Women' entirely, and focuses her attention instead on the 'pure and perfect beauty' of 'Fountain of Tears'. From *Lays of France* she singles out 'Chaitivel', but excerpts it to a single love song, omitting the more shocking elements of the poem, including infidelity, corpses rising from the dead, and suggestions of necrophilia.[83] From *Songs of a Worker* she focuses her praise on the devout 'Christ Will Return', and rejects the aestheticist sequence 'Thoughts in Marble', though it forms the bulk of the volume. It is the 'delicate lyrics' that Moulton wished to preserve, thereby denying O'Shaughnessy's identity as an aesthete and a rebel against Victorian moral standards.

Moulton's volume was followed in 1923 by the work of yet another American: *Poems of Arthur O'Shaughnessy*, edited by W.A. Percy. Percy recounts how he first encountered O'Shaughnessy's poetry in Palgrave's *Golden Treasury*, highlighting the importance of the anthology in O'Shaughnessy's early afterlife. Percy's selections are even more idiosyncratic than Moulton's. He prints 'Fountain of Tears', 'A Whisper from the Grave', and 'Love after Death', from *An Epic*, and while he does not entirely excise the 'Epic', he selects only 'The Daughter of Herodias', and even then, breaks the lengthy poem down into two 'lyrics', which he entitles 'John the Baptist' (four stanzas) and 'Salome' (eight stanzas). In his introduction he asserts that the poem 'in spite of many stanzas haunting in sound and color, is structurally appalling', and thus justifies his choices.[84] From *Music and Moonlight* Percy selects several short lyrics – 'I made another garden, yea', 'Has summer come without the rose', and 'I went to her who loveth me no more' – which have cemented O'Shaughnessy's reputation as a Victorian 'love poet'. However, unlike Moulton, Percy prints the entirety of 'Chaitivel' from *Lays*, with the result that of the 99 pages of his volume dedicated to the poetry, 34 are taken up by 'Chaitivel'. By allowing this poem to dominate the volume, Percy shifts the impression of O'Shaughnessy's verse somewhat away from that created by Moulton, giving the reader a sense of his more daring, experimental,

---

[82]   Moulton, p. 23.

[83]   See my discussion of 'Chaitivel' in Chapter 6 of this work.

[84]   Percy, p. 4.

18 *Arthur O'Shaughnessy, A Pre-Raphaelite Poet in the British Museum*

and erotic poetry. From *Songs* he includes two of O'Shaughnessy's translations – both of Sully Prudhomme – another interesting choice, given his limited space.

In the 1960s W.D. Paden of the University of Kansas gave O'Shaughnessy some attention in two biographical articles, the first considering O'Shaughnessy's ancestry, and the second taking an in-depth look at his crisis of employment within the British Museum. Paden's articles are very informative, but are, oddly enough, exclusively focused on the biography of the poet, rather than his body of work, never mentioning a single poem.

Paden's biographical interest follows on from a 1933 biography written in German by Oskar Brönner, as well as a curious volume produced in 1916 by Clement Shorter, the journalist and literary critic. In *A Pathetic Love Episode in a Poet's Life: Being Letters to Arthur W.E. O'Shaughnessy, Also a letter from him containing a dissertation on Love*, Shorter compiles the correspondence between O'Shaughnessy and Helen Snee, documenting their affair and her later breakdown and trial for attempted murder of herself.[85]

Since Paden, O'Shaughnessy has been mentioned only in passing in accounts of the 'major' Pre-Raphaelites. No critical work has focused exclusively on O'Shaughnessy until now, as another American joins those apparently drawn to O'Shaughnessy's 'American earnestness of manner'.

III.

Vernon Lee's caricature of O'Shaughnessy emphasizes his status as a 'minor poet', a figure that is often perceived as inherently ridiculous. O'Shaughnessy's proximity to poets such as Dante Gabriel Rossetti, William Morris, and Algernon Charles Swinburne has kept him in the public eye – as a 'minor' Pre-Raphaelite, mentioned in books and articles about these 'major' poets – but has simultaneously overshadowed his poetry's own merits.

In his essay 'What is Minor Poetry?' (1957), T.S. Eliot defined O'Shaughnessy as the quintessential minor poet. Eliot selected O'Shaughnessy as the definitive example of a category of minor poets 'who have written just one, or only a very few, good poems: so that there seems no reason for anybody going beyond the anthology'.[86] The poem in question is O'Shaughnessy's 1874 'Ode' which begins:

> We are the music makers,
>   And we are the dreamers of dreams,
> Wandering by lone sea breakers,
>   And sitting by desolate streams –
> World-losers and world-forsakers,
>   On whom the pale moon gleams:

---

[85] See Chapter 5 for more details.

[86] T.S. Eliot, *On Poetry and Poets* (London: Faber, 1957), p. 44.

Introduction 19

Yet we are the movers and shakers
Of the world for ever, it seems.[87]

This poem has been in print continuously since its composition, a staple of anthologies of English verse. As early as 1925 Gosse recognized the potential longevity of this poem, stating, '[O'Shaughnessy] appears in the anthologies, from which he will never be dislodged.'[88] In fact, the poem's legacy stretches far beyond even the man who produced it. In 1912 Edward Elgar set the ode to music in 'The Music Makers, Op 69', and online searches for the poem's opening lines bring up more mentions of Elgar than their actual author. The 'Ode' entered pop-culture lexicon in 1971, as Gene Wilder spoke its opening lines in the popular children's film *Willy Wonka & the Chocolate Factory*.[89] Since then, these two lines have been quoted in a very diverse selection of contemporary music and entertainment. Even more enduring, perhaps, is the coinage of the term 'movers and shakers' in this poem, a phrase now far more ubiquitous than O'Shaughnessy himself.

The unlikely concept that a man could write one good poem with such a long-lasting cultural impact, yet nothing else worth reading, is one of the ideas that drew me to a study of O'Shaughnessy.[90] Eliot dismisses the remaining 116 published poems by O'Shaughnessy, though many of them have drawn enthusiastic critical praise, both at the time of publication and since. Furthermore, O'Shaughnessy's verse can be seen to engage with many the major poetic innovations of the period: Pre-Raphaelitism, decadence, and aestheticism. He experiments with poetic style and form quite extensively throughout his four volumes of poetry, and in his unpublished papers we find attempts at prose narratives in addition to poetry, spanning from fantastical fairy tales to anthropological accounts of tribal behaviour in North America.[91]

Although New Historicist scholars have reclaimed many minor poets in recent decades, their work tends to focus on writers excluded from the canon because of gender, race, or class. While important, this kind of scholarship largely does not help to reclaim O'Shaughnessy. O'Shaughnessy is in the unique position of being a white, middle-class man, who during his lifetime socialized with poets as esteemed as Alfred Tennyson and Robert Browning. We must, then, look for other reasons for his continued obscurity. During his lifetime, O'Shaughnessy blamed his

---

[87] O'Shaughnessy, 'Ode', *Music and Moonlight* (London: Chatto & Windus, 1874), pp. 1–5.

[88] Gosse, *Silhouettes*, p. 174.

[89] *Willy Wonka & the Chocolate Factory*. Screenplay by Roald Dahl. Dir. Mel Stuart. Gene Wilder, Jack Albertson, and Peter Ostrum. Paramount Pictures, 1971.

[90] Even Eliot notes how unlikely the 'one-hit wonder' poet is, stating: 'But the number of poets of whom we can say that it holds true for all readers that they left only one or two particular poems worth reading, is actually very small: the chances are that if a poet has written one good poem, there will be something in the rest of his work which will be worth reading' (44). Nevertheless, for Eliot, O'Shaughnessy's 'Ode' is the only poem of worth in his whole body of work.

[91] See 'Ina's Tale', Queen's, MS 8/17, and 'The Miamis', MS 8/19.

20   *Arthur O'Shaughnessy, A Pre-Raphaelite Poet in the British Museum*

middling literary career on the necessity of 'earning a living' at the Museum, which necessitated divided focus and interests. This present work, then, will account for O'Shaughnessy's minority in terms of the working life of the petty bourgeoisie.

O'Shaughnessy's interest in and experimentation with decadence, socialism, and Darwinian theory in his poetry can all be traced back to his career at the British Museum, and the perceived burden of earning a wage, which marked him as different from much of the Pre-Raphaelite literary circle – men like Morris and Swinburne who were from the monied classes. O'Shaughnessy's day job at the museum, and the supposed disparity between this employment and his 'poetic nature', underpin my reading of O'Shaughnessy's oeuvre and his place within the canon of nineteenth-century poetry. His work as a naturalist obviously lends itself to considerations of the cultural impact of Darwinism, and the encroachment upon public life by the sciences in the nineteenth century. However, the reality of his position as a junior assistant and clerk also shapes O'Shaughnessy's thoughts on work and labour, and lead to his formulation of the proto-socialist 'art for humanity' political theory. His concerns regarding the social impact of Darwinism manifested as a strain of decadent naturalism in his verse, and mark him as one of the first importers of decadence from France. The influence of the French *Romantiques* on his poetry, and O'Shaughnessy's own influence in bringing the aestheticism of the Parnassians to England in the 1870s, highlights O'Shaughnessy's importance, alongside Swinburne, in crafting a bridge between Pre-Raphaelitism and the aestheticism of the later Victorian period. This work, therefore, reveals that rather than being a 'satellite' to major writers, O'Shaughnessy was an innovative and dynamic poet in his own right.

IV.

I have undertaken extensive archival research into O'Shaughnessy's personal and professional correspondence, his unpublished manuscripts, and his notes on both science and literature. These materials are spread among Queen's University, Belfast; Duke University, North Carolina; Columbia University, New York; and the archives of the British Museum and the Natural History Museum South Kensington, in London. Many of these materials have not been viewed since their acquisition. Duke's collection centres on O'Shaughnessy's poetic career, including extensive correspondence with his publishers, John Camden Hotten, Ellis & Green, and finally Chatto & Windus, which divulges details of the business of being a poet, the banal, everyday aspects of the life of an artist. Correspondence with prominent literary figures of the day, including D.G. Rossetti, Joseph Knight, and Westland Marston, details the reception of O'Shaughnessy's poetry, as well as his attempts to join the ranks of London's literary elite. The museum collections help to illustrate O'Shaughnessy's professional life as a naturalist, in correspondence with his superiors at the British Museum, as well as the record of a probationary hearing that occurred in 1870, discussed at length in Chapter 1. O'Shaughnessy's personal life is brought into focus by the Columbia collection, consisting of correspondence with his wife, Eleanor Kyme Marston, before and after their

Introduction 21

1873 marriage. These letters reveal ordinary details of their married life as well as ample discussion of his poetic career and the critical reception of his work. Finally, the O'Shaughnessy manuscript collection at Queen's University, Belfast, consists of 26 unpublished notebooks, containing prose and verse works, drafts of his published material, notes on his reading and research, and professional notes regarding his taxonomic work at the British Museum. These materials offer a new and more complete picture of O'Shaughnessy as poet and a naturalist.

Because of the varied nature of O'Shaughnessy's body of work, this study does not consider his poetry volume by volume. Rather, it traces the narrative of O'Shaughnessy's poetic growth through several large themes that recur in each of his four volumes. Each thematic strand culminates in his final volume, *Songs of a Worker*, which contains O'Shaughnessy's most mature and compelling work.

Chapter 1 focuses is on O'Shaughnessy's 'day job' as a taxonomist in the Departments of Natural History at the British Museum and the impact of this work on his poetry. The chapter begins with a biographical account of O'Shaughnessy's time at the Museum, centring on a probationary hearing that O'Shaughnessy faced in 1870. Having considered the difficulties O'Shaughnessy found in his scientific career, I demonstrate that in his early poetry the 'realm of art' was conceived as the antithesis of natural history at the Museum. Henri Lefebvre's theory of the divided man is employed to examine O'Shaughnessy's poetic attempts to escape the everyday, represented by his career at the Museum, and their inevitable failure. O'Shaughnessy's nature poetry, particularly 1870's 'Palm Flowers', 1874's 'Azure Islands', and 1881's 'Lynmouth', is used to explicate this section. I then turn to the broader scientific debates of the day and their impact on O'Shaughnessy's verse. Here my argument focuses particularly on 1870's 'Bisclavaret' and 1881's 'Eden', through which O'Shaughnessy's gradual acceptance of Darwinian theory can be traced. By identifying the ways in which O'Shaughnessy's verse critically engages with the more challenging aspects of Darwinian theory, we form a dynamic picture of the Darwinian debates at the time, heretofore overlooked in relation to O'Shaughnessy's poetry.

Chapter 2 turns to larger nineteenth-century theories of work and leisure in an exploration of O'Shaughnessy's conceptualization of the 'world of art' as a realm apart from, and opposed to, the everyday. Marx's notion of 'estranged labour' and Lefebvre's theory of alienated life are used to explicate the disconnect between the everyday and the ideal in O'Shaughnessy's poetry, and his conception of himself as an 'alien' in his own life. The poems 'A Discord', 'Seraphitus', 'Exile', and 'Nostalgie des Cieux' reveal O'Shaughnessy as a divided man. This chapter looks closely at nineteenth-century ideas of utility and aesthetics, as we see O'Shaughnessy struggle with the purpose of the artist in society. Through this lens, I consider his most famous poem, his 'Ode' of 1874. We can see, in this section, proto-socialist leanings in O'Shaughnessy's verse, giving lie to the notion, put forward by F.R. Leavis, that O'Shaughnessy was the archetype of the socially removed Victorian poet. It is in the idea of work as creation that we see O'Shaughnessy's reconciliation of the ideas of work and leisure, in order to attain Morris's notion of work-pleasure, culminating in the 1881 'Song of a Fellow-Worker'.

22   *Arthur O'Shaughnessy, A Pre-Raphaelite Poet in the British Museum*

Chapter 3 examines O'Shaughnessy's experimentation with formalism in relation to the bourgeois call for 'moral art' in this period. This chapter considers Robert Buchanan's infamous attack on the Pre-Raphaelites, including O'Shaughnessy, in his 'Fleshly School of Poetry'. O'Shaughnessy turned to formalism in order to circumvent the demand for morality in art, by embracing form over content. This is reflected both in his experimentations with French fixed forms of poetry and his use of ekphrasis in poems about art objects. I consider O'Shaughnessy's much-criticized 'Epic of Women' (1870) and demonstrate that rather than misogynistic shock-poetry, this sequence serves as an aestheticist manifesto, demanding that art be freed from moralistic criticism. I conclude with a discussion of O'Shaughnessy's posthumous 'Thoughts in Marble', which naturally follows on from Pater's 1873 *The Renaissance* in its embrace of classism in order to reject bourgeois morality. Here, 'Thoughts in Marble' can be seen to bridge the aesthetic theories of Pater in 1873 and Wilde in the 1890s, explicating the shift to Decadence and Aestheticism that occurred in this period.

Chapter 4 gives a more thorough account of the influences of French literature upon O'Shaughnessy's poetry. His correspondence with young French poets as well as his professional relationship with *Le Livre* in Paris help to draw parallels between the work being produced in France at the time and O'Shaughnessy's own poetry. Returning to Lefebvre's notion of the idealized leisure time as artificial and escapist, this chapter examines O'Shaughnessy's engagement with French decadence, particularly his works modelled on the poetry of Théophile Gautier and Charles Baudelaire. In tracing the influence of decadent verse throughout his career, we find in O'Shaughnessy's final collection, particularly in the poem 'Colibri', a reconciliation of the real and the ideal in the form of a naturalistic decadence that incorporates, rather than imitates, the generic markers of the French decadent movement.

Chapter 5 turns to O'Shaughnessy's participation in the popular medieval revival of the Victorian period in his second volume of poetry, *Lays of France* (1872). It will analyze O'Shaughnessy's participation in this trend in the light of the medievalism practised by Rossetti, Morris, and Swinburne, identifying the original niche O'Shaughnessy occupied within this movement. Questions of translation, adaptation and interpretation will be central to this chapter, as I consider the relationship of O'Shaughnessy's 'lays founded on Marie' to the original *lais* of Marie de France. Notions of failure and intent will be especially important to this discussion, as I interrogate the critically accepted notion that these poems are failed translations, by positing that the idea of translation is employed as a clever mask for a kind of eroticism usually condemned by the literary press. Medievalism is often theorized as an escape from the everyday (or, rather, an escape from modernity and its everyday concerns), but here we can see O'Shaughnessy employing medievalism to elevate the everyday. Specifically, we can trace the impulse for the *Lays of France* to an effort to ennoble his own love affairs, with the language of chivalry used to disguise the potentially tawdry aspects of modern infidelity.

Chapter 1

'Dreary Creeds' and 'Sham Wits': O'Shaughnessy's Poetic Representations of Nature and Science

Arthur O'Shaughnessy's professional life as a naturalist in the British Museum had an undeniable effect on his poetry, yet throughout his life he attempted to maintain a strict divide between his professional career and his artistic ambitions. This self-inflicted divide stemmed largely from the dissatisfaction he felt in his job at the British Museum – he faced conflict with colleagues and superiors, and often found himself caught up in the bureaucracy of the inner workings of the Museum. These were difficulties he could have faced in any office environment, but they caused O'Shaughnessy to attempt to reject 'science' in general – as a blanket term for the naturalism practised at the Museum, and the taxonomy he particularly performed. O'Shaughnessy saw his artistic career as fulfilling and creative where his work as a naturalist was unproductive and stultifying, and he thus sought to assert the one by denigrating the other. Despite the divide between science and art that he fervently proclaimed in his poetry, however, we can see many instances in which his scientific career seeped into his verse, in setting and subject matter, as well as evidence of an engagement with broader nineteenth-century science – specifically Darwinian theory.

I.

Arthur O'Shaughnessy worked at the British Museum from the age of 17 until his death in 1881. Both his initial appointment to the Museum and his subsequent promotion to the Natural History Departments were tainted by hints of scandal. O'Shaughnessy came to the museum on the recommendation of Edward Bulwer-Lytton, the popular novelist and member of the peerage. Nomination by a trustee was the only way to secure a coveted civil service position at that time, so Lord Lytton asked his friend, the Rt. Hon. John Evelyn Denison, Speaker of the House of Commons, and trustee to the British Museum, to nominate O'Shaughnessy. Although this was the normal way of obtaining this kind of position, rumours of unfair partiality began to swirl almost immediately. Gossip in the museum declared Lord Lytton O'Shaughnessy's natural father. In 1925 Clement Shorter reported:

> For him now and again, when the office hours had ended, there called a veiled lady in a well-appointed carriage with liveried servants. This veiled lady was always believed at the time to be O'Shaughnessy's mother. Certainly there was

24 *Arthur O'Shaughnessy, A Pre-Raphaelite Poet in the British Museum*

no doubt whatever in the minds of his fellow clerks at the Museum that Edward Bulwer Lytton, the novelist, was his father. The name "O'Shaughnessy" the poet owed to the old Irishwoman who brought him up. His mother may have been an Irishwoman, but her nationality has never been revealed.[1]

Edmund Gosse believed O'Shaughnessy confirmed the nature of his kinship to Lytton in 1873; he reported witnessing O'Shaughnessy's grief at the death of Lytton, and recounts his tearful exclamation of, 'No one will ever know what he was to me!'[2]

In fact, O'Shaughnessy was correct; his contemporaries never guessed his true connection to Lytton. It was not O'Shaughnessy's mother, but rather his aunt – Laura Deacon, the 'veiled lady' of Shorter's report – who was Lytton's mistress. Following Lytton's separation from his wife, Rosina, in 1835, he began a long-term affair with Laura that, according to his son the second earl Lytton, was 'not a mere passing flirtation but a relationship in all respects equivalent to marriage except the legality of the tie'.[3] Laura bore Bulwer-Lytton four children, and the family was established in fashionable accommodations in Grosvenor Square under the name Grant.

Nevertheless, Gosse remained convinced all his life that O'Shaughnessy was Lytton's illegitimate child, despite protests from the poet's cousin, Alfred Deacon. Following O'Shaughnessy's death, Deacon wrote to Gosse, asking him to clear any rumours of O'Shaughnessy's parentage by including O'Shaughnessy's father, Oscar, in any biographical accounts of the poet:

> My reason for this request is that several persons have written to me & asked if it was not true that my cousin O'Shaughnessy was an illegitimate son of the late Lord Lytton!! I need hardly say that the statement is a pure fabrication, but it is never the less widely spread, by many, as a truth, hence my anxiety that his father's name & profession should have been stated. Lord Lytton was always kind to him having been an old friend of our family & for a reason which until I see his son's (the Earl of Lytton's) memoir I am unable to state – as it was a matter of interest in Lord Lytton's life. When we meet I may perhaps be able to mention it – It is known but to two or three persons, besides myself.[4]

In an effort to preserve the reputations of everyone involved – in print, at least – Gosse's official obituary for O'Shaughnessy suggested that Lytton helped the poet secure his position at the Museum because he had been 'struck by the boy's talent'.[5]

---

[1] Shorter, p. 3.

[2] Edmund Gosse, *Silhouettes*, Essay Index Reprint Series (Freeport, NY: Books for Libraries Press, 1971), p. 175.

[3] Paden, 'Ancestry', p. 437, quoting *The Life of Edward Bulwer* (1913), by V.A.G.R. Lytton, second earl Lytton.

[4] Paden, 'Ancestry', p. 445.

[5] Edmund Gosse, 'Obituary: Arthur O'Shaughnessy', *The Academy* 457 (5 February 1881): 98–9 (p. 98). That Lytton did serve as a mentor for young writers of the day – whose literary reputations have outlived his own – is evidenced by a letter Swinburne wrote to

This fallacy was repeated as late as 1953, with one critic asserting that 'Lord Lytton, a friend of his mother, had liked the boy's early verses and in 1861 had brought about his appointment as a junior assistant in the Department of Printed Books'.[6] Despite his current rather tarnished reputation, at the time Bulwer-Lytton was one of the bestselling novelists in England; it was a flattering suggestion, then, that O'Shaughnessy might have been his literary protégé. Although Lytton was supportive of O'Shaughnessy's poetic career – writing enthusiastically that his poetry inspired 'unmistakable delight' – it is quite clear that Lytton's true interest in O'Shaughnessy was familial, rather than literary.[7]

In *Miss Brown*, Vernon Lee suggests that O'Shaughnessy may not have discouraged the gossip as firmly as Deacon did. Cosmo Chough, Lee's caricature of O'Shaughnessy, is depicted as being ridiculous in his pretensions, established early on with a reference to his parentage. Walter Hamlin says of Chough:

> "His only weakness is that he is a great republican and democrat, but would like to be thought the son of a duke."

> "Oh, the natural son, of course – forgive me, my dear," said Mrs. Macgregor. "People nowadays like anything illegitimate – it's a distinction. It wasn't in my day, but things have changed; and Mr Cosmo Chough would dearly like to be thought a bastard, especially a duke's."[8]

Here Lee suggests that O'Shaughnessy embraced the rumours of his relationship to Lytton in order to make himself seem more at home in the bohemian poetic circles in which he moved. In Volume 2 of the novel, it is revealed that Chough's father, far from being a duke, was 'an apothecary at Limerick'.[9]

The minor scandal of O'Shaughnessy's appointment to the Department of Printed Books in 1861 was soon to be overshadowed by his promotion to the Departments of Natural History, a sector of the museum which was rapidly expanding thanks to the Victorian rage for specimen collection.[10] Hundreds of thousands of specimens arrived from the far reaches of the British Empire, waiting to be identified and catalogued. Nicolaas Rupke describes the influx:

> All too soon, however, a stream of new objects, antiquities, ethnographic items, dried plants, stuffed animals and fossils, from private collectors, from Near

---

him in 1866, asking for advice on how to deal with problems with his publisher, as well as the moral censure of the reading public that followed the publication of *Poems and Ballads*. *The Swinburne Letters*, ed. Cecil Y. Lang (New Haven: Yale University Press, 1959), vol. 1, pp. 170–73.

[6] Hoxie N. Fairchild, 'Rima's Mother', *PMLA* 68, no. 3 (June 1953): 357–70 (p. 368).

[7] Duke, letter dated 19 October 1870.

[8] Lee, vol. 1, p. 279.

[9] Ibid., vol. 2, p. 270.

[10] O'Shaughnessy was appointed to the department on 5 August 1863. BMSCM, C.10440/1.

26   *Arthur O'Shaughnessy, A Pre-Raphaelite Poet in the British Museum*

Eastern excavations, African expeditions and colonial surveys had congested the Bloomsbury temple, even its basement, stairs and portico.[11]

All of these specimens needed to be catalogued, but as Dr Edward Gray came to the keepership of the department of Zoology, he had only four assistants and eight attendants. Thus, expansion was called for. As the Keeper of Printed Books, John W. Jones, asserted:

> Either this great national establishment must become a gigantic warehouse of unpacked goods, or it must be enormously enlarged, or there must be some division of its multifarious contents, and a single building be no longer made the receptacle for almost everything which man has executed and nature produced from generation to generation and from one end of the earth to the other.[12]

It was assertions like these which paved the way for the future Natural History Museum at South Kensington.

O'Shaughnessy's appointment as a Junior Assistant in the Departments raised hackles because a far more qualified candidate was passed over for the position – the explorer and naturalist Walter Henry Bates, recently returned from a voyage up the Amazon with Alfred Russell Wallace, co-discoverer of the theory of natural selection.[13] Bates's application was unusual, as the Museum was predisposed to promote from within,[14] but the recent publication of the account of his travels, *A Naturalist on the River Amazons* (1863), had gained him the support of such prominent men as Joseph Hooker, the botanist, and Charles Darwin.[15]

---

[11]   Nicolaas A. Rupke, *Richard Owen: Victorian Naturalist* (New Haven and London: Yale University Press, 1994), p. 32.

[12]   Rupke, p. 32. This expansion meant that by 1875 the department had gained an additional five employees, and by 1895 the total staff had risen to 34.

[13]   In 1858, Wallace sent a paper outlining his ideas of evolution by means of the struggle for survival to Darwin. The ideas were strikingly similar to Darwin's own work. Because they had come to the ideas independently, Darwin and Wallace sought a compromise to avoid conflict in publication. They submitted two extracts from Darwin's work and Wallace's paper to the Linnean Society, which was thereafter published as a single article entitled 'On the Tendency of Species to Form Varieties; and on the Perpetuation of Varieties and Species by Natural Means of Selection' in the *Proceedings of the Linnean Society* in 1858.

[14]   As W.D. Paden notes, Bates's application was 'irregular, for posts within the Museum were usually filled by promotions within the staff, to which entrance could be gained (as has been mentioned) only through nomination by a Trustee'. 'Arthur O'Shaughnessy in the British Museum: or, the case of the misplaced fusees and the reluctant zoologist', *Victorian Studies* 8, no. 1 (September 1964): 7–30 (p. 11).

[15]   Bates writes, 'I became acquainted with Mr Darwin, who, having formed a flattering opinion of my ability for the task, strongly urged me to write a book, and reminded me of it months afterwards, when, after having made a commencement, my half-formed resolution began to give way.' *The Naturalist on the River Amazons: A Record of Adventures, Habits of Animals, Sketches of Brazilian and Indian Life, and Aspects of Nature under the Equator during eleven years of Travel*, 2 vols (London: John Murray, 1863), vol. 1, p. v.

The disparity in qualifications between the two candidates is almost laughable. O'Shaughnessy was a 19-year-old boy who had worked in the Department of Printed Books for two years as a transcriber and had never before expressed an interest in natural history. Bates had just returned from 11 years in the remotest parts of South America, during which he had collected large numbers of specimens for the British Museum.[16] Bates came to the Museum with the backing of the most renowned naturalists of the day; in fact, The Entomological Society was so outraged by the slight to Bates that it filed a complaint, with the backing of the Royal Society. The dispute between the Museum and the Entomological Society lasted for over a year, and was partially carried out in the popular press.[17] Nevertheless, O'Shaughnessy retained the position.

It is doubtful that the rejection of such a qualified applicant was based solely on nepotism, despite Lytton's support of O'Shaughnessy. For such a subordinate position – Junior Assistant, Second Class – the Museum simply didn't require someone as qualified as Bates. O'Shaughnessy characterized the nature of his own employment at the Museum, saying, 'The conditions of Mr. O'Shaughnessy's employment in the Spirit Room as stated to him by Professor Owen were: That Dr. Günther had need of a person sufficiently educated & qualified to *write* for him, *his own hands being* engaged in the *dissection or manipulation of specimens in spirit* & not in a fit state to do so conveniently' (emphasis his).[18] O'Shaughnessy's workload primarily included clerical duties and catering to the needs of visiting researchers, and therefore his experience as a transcriber was enough to qualify him. The skills Bates possessed were unnecessary for such menial work.

However, it is also quite likely that the Departments, headed by Richard Owen and J.E. Gray, did not want such a staunch Darwinist in their midst. This is the conclusion W.D. Paden comes to, stating, 'Darwin was Bates' other supporter, but he was also the man who, by suggesting the transmutation of species, had shaken the foundation of Dr. Gray's concept of zoology as taxonomy.'[19] Richard Owen has long been thought of as Darwin's main opponent in the evolutionary debates of the 1860s, and thus it follows that he would not have wanted a friend and supporter of Darwin in his department.

The Departments soon found that even within the limited duties of the Junior Assistantship, someone more qualified was required. Although O'Shaughnessy received the necessary qualifications for his post – the Report and Certificate of Civil Service Examination on General Subjects and Report and Certificate of Examination in Systematic Zoology – his overall expertise was found lacking.[20]

---

[16] Bates's relationship with the Museum continued long after he was passed over for this position. See, for instance, a purchase of zoological specimen from Bates for £12 authorized on 12 June 1869 (BMSCM, C.11679) or another purchase of £34 of specimen, on 9 July 1870 (C.11931).

[17] The resolution regarding the complaint was printed in the *Athenaeum*, 18 July 1863. BMSCM, 11 July 1863, C.10372.

[18] Letter dated 11 November 1870, BMOP.

[19] Paden, p. 11.

[20] Letter to Mr Winter Jones, 11 November 1870, BMOP.

28 *Arthur O'Shaughnessy, A Pre-Raphaelite Poet in the British Museum*

He began his employment in the Entomology Department, but it quickly became apparent that his weak eyesight was too great a disadvantage for that kind of minute work. He was then transferred to the Geological Department, to assist Richard Owen in his paleontological research.[21] Just as quickly, he was transferred back to the Zoology Department, this time placed under Albert Günther, to assist in the catalogue of fish. It seems that O'Shaughnessy was initially enthusiastic about the work granted to him and the opportunity to publish his scientific findings, but soon became discouraged by the exacting nature of taxonomic classification. Günther describes some of O'Shaughnessy's failures within the Department:

> In the middle of last year I proposed to him to concentrate his study upon a small group of lizards of which we possess numerous examples, so to subject them to a thorough examination. He engaged with zeal in this work, so much so that he even expressed his intention of publishing a series of articles on the subject. Unfortunately, his want of experience in zoological literature, led him at the beginning into a mistake & subsequent controversy with a foreign zoologist, in consequence of which he discontinued the work. Finally I made an attempt to profit by his assistance and have certain specimens of sharks named by him, previously to my own examination. In this he failed entirely, although provided with ready means for their determination. For some he simply adopted the names previously attached to them; others were misnamed, & others left unnamed.[22]

Implicit within Günther's testimonial is O'Shaughnessy's difficulty with authority – the challenge of the 'foreign zoologist' was enough to put him off his work entirely. Günther's account also suggests an unwillingness in O'Shaughnessy to learn his new trade. His position required study and experience to gain the requisite understanding of taxonomy and zoology, but it seems O'Shaughnessy was averse to putting in the effort. Apparent from his correspondence during this time is the fact that he was entirely concentrated on his poetic career; the work of a naturalist was secondary to his art, and suffered in consequence. Notebooks dated from 1863 – the year he began work in the Natural History Departments – contain hundreds of pages of poetry. These early works evince O'Shaughnessy's dedication to the craft of poetry; they contain multiple revisions and drafts, with poems being revisited time and again as he struggled to find the right words to fit his vision. In contrast, he approached his work at the Museum only as the means to achieve an end – namely, providing a living wage so that he could write poetry.

While many critics choose to describe O'Shaughnessy as an 'expert' or an 'authority' in reptiles when he died – the *Athenaeum* asserts, 'he had gained such proficiency in subjects belonging to his department that several of his papers in connexion with them have excited much attention and approval' – others seem to revel in the struggles he faced in the zoology department, playing up

---

[21]   Owen (1804–1892) was the leading paleontologist of the day, and is perhaps most famous for coining the word *Dinosauria* in 1842.

[22]   Letter from Albert Günther to J. Winter Jones, Principal Librarian of the British Museum, 4 November 1870. BMOP, 11400.

his incompetence in his taxonomical work.[23] Thus Gosse repeats an apocryphal tale regarding O'Shaughnessy's clumsy ineptitude: '[I]ndeed, it used to be said that, having been the victim of an accident, he fitted the tail of one broken fish to the head of another so deftly that a German savant was deceived, and wrote a sensational memoir of a wholly new species.'[24] In Günther's account of O'Shaughnessy's troubles in the Department, quoted above, we can find the grain of truth that grew into this sensational – albeit humorous – anecdote; however, the mistake O'Shaughnessy made was misidentification of a poorly preserved specimen (of a lizard, in fact), not the gross incompetency Gosse reports with such relish. A similar and equally untrue story was repeated by the *Dundee Courier* a full year and a half after O'Shaughnessy's death, except in the place of fish were butterflies, and it was an entire conference of entomologists who discovered his mistake, rather than a single German zoologist:

> One day, shortly after his entrance upon the duties, the youthful bard accidentally sat down on a number of exceedingly rare South American butterflies which had just arrived at the Museum. Horrified at the disaster, he proceeded secretly and hurriedly to repair damages, but being in truth ignorant of butterflies, as he was indeed on natural history generally, he got the insects very much mixed up, glueing wings on the wrong bodies in the most reckless manner. Great was the astonishment of the wise men when they came to contemplate and classify the new contributions. Such species had never been seen before; the insect world and its history were revolutionised. Many were the solemn discussions that took place before Mr O'Shaughnessy's awful misadventure and skilful glueing were discovered. Then there was a wrathful conference of scientists, and the young man would have been dismissed had not Lord Lytton used his influence.[25]

Underlying all of these reports and comments is the same intimation: the idea of a poet working as a taxonomist is comically incongruous, a source of amusement that at times undermines his successes in both careers.

An incident that occurred in 1870 gives us a great deal of insight into O'Shaughnessy's acclimatization to the Natural History Departments. In the fall of that year O'Shaughnessy was officially reprimanded by the Museum for having a box of matches in the Spirit Room – an obvious danger – and was placed on probation.[26] O'Shaughnessy mishandled the initial reprimand, and a

---

[23]   'Mr. Arthur O'Shaughnessy', *Athenaeum* 2780 (5 February 1881), p. 197.

[24]   Gosse, *Silhouettes*, p. 175.

[25]   *The Dundee Courier*, 26 May 1882. The report continues: 'Warned by his blunder, O'Shaughnessy undertook the study of natural history, and now there is no one in the museum better skilled in the department,' an assertion which is as untrue as the apocryphal story of the butterflies. While O'Shaughnessy did overcome many of his initial shortcomings to become a valuable employee to the Museum, he was never an 'expert', and certainly not the best natural historian employed by the British Museum.

[26]   So obvious a danger, in fact, that a report had been issued to the Board of Trustees by the Principal Librarian, regarding the dangers of 'the large quantities of Spirit kept in

full-scale investigation into his work habits was launched. Rather than accepting the admonition from his superiors, O'Shaughnessy had his friend J.T. Nettleship (illustrator of his first volume of poetry) write a letter to the Board, claiming ownership of the box of matches and taking full responsibility for their presence in the Spirit Room.[27] Unfortunately for O'Shaughnessy, it was easy for John Winter Jones (Principal Librarian) to verify this claim. In a letter to the Trustees, Winter Jones writes:

> In consequence of the discrepancies between Mr. O'Shaughnessy's statements and those of the gentlemen under whom he was employed Mr. Jones felt it his duty to make further enquiries ... It is the duty of the Attendant Tomlinson to dust Mr. O'Shaughnessy's room and table and from him Mr. Jones learnt that in fetching things from Mr. O'Shaughnessy's table and in putting it as far as he could in order he had frequently seen the fusee-box lying amongst the papers on the table for five or six weeks past ... Mr. Jones, finding how untrustworthy Mr. O'Shaughnessy was, requested Professor Owen, Dr. Gray and Dr. Günther to state for the information of the Trustees the nature and value of Mr. O'Shaughnessy's services.[28]

Reports were requested from Albert Günther, O'Shaughnessy's immediate supervisor, John Edward Gray, the Keeper of the Department of Zoology, and Richard Owen, Superintendent of the Departments of Natural History. From these reports we are able to gain a picture of O'Shaughnessy's professional life at the Museum. He had been in the employ of the Natural History Departments for seven years at that point, and yet it is clear that he had never settled into the life of a naturalist.

The first set of reports issued following the reprimand was not encouraging for O'Shaughnessy. Richard Owen wrote: 'The only work in which I have had occasion to avail myself of the services of Mr. O'Shaughnessy has been that of a transcriber: I am glad to be able to say that he has done such work always readily, promptly and to my satisfaction.' Owen is certainly damning O'Shaughnessy with faint praise, and went on to note, 'he does not appear to have mastered any special branch or department of Natural History to do effective technical service therein.'[29]

Günther, with whom O'Shaughnessy worked most closely, provided the longest report on his progress at the Museum. It appears that Günther was trying to be kind towards O'Shaughnessy, yet he could not help but admit that the poet was inept in his position. He summarizes:

> I attribute these failures to the circumstance that Mr. O'Shaughnessy never entered into a methodical study of Reptiles & Fishes; his knowledge of zoological literature remains very imperfect; he has not acquired the necessary

---

the basement of the Zoological Department' in December of 1865. BMSCM, 9 December 1865, C.10900.

[27] BMOP, C.11068.

[28] Report of 9 November 1870, BMOP.

[29] BMOP, 2 November 1870, 11328.

'Dreary Creeds' and 'Sham Wits' 31

amount of experience in applying descriptions to the objects before him; he has no judgement of his own with regard to specific or generic distinctions; he has difficulties in arranging a series of objects in systematic order; & he is unable to make a proper examination of structures of small size.[30]

The report from J.E. Gray, Keeper of the Department, was the most unforgiving. He writes:

I am sorry I cannot say anything in his favour. Very soon after he was transferred to the Zoological Department I discovered that the defect in his vision and the want of aptitude in manual dexterity rendered him very unfit for the occupation there, and I thought that I observed a want of desire to remedy so far as he was able these imperfections.[31]

Gray continued, 'the fact is that besides being incompetent for the duties of an Assistant, he is so unwilling to exert himself and so full of excuses for his idleness that he has entirely lost my confidence, and I consider him not only nearly useless in the Department, but a detriment to it, as he fills a place that might be occupied by an efficient Assistant'.[32]

At these harsh words the Trustees were forced to take notice. Winter Jones writes:

The strong opinion expressed by Professor Owen, Dr. Gray and Dr. Günther as to his incompetency after being more than seven years in the Departments of Natural History gives much weight to Dr. Gray's remark that Mr. O'Shaughnessy is a detriment rather than an Assistance. These results of the enquiry which Mr. Jones has felt it to be his duty to institute as to Mr. O'Shaughnessy's conduct and qualifications are of so grave a nature that Mr. Jones has no alternative but to submit them to the consideration of the Trustees.[33]

Although Gray pushed for O'Shaughnessy's termination, the Board decided instead to place him on probation, barring him from standard annual salary increases, until he showed improvement. This clemency is mostly likely due, once again, to the intervention of Lord Lytton. Having been informed of the incident by O'Shaughnessy, Lytton wrote to Sir Roderick Murchison, a member of the Board of Trustees, requesting his 'lenient consideration' of O'Shaughnessy's case.[34]

---

[30] BMOP, 4 November 1870, 11400. O'Shaughnessy's poor vision was the reason he was unable to study the smaller specimens – an obvious disadvantage in the profession.

[31] BMOP, 2 November 1870, 11280.

[32] Ibid.

[33] BMOP, 9 November 1870, C.11996.

[34] As per Lytton's suggestion, O'Shaughnessy was reprimanded rather than dismissed (8 November 1870, 11725). O'Shaughnessy was finally taken off probation in July of 1871 (C.12225), and was granted regular salary increases again beginning in February of 1872 (C.12339).

32   *Arthur O'Shaughnessy, A Pre-Raphaelite Poet in the British Museum*

The timing of the initial reprimand and the subsequent investigation and probation happened to coincide exactly with the publication of O'Shaughnessy's first volume of poetry, *An Epic of Women*. Quick to shift the blame away from himself, O'Shaughnessy speculated that the reason for the animosity towards him in the department was 'jealousy' over his literary success. He wrote to Lytton saying, 'I fear I have now lost that position – in the Museum – through one unfortunate circumstance & the envy & ill-will of those who had the power to harm me.'[35] He continues on to voice his suspicions:

> At the same time the ill-will against me has been manifested, & curiously enough on *the very day* of the publication of my book a report was got up concerning me of the most ill-natured and virulent kind signed by Dr. Gray ... Numbers of people have exclaimed at the spite & ungentlemanliness of the treatment & a clerk in the Secretary's Office told me "*it was all about my book*". I am told it is probably owing to some such jealousy.[36]

While O'Shaughnessy may have been jumping to conclusions regarding the impact his slim volume of poetry had on the Natural History Departments, from the reports issued it seems clear that he was correct on one point: Gray appears to have been unfairly targeting him. Although he did not work closely with O'Shaughnessy, as Günther and Owen did, Gray's reports were the harshest in their criticism of the poet. In a progress report written in February in 1871, Gray wrote that he had difficulty finding work that O'Shaughnessy was capable of doing, that O'Shaughnessy's manner was unpleasant, that he was an 'encumbrance' to the Department, and that he served as a 'bad example' to the other assistants. Given the extreme nature of this report, Richard Owen felt the need to refute it himself. He countered Gray's report, saying that all the work O'Shaughnessy had been given had been 'performed punctually & satisfactorily', that his manner was 'uniformly agreeable, gentlemanly, manifesting every disposition to office & to give satisfaction', that 'so far from having found him or thought of him as an encumbrance, the Superintendent would feel regret in losing the opportunity of turning to account qualifications which Mr. O'Shaughnessy possesses, on the completion of the proposed Museum of Natural History', and finally that 'the Superintendent has had no reason from observation of, or intercourse with, the Junior Assistants, to believe or suspect that Mr. O'Shaughnessy ... influences the better gifted Assistants as a "bad example"'.[37]

It is impossible to say why Gray took such a strong dislike to O'Shaughnessy. W.D. Paden posits that Gray, having gone out of his way to ensure O'Shaughnessy's appointment in order to keep the position from Bates, was embarrassed to find how unsuited O'Shaughnessy was for the job. Whatever the reason, this animosity from one of his superiors clearly contributed to O'Shaughnessy's feelings of exclusion

---

[35]   Paden, p. 17.

[36]   Ibid., p. 18.

[37]   BMOP, 9 February 1871, C.12082.

and isolation at the Museum, with the constant surveillance by his superiors labelling O'Shaughnessy as a delinquent within the disciplinarian system of the Museum. Once branded as such, it seems there was little O'Shaughnessy could do to improve his reputation. Thus, *The Dundee Courier* was able to print the 'anecdote' quoted above, characterizing O'Shaughnessy as clumsy, ignorant, and reckless, even after his death. Despite this reputation, by all accounts he was a competent taxonomist in his later career.[38] In the years that followed his initial reprimand, we can thus see O'Shaughnessy embracing the deviant identity that was thrust upon him by the Museum bureaucracy, allowing it to feed into his image of himself as outsider poet like his idol, Baudelaire. The negative environment of the Museum encouraged him to conceive of his poetic career as the opposite of his Museum career, fulfilling where the other was stultifying, inclusive where the other was exclusive.

The Lefebvrian theory of the divided spheres of life – in which the worker is 'atomized' between labour and leisure – helps to explicate O'Shaughnessy's feelings of alienation within the museum.[39] According to Lefebvre, work culture is an 'oppressive power' in the worker's life, a 'mysterious punishment' the worker must undergo in order to 'earn a living'.[40] We know that O'Shaughnessy only took the job at the museum in order to support himself – he had little interest in the work itself. As he began to conceive of himself as an outsider poet, temperamentally unsuited to the environment of the British Museum, he further conceived of the two as completely separate, and in fact opposed, within his life. We can see here Lefebvre's theory in practice: 'the worker craves a sharp break with his work, a compensation. He looks for this in leisure seen as entertainment or distraction. In this way leisure appears as the non-everyday in the everyday.'[41] Lefebvre insists that labour must result in pleasure, or else it loses its meaning.[42] Similarly, O'Shaughnessy embraced his poetry as his 'true' career – the one that brought him pleasure – and rejected his career at the Museum as tainted by the negativity generated by his unwilling place within the bureaucratic system. Lefebvre posits intellectual escapism to 'the marvellous', particularly in the man of '*belles-lettres*' of the nineteenth century, in reaction to the oppressive force of the labour market:

---

[38] In his *History of the Collections Contained in the Natural History Department of the British Museum* (London, 1904–1912), Albert Günther said: '[O'Shaughnessy] acquired considerable knowledge of the classes, and proved very efficient in his duties' (Appendix, p. 41). Following the reading of his final scientific paper, 'An account of a collection of lizards made by Mr. Buckley in Ecuador', at a meeting of the Zoological Society on 1 February 1881 (a mere two days after O'Shaughnessy's sudden death), his colleagues of the society honoured his memory by naming the new species identified in the paper *Enyalius O'Shaughnessyi*. *The Athenaeum*, 12 February 1881, p. 237.

[39] Henri Lefebvre, *Critique of Everyday Life*, trans. John Moore (London: Verso, 1991), vol. 1, p. 32.

[40] Ibid., p. 39.

[41] Ibid., p. 40.

[42] Ibid., p. 191.

34 *Arthur O'Shaughnessy, A Pre-Raphaelite Poet in the British Museum*

> Under the banner of the marvellous, nineteenth-century literature mounted a sustained attack on everyday life which has continued unabated up to the present day. The aim is to demote it, to discredit it. Although the duality between the marvellous and the everyday is just as painful as the duality between action and dream, the real and the ideal – and although it is an underlying reason for the failures and defeats which so many works deplore – nineteenth-century man seemed to ignore this, and continued obstinately to belittle real life, the world "as it is".[43]

It is here, in the false dichotomy between the marvellous and the everyday, that we can situate much of O'Shaughnessy's early poetry. He turned to an idealized world of art and nature as an escape from the prosaic world of the museum, but, as we will see, rather than being an escape from the everyday, O'Shaughnessy's marvellous was often only a reflection of his time at the museum.[44]

II.

Although O'Shaughnessy spent the entirety of his adult life working in the British Museum, his poetry has never been considered in the context of this career. I suggest that this is because of the boundaries he attempted to erect between the two in his own life, rigidly policing the divide between his art and his work. Thus, critics during his lifetime never mentioned his career at the Museum in relation to his poetry and later critics often merely repeated the assessments of those writing during O'Shaughnessy's life. Furthermore, during the majority of the twentieth century, critical work on the intersection of literature and science in the nineteenth century focused on literature *about* science – much attention was given, for instance, to Tennyson's *In Memoriam* or 'Lucretius'. This critical field was very much shaped by Lionel Stevenson, early in the twentieth century, and his model of discussing works of literature that dealt with scientific theory explicitly.[45] Until Gillian Beer's seminal *Darwin's Plots*, this was the principal way of critically discussing the influence of science upon literature – a one-way street of scientific concepts incorporated into fiction. Because O'Shaughnessy's poetry does not explicitly appear to be *about* science, it has never been considered from this angle, and no work has been done on O'Shaughnessy since Beer and

---

[43] Ibid., p. 105.

[44] As Lefebvre says, 'We cannot step beyond the everyday. The marvellous can only continue to exist in fiction and the illusions that people share. There is no escape. And yet we wish to have the illusion of escape as near to hand as possible. An illusion is not entirely illusory, but constituting a 'world' both apparent and real (the reality of appearances and the apparently real) quite different from the everyday world yet as open-ended and as closely dovetailed into the everyday as possible' (40).

[45] See, for example, Lionel Stevenson's 1932 *Darwin Among the Poets*, which helped shape the interdisciplinary field of science and poetry, or, later, U.C. Knoepflmacher and G.B. Tennyson's *Nature and the Victorian Imagination* (1977).

her contemporaries revitalized the field in the 1980s and 1990s. O'Shaughnessy's career at the Museum encompassed the whole of his adult life, and the practices and theories he was exposed to there greatly influenced his poetic works. Reading his poetry through the lens of his scientific career offers new insight into works that have often been dismissed as 'obscure' or 'unintelligible'. Within his poetry O'Shaughnessy tried to erect rigid boundaries between science and art, yet his two careers perpetually influenced one another.

> Yea, with their dreary creeds, their life's pale
> > bloom,
> > Their science, all of matter, that just plays
> > With the eternal slough as it decays,
> Left by some risen spirit near his tomb, –
> They seem indeed to dwell in lower gloom
> Of mansions, through whose every upper room,
> > Made wonderful with full and cloudless rays,
> > My winged soul passed in splendid former days.[46]

In this stanza from 'Nostalgie des Cieux' (1874) we can see the worlds of art and science contrasted, one soaring free, and the other imprisoned in a darkened tomb. The dark imagery of this poem, in which science is equated with a basement tomb, is quite literally reflected in O'Shaughnessy's professional life. The Natural History Departments operated in the basement of the Bloomsbury location of the British Museum, and all reports suggest that the spirit room – where O'Shaughnessy did most of his work – was a dark, damp, cold, and unpleasant work environment. Albert Günther once described it, saying, 'the conditions of light and temperature were most suitable for the preservation of the specimens, but less so for the comfort and health of the persons compelled to work in that locality.'[47] The physical reality of O'Shaughnessy's work environment might be suggested by 'Nostalgie', but it is the work itself that faces the most censure. In this poem, 'science' is defined by its materialism – he describes it as concerned only with the 'matter' of the earth, subtly drawing attention to the more important matters that science ignores. In defining science by its adherence to 'dreary creeds', O'Shaughnessy suggests a surprising overlap between science and religion, in which the central tenets are taken on faith and never challenged. He insinuates a lack of intellectual curiosity, predicated on the mundane work he personally performed at the Museum.

The restrictive nature of the Museum environment is also suggested in O'Shaughnessy's 1870 poem 'A Neglected Harp'.

> O hushed and shrouded room!
> O silence that enchains!

---

[46] O'Shaughnessy, *Music and Moonlight: Poems and Songs* (London: Chatto & Windus, 1874), pp. 156–7.

[47] William T. Stearn, *The Natural History Museum at South Kensington: A History of the British Museum (Natural History) 1753–1980* (London: Heinemann, 1981), p. 166.

O me – of many melodies
    The cold and voiceless tomb;
What sweet impassioned strains,
What fair unearthly things,
Sealed up in frozen cadences,
Are aching in my strings![48]

Here O'Shaughnessy self-consciously echoes one of the most famous poems of the Romantic period – Keats's 'Ode on a Grecian Urn', which also considers an art object in a museum setting.[49] He deliberately draws the comparison, asking 'What sweet impassioned strains, / What fair unearthly things', echoing the language Keats employs in the first stanza of the 'Ode' ('What leaf-fringed legends', 'What men or gods', 'What mad pursuit', 'What pipes').[50] The deliberate invocation of 'melodies' suggests Keats's poem and highlights the way O'Shaughnessy's poem reverses the optimism of Keats's work. 'Ode on a Grecian Urn' expresses the eternal potential of art, but O'Shaughnessy reinterprets the act of looking at a frozen art object (here, an unplayed harp, rather than a fully realized urn) to suggest the despair of unfulfilled potential. Keats insists, 'Heard melodies are sweet, but those unheard / Are sweeter'.[51] The melodies O'Shaughnessy writes of are also unheard, but the tone of his poem is drastically different. In Keats's poem, art freezes moments into eternal anticipation and pleasure; O'Shaughnessy, in contrast, depicts art frozen by outside forces. Thus, O'Shaughnessy's harp is not just frozen, it is 'up-pent', 'muffled' and 'prisoned'. In the museum setting the harp can only be looked at, never played. O'Shaughnessy rejects the impulse, represented by museums, to collect and catalogue, but never touch or enjoy.

Furthermore, the harp can be read as a reflection of O'Shaughnessy's own artistic impulses; thus, the outside force that stifles the potential for art is O'Shaughnessy's working life. As in many of his poems, the moment of art comes 'at eve' with the 'setting sun', i.e., at the end of the workday. In 'A Neglected Harp', the strings swell with unplayed music every evening, but the melody never comes. The fear at the heart of this poem is that unrealized art will 'languish'. Here we can see a reflection of the way O'Shaughnessy pitted his scientific and artistic careers against each other; the more the one thrives, the poem implies, the more the other fails. The poem suggests a Marxian critique of the swelling

---

[48] O'Shaughnessy, *An Epic of Women and Other Poems* (London: John Camden Hotten, 1870), p. 13.

[49] In his correspondence O'Shaughnessy discusses Keats with both Helen Snee and May Doyle. *A Pathetic Love Episode in a Poet's Life, being letters from Helen Snee to Arthur W.E. O'Shaughnessy. Also a letter from him containing a dissertation on Love*, ed. Clement King Shorter (London: printed for private circulation, 1916), p. 17; and a letter dated 24 October 1879 from May Doyle, Duke University Manuscript Collection, 6th 11:A Box 1, c.1.

[50] John Keats, 'Ode on a Grecian Urn', *The Poetical Works of John Keats*, a new edition (London: Edward Moxon, 1847), p. 211, lines 5–10.

[51] Ibid., line 11.

work 'day', which depletes leisure time by the endless demand for labour, and eventually precludes all other activities:

> It has been seen that to these questions capital replies: the working day contains the full 24 hours, with the deduction of the few hours of repose without which labour-power absolutely refuses its services again. Hence it is self-evident that the labourer is nothing else, his whole life through, than labour-power, that therefore all his disposable time is by nature and law labour-time, to be devoted to the self-expansion of capital. Time for education, for intellectual development, for the fulfilling of social functions and for social intercourse, for the free-play of his bodily and mental activity, even the rest time of Sunday (and that in a country of Sabbatarians!) – moonshine![52]

However, even as O'Shaughnessy depicts art and science as opposed, by alluding to Keats's 'Grecian Urn' O'Shaughnessy collapses the categories into one another. The fact that he adopts the language of high art poetry to discuss his scientific career implies that O'Shaughnessy is unable to fully separate the two – science is forever in conversation with the other aspects of O'Shaughnessy's life, including art and poetry.

'A Neglected Harp' anticipates the comparison of the Museum to a tomb that we saw in 'Nostalgie', quoted earlier. This recurring motif helps to explicate one of O'Shaughnessy's greatest complaints about the Museum and the work he performed there. As a professional taxonomist, O'Shaughnessy only ever saw his specimens as just that – specimens in jars. Unlike Bates and the other explorers who collected the plants and animals catalogued at the British Museum, O'Shaughnessy never saw his specimens in nature – or even alive.[53] This divide between collector and cataloguer was a source of great frustration for him, evinced in an early article published in *The Annals of Natural History*:

> The great disadvantage which one has to contend with in studying the lizards of the group *Anolis* is, that their brilliant and varied metallic colours, which are so important a characteristic of their species, fade, and even vanish completely, in the preserved states of the specimens. A person able to test the accuracy of the present determinations of species in this group by continual observation of the living or fresh animal, would of course be in a position to speak more confidently than one who has only specimens in spirits to judge from.[54]

---

[52]   Karl Marx, *Capital: A critical analysis of capitalist production*, translated from the 3rd German edition by Samuel Moore and Edward Aveling, and edited by Frederick Engels (London: Swan Sonnenschein, Lowrey, & Co., 1887), vol. 1, p. 249.

[53]   As Nicolaas Rupke tells us, the British Museum relied solely on amateur or self-funded naturalists for their specimen – as compared to a museum like the Jardins des Plantes in Paris, which employed eight 'Naturalists Voyageurs' at around this time. Richard Owen made use of the navy, civil servants, missionaries, Colonial Governors, settlers, and travellers as a source for specimens from abroad. Nicolaas A. Rupke, *Richard Owen: Victorian Naturalist* (New Haven and London: Yale University Press, 1994), p. 77.

[54]   Arthur O'Shaughnessy, 'Notes on Lizards of the Group Anolis', *Annals and Magazine of Natural History* 4, no. 3 (1869): 183–92 (p. 183).

38   *Arthur O'Shaughnessy, A Pre-Raphaelite Poet in the British Museum*

O'Shaughnessy's poor health, poor vision, and lack of independent means prevented him from travelling the world and seeing the animals he studied in their natural habitats. Instead, he spent his days in the small, dark spirit room in the basement of the British Museum. There, he constantly battled with badly preserved specimens, rotting before his very eyes. For O'Shaughnessy these conditions only heightened the sepulchral feel of the Museum. It is no wonder he felt he was just 'playing with the slough' of the earth, dead matter he contrasted sharply with the vitality of the world of art.

O'Shaughnessy's dissatisfaction with his daily life at the Museum manifests in his poetry as a recurring fantasy of escape. Surprising, however, is the form these fantasies take. He dreams of an escape from his life as a naturalist *to* nature – but nature freed from the demands of scientific enquiry. His poetry is haunted by the trope of the Museum as a mere charnel house for the corpses of the natural world, an image which is continually contrasted with 'real' nature, which for O'Shaughnessy is equated with the freedom of art. In his poetry Art embraces nature in its own habitat, celebrating the profusion of life; Science, on the other hand, seals it up in jars and tucks it away in dark corners. At the Museum nature is not only dead but completely removed from the context that makes it beautiful.

The professionalization of science during this period made the work of a naturalist into a career, bringing with it all the minor annoyances of an office environment: the disagreements with colleagues, the expectations of superiors, the paperwork to be filed, the people to be appeased.[55] We can see this all reflected in the myriad reports filed regarding the incident with the box of matches. Furthermore, it was the specialization of science that led to the divide between the collectors and cataloguers that O'Shaughnessy so lamented, which meant that while some men experienced nature, others merely catalogued it. Thus, Bates could write of his explorations in Brazil:

> The whirring of cicadas; the shrill stridulation of a vast number and variety of field crickets and grasshoppers – each species sounding its peculiar note; the plaintive hooting of tree frogs, all blended together in one continuous ringing sound – the audible expression of the teeming profusion of Nature.[56]

Bates experienced a vital, living nature, teeming with sound and motion, whereas O'Shaughnessy was left with the silent, decaying forms sent over thousands of miles to London; hence, the emphatic silence that pervades 'A Neglected Harp'. Richard Owen, himself never a field naturalist, categorized this divide, saying:

---

[55]   As Marx says of the nineteenth century: 'The bourgeoisie has stripped of its halo every occupation hitherto honoured and looked up to with reverent awe. It has converted the physician, the lawyer, the priest, the poet, the man of science, into its paid wage labourers.' *Manifesto of the Communist Party*, from the English edition of 1888, ed. Friedrich Engels, p. 15.

[56]   Bates, vol. 1, p. 6.

> The naturalist of one order goes forth to the far wilderness, it may be, or the trackless forest, the denizens of which he finds in the full exercise of their faculties, unchecked by the encroachment and unmodified by the influence of civilized man ... The museum-naturalist has a narrower walk of research, but his more finished labours, again, are essentially ancillary to the other's rough draughts from living Nature. Calm and sedentary, in the close atmosphere of the cabinet he scrutinizes the dried and stuffed skins of birds and beasts, and the analogous exuviae of other animals.[57]

While Owen might have been content with the 'more finished labours' of the museum naturalist, O'Shaughnessy, whose work ranked so much lower than that of Owen's, was not satisfied with the narrow walk of life that left him with the exuviae of animals. In 1880, Ray Lankester dismissed the work of taxonomists, saying, 'It is a common mistake to consider all knowledge of raw products, of living objects or other natural objects, as necessarily "science". The truth is, that a man may have great knowledge of these things as so many facts, and yet be devoid of "science".'[58] For Lankester, 'the mere inspection and cataloguing of natural objects' could not be mistaken for that 'truly scientific attitude which consists in assigning the facts which come under our observation to their causes'.[59] O'Shaughnessy seemed to agree with this divide between the work he performed at the Museum and useful scientific pursuits. Thus, it is not science as knowledge or even a way of viewing the world that he rejects in these poems, but the science he performed at the museum, the set of practices that encompassed the science of taxonomy.

O'Shaughnessy's desire to experience nature as the field naturalists did helps to explain why he turned to *nature* when displeased with Museum *naturalism*. O'Shaughnessy primarily worked on specimens from the tropics, and the majority of his escapist poems are set in tropical environs. Poems like 'Palm Flowers', 'Song of Palms', and 'Azure Islands' all employ tropical settings as a foil for the British Museum, the profusion of colour and life a contrast to the gray, dead world of the Museum. 1870's 'Palm Flowers' indulges a fantasy of escape from the Museum, with the final stanza enacting a moment of 'awakening' from the dream of the poem:

> O that land where the suns linger
>   And the passion-flowers grow
> Is the land for me the Singer:
>   There I made me, years ago,
>
> Many a golden habitation,
>   Full of things most fair to see;

---

[57] Quoted by Rupke, p. 81.

[58] E. Ray Lankester, *Degeneration: A Chapter in Darwinism* (London: Macmillan and Co., 1880), p. 5.

[59] Ibid., p. 2.

40   *Arthur O'Shaughnessy, A Pre-Raphaelite Poet in the British Museum*

And the fond imagination
  Of my heart dwells there with me.

Now, farewell, all shameful sorrow!
  Farewell, troublous world of men!
I shall meet you on some morrow,
  But forget you quite till then.[60]

In these final lines we learn that the exotic landscape and the freedom offered by the poem are nothing more than the fantasy of a man who is unhappy in his daily life, sustained only by the dream of nature. A similar 'awakening' is enacted in 'Azure Islands' (1874). The final stanza of this poem is set off by three asterisks, representing the divide between dreams and real life, which brings the fantasy of an escape to nature to an abrupt halt.[61]

But I, whose freed soul voyages far,
  Do pass my working day
'Mid hardened lives, where no dreams are,
  In straitened speech and way:
Therefore that bark, O shipmen, stay not,
  But let it sail securely,
For – ceased *that* voyage – I, who may not,
  Should die or go mad surely.[62]

The daydream of nature, contrasted with the naturalism performed in the urban space of the Museum, enacts a discursive protest against the objectivity and specificity demanded in scientific writing, as he complains of 'straitened speech and way'. A first-hand and subjective experience of nature is privileged in 'Azure Islands': 'my soul dwells there ecstatic, / Knowing each palm tree and each flower, / Gorgeous and enigmatic'.[63] The knowledge described in this stanza is not the kind

---

[60]   *Epic*, p. 77.

[61]   O'Shaughnessy's correspondence evinces a deep concern with the *appearance* of his volumes (from illustrations to bindings) and thus we are not surprised to find that he was concerned with the shape of the words on the page, and made use of asterisks in this way. 'A Neglected Harp' also has a divide between the bulk of the poem and the final stanza, there with the asterisks arranged into a triangle formation. In 'Azure Islands' the asterisks clearly represent the line between dream and reality, while in 'A Neglected Harp' they separate the voice of the harp from the external narration, as a faceless narrator hears the cry of the harp (the speaker for the majority of the poem).

[62]   *Music and Moonlight*, p. 77. Interestingly, in his 1923 collection of O'Shaughnessy's poems, William Alexander Percy abridged 'Azure Islands' to just the first seven stanzas (*Poems of Arthur O'Shaughnessy* [New Haven: Yale University Press, 1923]). By leaving out the final stanza, Percy removes the entire subject matter of the poem (dreams vs. reality), leaving stanzas that Edmund Gosse characterized as 'being quite unworthy of the poet in every way'. *The Academy*, 4 April 1874, p. 360.

[63]   *Music and Moonlight*, p. 74.

'Dreary Creeds' and 'Sham Wits' 41

gained at the Museum, studying dead specimens, but rather a sensuous experience that maintains the enigmatic quality of the natural world.

Although Gillian Beer has focused on the fictive qualities of Darwin's prose, she acknowledges the conflict between scientific and metaphorical language, saying of Darwin's revisions to subsequent editions of *Origin*: 'Such labour came hard to him. The exuberantly metaphorical drive of the language of *The Origin* was proper to its topic. The need to establish more parsimonious definitions and to combat misunderstandings may help to account for that dimming of his imaginative powers which he so deeply regretted.'[64] As Paul Ricoeur has suggested, scientific language is defined by the elimination of ambiguity in language – an increased specificity of signs and symbols in order to eliminate the possibility of misinterpretation.[65] In contrast, Ricoeur suggests, poetic language works to preserve ambiguity, to allow a multiplicity of meanings and interpretations.[66] Turning to his scientific writings, we can see that O'Shaughnessy's work at the museum was driven by specificity and precise, objective descriptions. In an 1873 article, O'Shaughnessy writes:

> Head broad posteriorly; supranasals two pairs, oblique, unsymmetrical; internasal wide, transverse; fronto-nasals large and broadly in contact along the median line. Scales of back keeled, moderate, in forty-eight transverse series from occiput to tail, thirty-two between axil and groin; in fourteen longitudinal series; ventral plates in twelve longitudinal series. Limbs short, not meeting. Tail once and a half the length of head and body.[67]

In considering the poetry written by scientific practitioners, Erika Behrisch has suggested: 'While scientific discourse called for detailed descriptions of, and unquenchable curiosity for, exploring the surrounding world, it elided the individuality of the observer, as well as the emotion inherent in the experience of discovery, in favour of a series of "objective" observations.'[68] Objectivity, George Levine has asserted, is a 'nonhuman condition'.[69]

In 'Nostalgie des Cieux', we can see an attack on the taxonomic specificity demanded of O'Shaughnessy at the Museum and reflected in the passage quoted above.

---

[64] Gillian Beer, *Darwin's Plots: Evolutionary Narrative in Darwin, George Eliot and Nineteenth-Century Fiction* (Cambridge: Cambridge University Press, 2000), p. 38.

[65] Paul Ricoeur, 'The Power of Speech: Science and Poetry', *Philosophy Today* 29, no. 1 (Spring 1985): 59–70 (p. 63).

[66] Ibid., p. 67.

[67] O'Shaughnessy, 'Herpetological Notes', *Annals and Magazine of Natural History* 4, no. 12 (1873): 44–8 (p. 47).

[68] Erika Behrisch, '"Far as the eye can reach"; Scientific Exploration and Explorers' Poetry in the Arctic, 1832–53', *Victorian Poetry* 41, no. 1 (Spring 2003): 73–91 (p. 73).

[69] George Levine, *One Culture: Essays in Science and Literature* (Madison: University of Wisconsin Press, 1987), p. 12.

42   *Arthur O'Shaughnessy, A Pre-Raphaelite Poet in the British Museum*

> I hate the heavy sham of wits, that find,
>   Examine, lose, and refind that sole grain
>   Of rarest gold-dust on a golden plain,
> Their science – leaving thousand-fold behind
> Mysterious tracts of knowledge, that my mind
> Scans with some inner vision not yet blind.[70]

This stanza can be read as an attack on the work performed at the Museum, which pretends that the grain is the 'rarest gold-dust' even though it comes from a 'golden plain'. We can further read a critique of the process of species classification as the scientists in the poem 'find, lose and refind' the same 'rare' grain. O'Shaughnessy suggests that taxonomists are so focused on tiny particulars that they miss the big picture – they can't see the gold plain for the sole grain. As in 'Azure Islands', here 'mysterious tracts of knowledge' are privileged over the knowledge gained at the Museum, their paradoxical unknowability making them all the more desirable.

The taxonomic identification O'Shaughnessy performed at the Museum decentred the human experience of nature by reducing it to nothing but recorded data, a series of measurements. In his poetry, then, O'Shaughnessy rejects the museum environment in favour of nature itself in order to reposition himself and his own sensual, visceral reactions to nature at the fore. These verses can be read as an attempt to re-imbue the natural world with a sense of enchantment that is lost in the recitation of bare facts. Unlike the mathematical, objective scientific writing he produced at the museum, O'Shaughnessy's poetry allows him to detail both the *experience* of nature, and his own place within it.

In 'Lynmouth' (1881), O'Shaughnessy writes:

> The green exuberant branches overhead
>   Sport with the golden magic of the sun,
> Here quite shut out, here like rare jewels shed
>   To fright the glittering lizards as they run.[71]

This is one of the few appearances of lizards within O'Shaughnessy's verse, and we can immediately see the sensual difference between the description of nature found here and those found in his scientific writing. There he reports that a new species of Skink has 'fifty-two scales in a longitudinal dorsal series, fifty in a ventral one; twenty-two scales in a series round the body; those on the back larger. Number of scales between fore and hind limbs about thirty-four'.[72] The delight O'Shaughnessy obviously found in nature has no place within his taxonomic writing. His scientific papers hint at his desire to be able to express himself more artistically – as in the article quoted earlier, in which he laments the 'brilliant colours' that have faded on his specimens. Or in another description of the lizard

---

[70]   *Music and Moonlight*, p. 156.

[71]   O'Shaughnessy, *Songs of a Worker* (London: Chatto & Windus, 1881), p. 59.

[72]   'Descriptions of a new species of Skink', *Annals and Magazine of Natural History* 4, no. 14 (1874), p. 35.

anolis, in which he notes: 'Colours prettily variegated. Ground-colour above apparently a lustrous brown, with blue and violet reflections; a series of glittering spots like arrow-heads pointing forwards along median line of back.'[73] This is the most expressive passage to be found in O'Shaughnessy's scientific writing, and we can sense the restrained longing to indulge his poetic impulse, as he chooses words like 'lustrous' and 'glittering' to describe the lizard's colouring, anticipating the language employed in 'Lynmouth'. But it is in his poetry, not his scientific work, that O'Shaughnessy reasserts his subjectivity, in order to detail the sensuous experience to be found in nature.

In his nature poetry, O'Shaughnessy generates life into his dead specimens by reimagining the natural worlds from which they came, but he also uses poetry to look beyond the physical reality of the world, present in his taxonomic work, to the greater metaphysical mysteries raised by science of the day. George Levine has suggested that in the nineteenth century, scientific imagination – particularly Darwin's – was seen as 'entirely corporeal', and therefore opposed to the 'mythic and moral'.[74] But implicit in this criticism (made by John Ruskin, among others) is the idea that there *should* be a space in which to discuss the moral and mythic qualities of science – a space O'Shaughnessy found in his poetry. Levine denies the idea that Darwin's corporeal imagination was limiting, suggesting that the ordinary was transformed into the extraordinary within Darwin's theory: 'The Darwinian gaze at the minute and the trivial – the little stones, the mud – transforms into the massive, the incomprehensibly vast and uncontainable. The ordinary becomes extraordinary even as Darwin is busy attempting to make the extraordinary comprehensible in terms of the working of ordinary nature.'[75] This is the grand, fictive quality of Darwin's theoretic writing to which Beer often refers. In contrast, O'Shaughnessy was mired in nothing but the minutiae of the world – it is here that we find justification for his complaint in 'Nostalgie' about 'sham wits'. In order to grapple with the 'incomprehensibly vast and uncontainable' ideas generated by science of the period, O'Shaughnessy turned to poetry, a space in which he could consider both the moral and mythic implications of science.

III.

As early as 1864, only a year after he joined the Natural History Departments, we can see O'Shaughnessy turning to poetry to grapple with the 'bigger picture' of new science, in poems such as the unpublished 'I mused upon the universe of things'.[76] In this lengthy poem, O'Shaughnessy self-consciously makes use of the

---

[73] 'List and Revision of the species of Anolidae in the British Museum Collection', *Annals and Magazine of Natural History* 4, no. 15 (1875): 270–81 (p. 280).

[74] Levine, 'Reflections on Darwin and Darwinizing', *Special Issue: Darwin and the Evolution of Victorian Studies* 51, no. 2 (Winter 2009): 223–45 (p. 236).

[75] Ibid., p. 241.

[76] Queen's University, Belfast, O'Shaughnessy Manuscript Collection, MS 8/10, pp. 34–48.

terms and ideas of physics, rendering this work explicitly a 'science poem'. Thus, he writes of 'a pencil of conveying streams of Light' and 'quivering nebula'. The poem contains stanzas that overtly deal with evolutionary theory (still a topic of fresh debate, five years after the publication of *Origin*):

> For where the Lamp of Science did assist,
> Its Earthly view; throughout the meaner world,
> In one infinite series closely curled,
> Life within life, a starting point displayed,
> Which Thought the step to mightier musings made.
>
> And from those first and lowest grades distinct,
> Up the great Ladder of Life, so subtly linked.[77]

And in the next stanza he speaks of mortals' rise from 'worms that crawl'. Although not specifically Darwinian, these lines address origins (the 'starting point' of life) and the 'Ladder of Life', an image commonly associated with evolution. This poem, then, self-consciously adopts the language and imagery of science in order to ponder the 'giant matter' of the universe. It muses whether science or imagination is the best way to conceive of the 'universe of things' – of the whole of the cosmos, including thought, consciousness, and morality. This was a much-debated issue during the period, as scientists wondered when, in the evolution of humanity, the soul became manifest.

> Upon that lofty, ever dauntless plight
> Of Fancy, fresh and buoyant, when the might
> Of slow and plodding Reason sinks and falls
> Exhausted back to Earth: – still Fancy calls,
> From far and distant heights, and seeks to lead
> The halting steps of Reason's cautious Steed;
> But Reason doubts its guide, and fears to mount
> The scaling-rope, whose steps it cannot count.[78]

In this stanza O'Shaughnessy appears to give primacy to 'Fancy' over 'Reason' and, perhaps, literature over science. However, the prominent place of science and reason in the world of men is never truly questioned within the poem. In the end, the conclusion O'Shaughnessy appears to come to is that the best way to conceive of the bigger picture of the world is through a combination of science and imagination, the two working in tandem to reach beyond where either would have stretched alone.

This poem, while very compelling, is muddled by the attempted scope of the work – O'Shaughnessy was just 20 when he wrote it – and, as it was never published, it is not clear how 'finished' it is. But within it, we can see O'Shaughnessy

---

[77] Ibid., pp. 36–7.

[78] Ibid., p. 47.

attempting to theorize science beyond the specific taxonomic work he performed at the Museum, and even beyond the biological work performed in the Zoological Department, adopting the language of physics to try and conceptualize the whole of the universe. While this work is more explicitly 'science poetry' than anything he actually published, we can see a similar attempt to theorize scientific discoveries of the time in several of his other works.

One of the biggest changes to nineteenth-century science came with the publication of Darwin's *On the Origin of Species* in 1859, which brought public focus to the potentially negative aspects of the natural world and man's place within it, including ideas of degeneration, atavism, and extinction. Even in poems that have not been considered 'scientific' in content, we can see O'Shaughnessy struggling with the changing understanding of the natural world at this time. 'Bisclavaret' (1870) can be seen to raise the concerns of the potential moral and social implications of the new reality revealed by Darwin's work.

In 1863 T.H. Huxley wrote:

> Ancient traditions, when tested by the severe processes of modern investigation, commonly enough fade away into mere dreams: but it is singular how often the dream turns out to have been a half-waking one, presaging a reality ... though the quaint forms of Centaurs and Satyrs have an existence only in the realms of art, creatures approaching man more nearly than they in essential structure, and yet as thoroughly brutal as the goat's or horse's half of the mythical compound, are now not only known, but notorious.[79]

Here, science is mythologized and myth is also given credence. These man-like beasts are creatures that truly existed, and perhaps, given the potential for degeneration raised by Darwinian theory, could exist again. In ancient myth the hybrid creatures – part human, part animal – were degraded and bestial, driven only by a desire for drink or sex. In these stories, satyrs, centaurs, and even the sirens, represent man's most animalistic nature. Apparent in both scientific and literary works of the later nineteenth century is the fear that the highly evolved European might be capable of slipping backwards on the evolutionary ladder, descending to the level of the 'savage' or even the animal.[80] Thus, Lankester writes:

> Does the reason of the average man of civilised Europe stand out clearly as an evidence of progress when compared with that of the men of bygone ages? Are all the inventions and figments of human superstition and folly, the self-inflicted torturing of mind, the reiterated substitution of wrong for right, and of falsehood for truth, which disfigure our modern civilisation – are these evidences of progress? In such respects we have at least reason to fear that we may be degenerate.[81]

---

[79] Thomas Henry Huxley, *Evidence as to Man's Place in Nature* (New York: D. Appleton and Co., 1873), p. 1.

[80] See, for example, Cesare Lombroso's *The Criminal Man* (1876) or *Crime, Its Causes and Remedies* (1899) and Max Nordau's *Degeneration* (1892).

[81] Lankester, p. 60.

This fear of degeneration appears not only in scientific debates of the time, but throughout popular literature, as writers tried to come to terms with the troubling ideas raised by evolutionary science. 'Bisclavaret', included in O'Shaughnessy's first volume of 1870, while not overtly a 'science poem', evinces a philosophical concern for the social and moral impact of new evolutionary theory.

The title 'Bisclavaret' is taken from Marie de France's twelfth-century *lai* of the same name, in which she relates the story of the Breton werewolf.[82] The obscurity of this source is in part responsible for the fact that, although almost universally considered to be one of O'Shaughnessy's best poems, 'Bisclavaret' is also seen as his most confusing.[83] At the time of its publication Dante Gabriel Rossetti complained of its 'obscurity' and 50 years later the conclusion was still that it 'baffled analysis'.[84] In responding to this work, critics never mentioned O'Shaughnessy's career at the Museum. In fact, this poem has never before been considered from a scientific standpoint. However, the obscurity of 'Bisclavaret' clears when viewed alongside Darwinian theory.

In fact, 'Bisclavaret' is an early example of a number of late Victorian works that address the duality inherent in man's animal nature. Like R.L. Stevenson's *Strange Case of Dr Jekyll and Mr. Hyde* (1886), Arthur Machen's *The Great God Pan* (1890), or H.G. Wells' *The Island of Dr Moreau* (1896), 'Bisclavaret' depicts man's inner animal released and run rampant. O'Shaughnessy's career as a naturalist helped him to anticipate these works of the 1880s and 1890s; his close ties to evolutionary theory brought him to the *fin-de-siècle* ideas of degeneration and decay as early as 1870. The duality apparent in these later works is, of course, inherent to the idea of the werewolf – of man turned into beast. However, one of

---

[82] The medieval story is usually spelled 'Bisclavret'. The spelling in O'Shaughnessy's epigraph from the *lai* is 'Bisclaveret' and for the title of the poem O'Shaughnessy has changed that first 'e' to an 'a' for the name to read 'Bisclavaret'. This is perhaps a quirk of translation, to aid English readers in pronunciation. However, this inconsistency means that the poem is spelled differently in nearly all reviews of *An Epic*.

[83] In their obituaries for O'Shaughnessy, both *The Academy* and the *Athenaeum* include 'Bisclavaret' among his best poems. L.C. Moulton and Alexander Percy, editors of the two short collections of O'Shaughnessy's work in existence, also both include 'Bisclavaret' among their selections, with Moulton saying that there was 'no more original' poem among O'Shaughnessy's work. *The Academy* (5 February 1881), *Athenaeum* (5 February 1881), and Louise Chandler Moulton, *Arthur O'Shaughnessy: His Life and Work with Selections from His Poems* (Cambridge and Chicago: Stone & Kimball, 1894), p. 26.

[84] In a letter dated 15 October 1870, Rossetti writes, 'I must confess – that after 2 careful readings it still remains obscure to me, much as it impresses the mind and stimulates conjecture.' Despite this, he praises the poem's 'beauty & apparent purpose', concluding that it 'dominates the whole series as regards sustained dignity of execution'. *Correspondence of Dante Gabriel Rossetti*, vol. 4, ed. William E. Fredeman (Cambridge and Rochester: D.S. Brewer, 2004), p. 543. In 1923, Alexander Percy wrote, '"Bisclavaret," usually regarded as standing apart from the rest of his work, baffles analysis.' William Alexander Percy, ed., *Poems of Arthur O'Shaughnessy* (New Haven: Yale University Press, 1923), p. 5.

the reasons that critics and commentators found Bisclavaret so baffling is that the title and epigraph – both taken from Marie – provide the only explicit reference to the concept of the werewolf.[85] A reader had to know the origin of the title and the subject matter of the medieval story in order to guess that O'Shaughnessy's poem dealt with the werewolf. Thus, the reviewer for the *Athenaeum* noted, 'Many readers of "Bisclaverit" [sic] will reach the last line without discovering that Mr. O'Shaughnessy has been alluding to the werewolf.'[86] While the medieval *lai* was a tale of a man cursed to bear the form of a beast, O'Shaughnessy's poem is far more abstract. There are references throughout to 'cloven footsteps', 'high-antlered crests', 'fierce manes', and 'unmeasured wings', but there is no specific mention of the werewolf – a creature that is, of course, not identified by any of the animal attributes just listed.[87] Rather, the poem is dominated by animalism in general, and the uncontrollable quality of the natural world.

The contrast between the source material and O'Shaughnessy's work helps to highlight the Darwinian influence on O'Shaughnessy's poem. The medieval story tells of a noble knight who happens to be cursed with lycanthropy. While this could make him into a monster, the affliction doesn't alter his integrity. Marie admits that 'a werewolf is a ferocious beast which, when possessed by this madness, devours men, causes great damage and dwells in vast forests', but that doesn't change the fact that '[Bisclavret] was a good and handsome knight who conducted himself nobly'.[88] Rather, the villain of the story is Bisclavaret's untrustworthy wife, who betrays the confidence of his curse, and traps him in his wolf form. The knight's humanity shows through his animal shape, however, and he is taken into the court of the King as a favourite pet. There he is able to expose the treachery of his wife and regain his human form.

The moral of the medieval story is that outward appearance bears no relation to inner nature – although Bisclavaret looks like an animal, he is still the same honourable man. However, that message can take on a new meaning in a Darwinian context. O'Shaughnessy twists the moral to assert that no matter how civilized man looks on the outside, it doesn't alter his true inner nature – which is that of an animal. In this Darwinian context, rather than a stark duality, man and beast blend into one. O'Shaughnessy dispenses with the plot and characters of Marie's *lai* in order to focus on Bisclavaret's state of mind.[89] There is no

---

[85] The epigraph is taken from the opening lines of Marie de France's *lai*, which translate as: 'Bisclavret is its name in Breton, while the Normans call it Garwall. In days gone by one could hear it tell, and indeed it often used to happen, that many men turned into werewolves and went to live in the woods.' Translation by Glyn S. Burgess and Keith Busby (London: Penguin Books, 2003).

[86] *The Athenaeum* (5 November 1870): 585.

[87] Thus, *The Academy* notes that 'the speaker, then, is a Werewolf, but even that a Werewolf of the poet's own invention ... not, as one gathers, in the common likeness of wolves'. *The Academy* (15 November 1870): 32–3 (p. 33).

[88] Marie de France, p. 68.

[89] Thus, Percy notes of 'Bisclavaret', 'Though a ballad in form, it tells no story' (p. 5). O'Shaughnessy does employ the standard 'ballad metre' of quatrains of octosyllable verse.

explicit curse in O'Shaughnessy's version, either. Rather, uncontrollable nature calls to all civilized men and women, luring them to 'slough' off their humanity and join in the animalistic fray. These changes transform the medieval fairy tale into a modern parable, exposing the potential implications of a post-Darwinian world. If evolutionary theory sparked the fear of physical degeneration into more primitive and animalistic types during the nineteenth century, Darwin's theory of natural selection fostered the fear of *moral* degeneration. The fear was that the revelation of Darwin's theory would impact man's behaviour, and this was enforced by philosophers like Herbert Spencer, who sought to apply the laws of nature to the interactions of men in his promotion of laissez-faire economics. It is this fear that we can see behind O'Shaughnessy's tale of the werewolf. There is no denying that the theory of natural selection, centred as it is on the struggle for existence, is disturbing to an image of natural harmony in the world. As Gillian Beer puts it, Darwinism 'is a daemonic theory, emphasizing drive, deviance, and the will to power. It is not a theory which readily accords with ideas of measure or reason'.[90] Furthermore, In Darwin's theory of natural selection, the struggle for existence is most intense between members of the same species – between a man and his neighbour.[91]

Even Darwin had trouble fully accepting the implications of his theory, and he tried throughout his career to maintain a positive view of natural selection. Thus, he ended *Origins* on an optimistic note, insisting, 'When we reflect on this struggle, we may console ourselves with the full belief, that the war of nature is not incessant, that no fear is felt, that death is generally prompt, and that the vigorous, the healthy, and the happy survive and multiply.'[92] Darwin acknowledges that humanity needs consolation in the face of his theory, but all he can offer are platitudes that are clearly false. The truth is, it is difficult to see the positive in a theory that embraces 'the survival of the fittest'. This phrase was, of course, not coined by Darwin himself, but rather by Herbert Spencer.[93] However, Darwin could

---

However, this standardized form is, as Percy noted, undermined by the non-standard narrative, almost a stream-of-consciousness, full of 'descriptions accurate and unreal' (p. 5).

[90]   Beer, p. 124.

[91]   Thus, Darwin points out: 'As in each fully stocked country natural selection necessarily acts by the selected form having some advantage in the struggle for life over other forms, there will be a constant tendency in the improved descendants of any one species to supplant and exterminate in each stage of descent their predecessors and their original progenitor. For it should be remembered that the competition will generally be most severe between those forms which are most nearly related to each other in habits, constitution, and structure.' Charles Darwin, *On the Origin of the Species by Means of Natural Selection: Or the Preservation of Favoured Races in the Struggle for Life*, 6th ed. (London: John Murray, 1872), p. 93.

[92]   Ibid., p. 72.

[93]   In *Principles of Biology*, vol. 1 (London: Williams and Norgate, 1864). 'This survival of the fittest, which I have sought to express in mechanical terms, is that which Mr. Darwin has called "natural selection", or the preservation of favoured races in the struggle for life' (p. 445).

'Dreary Creeds' and 'Sham Wits' 49

not help but admit the appropriateness of Spencer's turn of phrase, and 'survival of the fittest' was incorporated into the fifth edition of the *Origins*, published in 1869. Furthermore, in *Descent of Man* (1871), Darwin had to agree with Spencer that humanity faced biological decline, because charitable projects cushioned the 'unfit' from the impact of natural selection. A government that helps to care for the sick and the mentally unwell allows them to survive and procreate. This was counter to everything in Darwin's theory and was seized upon by those advocating a much harsher treatment of the 'unfit' in society. Thus, Spencer could write, in 1864, 'That the average vigour of any race would be diminished, did the diseased and feeble habitually survive and propagate; and that the destruction of such, through failure to fulfil the conditions to life, thus keeps up the average fitness to the conditions to life; are almost self-evident truths.'[94] While men like Spencer insisted that natural law could serve as a strong moral basis for human society, helping guide us to a future perfection, others were appalled at how it seemed to encourage men to turn on each other. To behave, as it were, like animals.[95] It is the anxiety that men will become 'beastly' and 'bestial' that O'Shaughnessy expresses in 'Bisclavaret'.

This poem explores a nightmarish world in which the veneer of civilization is peeled away from humanity, revealing the horror that lies beneath. It begins in a domestic setting, with a man seated beside a fire. The use of the word 'hearth' to describe the fire makes the strong connection to 'home'. Nature rages outside his door, in the form of a violent storm, yet there is an illusion of safety within that civilized fire. However, this illusion is almost immediately shattered.

> And sitting by the low hearth fires,
> I start and shiver fearfully;
> For thoughts all strange and new desires
> Of distant things take hold on me.[96]

In this poem the comfort of a cosy fire has been lost, because nature is no longer something that can be locked out of doors. The theory of evolution made man and nature one and the same, and thus there are no longer any doors to secure against the wild, since it exists within the very heart of men. Violent and threatening nature doesn't attack the man; rather it awakens something within him, and draws him out of civilization into the wilds of nature.

As previously mentioned, the medieval *lai* of the same name is a rather straightforward tale of cursed metamorphosis. However, in a post-Darwinian world, metamorphosis takes on a whole new meaning. John Holmes has suggested, '[in] Darwinian metamorphoses ... the human becomes something he or she already is:

---

[94] Spencer, *Principles of Biology*, vol. 1, p. 445.

[95] Cf. Mary Midgley's *Beast and Man: The Roots of Human Nature* (1978). Midgley provides a fascinating overview of humanity's conception of animal nature as a foil for our own 'higher' civility.

[96] *Epic*, p. 56.

50   *Arthur O'Shaughnessy, A Pre-Raphaelite Poet in the British Museum*

an animal.'[97] Rather than a true transformation into something new, these stories are of discovering one's animal nature, which was always lying just below the surface. As such, there is no actual metamorphosis or physical transformation in 'Bisclavaret'; this is probably one of the reasons O'Shaughnessy's friends found the poem so difficult to unravel. Instead of a man transforming into a beast, we see a man embracing the beast he already is. As shown by Social Darwinism and the later eugenics programmes that stemmed from it, men can be monsters without changing their forms. It is a rather obvious leap to read a poem about a werewolf as being about the potential for degeneration, but I would argue that more specifically, 'Bisclavaret' is about the potential for moral degeneration in the face of evolutionary theory. Critics of the resurgence of interest in the medieval period in the nineteenth century have suggested that it was a reaction to the Spencerian laissez-faire economics being practised at the time, a return to chivalry to combat the survival of the fittest.[98] In this we can find justification for O'Shaughnessy's choice of an obscure medieval tale in which to couch his concerns for modern society.

The potential for moral degeneration is reinforced by the illustration accompanying the poem. J.T. Nettleship provided illustrations for several poems in O'Shaughnessy's first volume of poetry, and his simple and yet disturbing line drawings call to mind Aubrey Beardsley's work 20 years later. Nettleship illustrated this poem with a swarm of naked bodies. Looking closer, one notes that though the forms are clearly human, the way the bodies are layered upon each other means no eyes or other humanizing features are visible. Instead, there are just endless rows of open, devouring mouths. It is this quality, humanity reduced to its basest needs and desires, that O'Shaughnessy captures in his haunting poem.

'Bisclavaret' explores the consequences of hedonistic self-indulgence. Although the poem shows man reduced to the state of a beast, it also shows how seductive the animal state can be. There is a sense of liberty inherent in the rejection of civilization. Although I argue that we can trace the inspiration for this poem back to the evolutionary ethics of Herbert Spencer, the struggle for the survival of the fittest is not represented here. O'Shaughnessy originally conceived of a more violent form of animalism, writing in an early draft of the poem, 'he shall delight to hurt & maim / the flesh with many a scar most foul'.[99] However, these lines were removed in favour of emphasizing a cruel sexuality. As mankind's most basic desires, lust and hunger are brought to the forefront in this poem:

> The wild thirsts and lusts they know,
> The sharp joys sating them at length,
> The new and greater lusts that grow.[100]

---

[97]   John Holmes, *Darwin's Bards: British and American Poetry in the Age of Evolution* (Edinburgh: Edinburgh University Press, 2009), p. 218.

[98]   See Alice Chandler's *A Dream of Order* (1971) or Mark Girouard's *The Return to Camelot* (1981).

[99]   Queen's University, Belfast, MS 8/3, p. 167. Dated approximately 1867.

[100]   *Epic*, p. 59.

The poem acknowledges the allure of hedonism, as the narrator questions, 'O who at any time hath seen / Sight all so fearful and so fair'.[101] This aspect of the poem is one of the reasons why it has never been given a scientific reading. In Alexander Percy's 1923 examination of the poem, after noting that it 'baffles analysis', Percy says, 'What that emotion[al impulse] is, I am not sure. My guess would be ... that spring storm within a man, vehement and undirected and lawless, which we usually term sex.'[102] Sex does dominate the poem; it is one of the base passions that civilization urges men to suppress, and thus one of the first that would rear its head if civilization were abandoned. Without the framework of Darwin and Spencer, this poem seems only to be about sexual passion, akin to the sado-masochistic revels of Swinburne's *Poems and Ballads* (1866). However, within the context of O'Shaughnessy's scientific background, it is impossible to ignore the implications of a man degenerating into a beast.

O'Shaughnessy takes a story about a single cursed man and transforms it into a narrative about a curse on all mankind. He uses a first person present-tense narration to create a sense of immediacy and urgency, but three-quarters of the way through the poem the pronouns become the plural and inclusive 'we' and 'our'. In addition to aligning the speaker with the 'demonic herd' of hedonistic revelers, these pronouns serve to implicate the reader as well.

> And loud, mid fearful echoings,
>   Our throats, aroused with hell's own thirst,
> Outbay the eternal trumpetings;
>   The while, all impious and accurst,
>
> Revealed and perfected at length
>   In whole and dire transfiguration,
> With miracle of growing strength
>   We win upon a keen warm scent.[103]

The universality of this curse is apparent: '*Our* throats' are 'aroused with hell's own thirst' and '*We* win upon a keen warm scent'. Our own animal nature is called out in these lines, making use of tangible sensations like thirst and scent to draw the reader into the 'splendid fearful herds'. This is not a single man, bearing a terrible curse, like the medieval *lai*, but something that lurks within all of humanity, clawing its way to the surface. The use of the word 'perfected', referring to the transfiguration of the once civilized man, may be a reference to the language used by the proponents of a progressive evolution, who saw mankind moving up the evolutionary ladder towards perfection. Here, then, O'Shaughnessy rejects an optimistic misreading of Darwin's theory, showing the 'perfection' that would come from adherence to survival of the fittest to be the 'accurst' and demonic

---

[101] Ibid., p. 58.

[102] Percy, p. 5.

[103] *Epic*, p. 61.

52 *Arthur O'Shaughnessy, A Pre-Raphaelite Poet in the British Museum*

creatures represented in this poem, slave to their passions, lusts, and hungers. Thus, this poem addresses not just the fear of our own animal nature inherent to criticism of Darwin's theory, but the system of ethics proposed by Herbert Spencer and the laissez-faire capitalism that dominated British industry. The question raised is not whether evolutionary theory is true, but how mankind will interpret that truth.

The bulk of 'Bisclavaret' revels in animalistic passion, indulging in the forbidden:

> I burn – as though keen wine were shed
> On all the sunken flames of sense –
> Yea, till the red flame grows more red,
> And all the burning more intense.[104]

However, unlike Swinburne's hedonistic fantasies, like 'Laus Veneris', 'Anactoria', or Faustine', O'Shaughnessy's poem never gives itself fully over to the passions it depicts. That this poem is not merely about man's sexual nature is evidenced by the harsh condemnation that comes at the end of the narrative. Although never denying the allure of giving in to one's animality, the poem calls to its readers to turn away from their animalistic nature and seek a higher consciousness, a deeper morality than the one proposed by Social Darwinists. O'Shaughnessy contrasts a morality based only on natural law, represented in his demon herd, with a religious man, 'The beadsman in his lonely cell … Kneeling before the open book'.[105] While this could be an assertion of the superiority of Christian morality over evolutionary ethics, it seems that here religion operates as a symbol for civilization at large, the realization of man's attempts to rise above his animal nature. The poem ends:

> We hold high orgies of the things,
> Strange and accursèd of all flesh,
> Whereto the quick sense ever brings
> The sharp forbidden thrill afresh.
>
> And far away, among our kin,
> Already they account our place

---

[104]   *Epic*, p. 56.

[105]   Ibid., p. 60. The mention of a 'beadsman' is most likely a reference to Keats's 'The Eve of St. Agnes' (1820), in which the cold cell of a beadsman is contrasted with the 'argent revelry' of a 'blood-thirsty race'. Keats's beadsman prays for the souls of the Baron and his revelers, who are fully absorbed in the pleasures of the flesh, an aspect of the poem that 'Bisclavaret' directly recreates. However, in 'The Eve of St. Agnes' the coldness of the beadsman's religion is negatively contrasted with the warm love felt by Madeline and Porphyro. Religion is presented as unfeeling and comfortless, just as the revelers' materialism is seen as heartless, both set against the exaltation of romantic love. It is the young lovers that O'Shaughnessy chooses not to replicate in his poem, perhaps suggesting what might be lost in a new world order, that pits man against his neighbour. 'The Eve of St. Agnes', *The Poetical Works of John Keats*, a new edition (London: Edward Moxon, 1847), pp. 148–60.

'Dreary Creeds' and 'Sham Wits'

> With all the slain ones, and begin
> The Masses for our soul's full grace.[106]

While there is a thrill in the forbidden, and an allure to the life of the flesh that the demon hordes engage in, the final stanza shows the consequences of this life. Not only the religious consequences, but also the inevitable alienation from the rest of mankind. One cannot live one's life by the mantra of 'survival of the fittest' and expect to be part of the fellowship of mankind. It is the sense of community, here, that the pleasure-seekers lose out on.[107]

Reading this poem in the context of O'Shaughnessy's career as a naturalist and his interest in scientific theories of the day sheds light on an otherwise rather obscure narrative. As O'Shaughnessy insisted to his friends, the key to the poem lies in the concept of the werewolf: man degenerated into beast.[108] This poem reflects O'Shaughnessy's thoughts not only on Darwin's theory but on the potential social applications of survival of the fittest.

O'Shaughnessy was clearly cognizant of the potentially negative social and ethical consequences of Darwinian theory. However, by the end of his career, we can see a sharp reversal from the position held in 'Bisclavaret'; in 'Eden', published in 1881, natural and civilized law are once again contrasted, but in this later poem, it is natural law that is favoured.[109] This shift reflects the change in the wider public perception of Darwinian theory – the fraught debates over the veracity of Darwin's claims had died down, and the public on the whole accepted evolution, if not the more specific details of natural selection.[110]

The title of 'Eden' suggests both an interest in beginnings and a lost golden age, but O'Shaughnessy's poem actually enacts a radical reversal of the Biblical story of the paradisal garden.[111] The poem begins at the point at which chapter 3 of the Book of Genesis ends – with exile. The Bible tells us, 'Therefore the

---

[106] *Epic*, p. 63.

[107] In the following year, Darwin published *The Descent of Man* (1871), which detailed the evolution of the social instinct as a counter to the selfish drive to survive, showing these two instincts to be forever in conflict.

[108] See the letter of Westland Marston to O'Shaughnessy, dated 12 November 1870, in which Marston refers to the 'were wolves' as the 'key' to the poem (Duke).

[109] 'Eden', *Songs of a Worker* (1881), pp. 63–7.

[110] Peter Bowler, *Evolution: the History of an Idea* (Berkeley: University of California Press, 1984), p. 184.

[111] While O'Shaughnessy was undoubtedly aware of D.G. Rossetti's 'Eden Bower' (1870), the poems are quite different. Rossetti's poem is a ballad and maintains archaic Biblical language throughout. 'Eden', in contrast, is less structured, and uses Biblical language only occasionally, to highlight the changes the garden has undergone. Most dramatically, while both poems present an erotic picture of the paradisal garden, Rossetti's poem revels in the wickedness depicted, while O'Shaughnessy's attempts to do away with the very definition of 'wickedness', instead showing the lovers' passions to be entirely natural.

54 *Arthur O'Shaughnessy, A Pre-Raphaelite Poet in the British Museum*

LORD God sent him forth from the garden of Eden, to till the ground from whence he was taken. So he drove out the man; and he placed at the east of the garden of Eden Cherubims, and a flaming sword which turned every way, to keep the way of the tree of life.'[112] In contrast to Adam and Eve, exiled from the garden, O'Shaughnessy's poem begins with two lovers exiled from civilization, seeking asylum outside of human society. They search for the lost paradise, 'Hoping the angel would be kind, / And let us pass the gate'.[113] This act of re-entry reverses the order of God and challenges the orthodoxy of mankind's Fall. Far from the carefully guarded gate they expect, the lovers find a 'lawless waste', without God, civilization, or man. In this poem, O'Shaughnessy rejects both the Christian myth of humanity's origins, and along with it, the idea of the past as a golden age to which the world can never return.

Nineteenth-century science helped to replace a literal reading of the Biblical story of creation with a naturalistic explanation for the world in which we live. While some people reacted negatively to this usurpation of the authority of the Bible, others embraced a narrative of humanity's past that replaced degeneration with progress. As Gillian Beer suggests:

> Evolutionary theory implied a new myth of the past: instead of the garden at the beginning, there was the sea and the swamp. Instead of man, emptiness – or the empire of mollusks. There was no way back to a previous paradise: the primordial was comfortless ... nostalgia was disallowed, since no unrecapturable perfection preceded man's history. Ascent was also flight – a flight from the primitive and the barbaric which could never quite be left behind.[114]

This 'new myth', however, required an optimistic understanding of evolution as progressive – and thus a misreading of Darwin's theory. Historian of evolution Peter Bowler explains:

> With natural selection there is no room for even an indirect form of design. The laws of nature operate without concern for future goals, and with an apparent disregard for the well-being of individual organisms. New characters appear more or less at random and are whittled down by a merciless struggle for existence to leave only those with survival value. This is evolution by trial and error, not by design.[115]

Evolution, the process of transmutation of species, allows for ideas of progress and purpose; Darwin's theory of natural selection does not. As Darwin himself admitted, 'which groups will ultimately prevail, no man can predict; for we know that many groups, formerly most extensively developed, have now

---

[112] Genesis, 3:23–4, KJV.

[113] *Songs*, p. 63.

[114] Beer, p. 127.

[115] Peter Bowler, *Monkey Trials and Gorilla Sermons: Evolution and Christianity from Darwin to Intelligent Design* (Cambridge, MA: Harvard University Press, 2007), p. 80.

become extinct'.[116] Thus, mankind could not see themselves continuously progressing towards perfection, because the possibility of extinction was always present.

However, viewing evolution as progressive is only a misreading of Darwin's theory from the perspective of a single species. Natural selection is a process to be feared solely from the point of view of the inferior life forms that will be slowly wiped out by its processes. As species become more fit for the world they inhabit, natural selection and evolution do lead to a better future – just not necessarily for humankind. The possibility of degeneration and extinction, once fully understood, haunts humanity, disallowing an optimistic view of evolution. It is these aspects of Darwin's theory that create the nightmare world of 'Bisclavaret'. However, once divorced from an anthropocentric perspective, Darwin's theory can be embraced as a positive force for the world as a whole.

Decentring the human from an understanding of evolution is naturally difficult. It was one of the aspects of the theory that Victorians found most troubling – once humanity was no longer a special creation of a benevolent God, it meant nature did not exist *for* us, but *in* us. *Genesis* promised that mankind would always be at the top of the food chain, but Darwinian theory gave the lie to that promise. The possibility of our usurpation was a difficult concept for many people at the time – and since. In 'Eden', O'Shaughnessy revisits the issue of man's origin and possible future, in a fantasy of this very usurpation.

In contrast to 'Bisclavaret', 'Eden' lays the charges of cruelty and brutality at society's doorstep, in its laws rather than its lawlessness. As compared to civilization, which persecutes the lovers at the centre of the poem, the garden is welcoming to all:

> Our hearts, o'erwhelmed with many a word
>   Of bitter scathing, human blame,
> Trembled with what they late had heard,
>   And fear upon us came,
> Till, finding the forbidden tree,
> We ate the fruit, and stayed to see
>   If God would chide our wickedness;
> No God forbade my love and me
>   In Eden wilderness.[117]

The laws of man – embodied here by arbitrary religious strictures – are not merely broken in O'Shaughnessy's poem; they are shown to be meaningless. The lovers in the poem initially seek solace in the paradise God created, hoping for forgiveness, but they find that their crimes are no longer crimes in this new and merciful world. There are no angels and no God in the Garden, only a riot of nature that has broken down the surrounding wall, laying the garden open to all who might come.

---

[116] Darwin, *Origin*, p. 96.

[117] *Songs*, p. 63.

56   *Arthur O'Shaughnessy, A Pre-Raphaelite Poet in the British Museum*

> We cross the flower-encumbered floor,
>   And wandered up and down the place,
> And marvelled at the open door
>   And all the desolate grace;
> And beast and bird with joy and song
> That broke man's laws the whole day long,
>   For all was free in Eden waste:
> There seemed no rule of right and wrong,
>   No fruit we might not taste.[118]

This lawlessness is celebrated in O'Shaughnessy's poem – it is not the brutal lawlessness that rules in 'Bisclavaret', but a joyful one, that rejects the cruel and unjust oppression of civilization.

Similar in its condemnation of society and its arbitrary laws is Émile Zola's *La faute de l'abbé Mouret*, published in 1875. It is entirely likely that O'Shaughnessy was familiar with Zola's novel – we know he was acquainted with Zola's works – and the similarities between the two are numerous.[119] Both depict a couple that would be kept apart by the laws of man finding refuge in a paradisal garden, which returns them to the idyllic, naturalistic state of the pre-fall. In both, however, it is not pre-, but rather post-civilization that is embraced: 'Eden' is not an idyll of nature untouched by man, but rather a celebration of nature overthrowing man; the focus of the poem is on the crumbling vestiges of civilization's hold on the land. O'Shaughnessy describes the 'ruined wall', the 'open door', and the 'overgrown' bower. Similarly, Zola writes:

> Nature left to herself, free to grow as she listed, in the depths of that solitude protected by natural shelters, threw restraint aside more heartily at each return of spring ... A rabid fury seemed to impel her to overthrow whatever the effort of man had created; she rebelliously cast a straggling multitude of flowers over the paths, attacked the rockeries with an ever-rising tide of moss, and knotted round the necks of marble statues the flexible cords of creepers with which she threw them down.[120]

Both gardens are coloured by the kind of extreme fecundity that drew censure upon Darwin's theory – in Beer's words, the 'daemonic drive' of the 'unassuageable

---

[118]   *Songs*, p. 64.

[119]   Many of O'Shaughnessy's friends and contemporaries in Paris, such as Stéphane Mallarmé and Catulle Mendès, were known to associate with Zola, and their brand of aesthetic decadence can be seen to stem from Zola's earlier decadent naturalism. O'Shaughnessy mentions Zola only once in his correspondence – in a letter to Edmund C. Stedman, dated 7 October 1880 (Duke), but this leaves no doubt as to his familiarity with the French novelist, and the similarities between 'Eden' and *La faute de l'abbé Mouret* cannot be ignored.

[120]   Émile Zola, *Abbé Mouret's Transgression*, trans. Ernest Alfred Vizetelly (New York: The Marion Co., 1915), p. 128.

passion of the sexes for each other'.[121] In both poem and novel, sex is dominant, and the naturalistic passages are highly eroticized. It is Love, or rather sex without censure, which returns to Eden in both works. The 'nuptial riot of the rose' rules here, and so the lovers 'need not fear to kiss'.

Stylistically, decadent naturalism defines O'Shaughnessy's poetic corpus, and in this he was most influenced by his French contemporaries, including Zola, in whom the style is perhaps most notable. However, Zola's brand of decadent naturalism is commonly regarded as a pessimistic reaction to Darwinian theory.[122] Although religion and the laws of man are attacked in *La faute*, natural law is also quite monstrous in its oppressive determinism. The two main characters – Albine and Serge – seem to have no free will under the power of natural law; when they succumb to passion, and therefore their ultimate downfall, it is stated that they 'yield to the demands of the garden'. 'It was the garden that had planned and willed it all. For weeks and weeks it had been favouring and encouraging their passion, and at last, on that supreme day, it had lured them to that spot, and now it became the Tempter whose every voice spoke of love.'[123]

Here Zola invokes the Biblical language of the Fall in his depiction of Albine and Serge's naturalistic downfall. In contrast, O'Shaughnessy overturns the language and the laws of God. In 'Eden', temptation is no longer shameful:

> And now we need not fear to kiss;
>   The serpent is our playfellow,
> And tempts us on from bliss to bliss.[124]

Unlike Zola's novel, O'Shaughnessy's poem fully embraces the rule of natural law, and suggests that had Zola's couple been allowed to stay in Paradise without the intrusion of civilization, they would have been happy. Because civilization still lurks outside the garden in Zola's novel, the lovers can never truly be together – in the end, Serge abandons Albine to the garden, returning to the ascetic life of the priesthood. Having found the metaphorical tree of life and consummated their relationship, knowledge descends upon Serge and Albine, as it did Adam and Eve, and they are ashamed of their naturalistic state of being: 'She had turned quite scarlet. It was new-born modesty, a sense of shame which had laid hold of her like a fever, mantling over the snowy whiteness of her skin, which never previously had known that flush.'[125] It is at this point that the joyful, naturalistic text turns dark, with the inevitable breakdown of Serge and Albine's relationship, and her eventual death. O'Shaughnessy rejects this negative outcome; his lovers happily eat the

---

[121] Beer, p. 124.

[122] Cf. *Decadence and the 1890s*, ed. Ian Fletcher (1979), and *Decadent Subjects; The Idea of Decadence in Art, Literature, Philosophy and Culture of the Fin de Siècle in Europe*, ed. Charles Bernheimer, T. Jefferson Kline, and Naomi Schor (2002).

[123] Zola, p. 185.

[124] *Songs*, p. 66.

[125] Zola, p. 189.

fruit of the tree of life and suffer no consequences. Nature is unable to damage the lovers in 'Eden'. It is only mankind and its restrictive laws – represented here by religion – that poses a threat. I suggest, then, that O'Shaughnessy's poem serves as a 'response' of a sort to Zola's novel – an alternative happy ending for the tragic couple at the heart of Zola's work.

> And while we joy in Eden's state,
> Outside men serve a loveless lord;
> They think the angel guards the gate
> With burning fiery sword!
> Ah, fools! He fled an age ago,
> The roses pressed upon him so,
> And all the perfume from within,
> And he forgot or did not know;
> Eden must surely win.[126]

'Eden', therefore, is reclaimed from Christianity; it comes to mean nature at its most primal, rather than the sheltered garden of God.[127] These lines do not only reject religion; they depict nature staging a violent coup against the institution. Religion is shown to be meaningless in a natural world, ruled by natural law.

In 'Bisclavaret', religion – as embodiment of man's efforts to civilize the world – is the only remaining oasis of humanity amidst the nightmarish rule of natural law. In contrast, in 'Eden' it is nature that is the gentle and comforting oasis amidst the cruelty of the world:

> The trees have joined above and twined
> And shut out every cruel wind
> That from the world was blown:
> Ah, what a place for love to find
> Is Eden garden grown![128]

In this poem it is the oppressive laws of mankind that are brutal and senseless, not those of nature.

The language O'Shaughnessy employs in 'Eden' is that of decadent ruin – things are 'desolate', 'overgrown', 'lawless', 'ruined', a 'waste' – and yet the tone is overwhelmingly positive. This *is* Darwin's tangled bank; without humans or God, nature has been allowed to run wild, and it is beautiful and exciting and

---

[126] *Songs*, p. 67.

[127] Fifteen years earlier, O'Shaughnessy drafted but never published another poem entitled 'Eden', this one a piece of bitter nostalgia for the lost golden age of human happiness. This 'Eden' is far more in line with the story of Genesis; the garden described is a place where there is no death or discord, and therefore divorced from Darwinian theory. With the loss of humanity, the garden itself is lost, sinking into the ocean, 'never to rise again'. Unlike the 'Eden' of 1881, nature itself is destroyed by humanity's absence. Queen's, MS 8/10, pp. 100–104.

[128] *Songs*, p. 65.

'Dreary Creeds' and 'Sham Wits'   59

welcoming to all. The joy of nature here is entirely divorced from a Christian God. The potential negativity of the loss of mankind is eclipsed here by the proliferation of superior life promised by Darwin's theory. 'Eden' is a return to the world's origins, but it is neither the unattainable perfection of the pre-fall offered by the Bible, nor the dark, primordial ooze that evolutionary optimists saw mankind as surmounting. Rather, it is simply the natural world, continuing on with or without mankind, past, present, and future.

Several critics of 'scientific poetry' have focused their work on finding nineteenth-century writers who evince a clear understanding of the reality of Darwin's theory – the negative, along with the positive. Thus, Tess Cosslett has defined the 'Scientific Movement' in poetry by an acceptance of the 'hard truths' of Darwinian theory, and John Holmes has focused his comprehensive *Darwin's Bards* on poets who reject the 'non-Darwinian' progressive evolution that was so popular during the nineteenth century.[129] It is in O'Shaughnessy's nature poetry of 1881 that we find both an understanding of the 'hard truths' of the natural world and an acceptance of Darwinian theory, not as something dangerous or potentially detrimental to mankind, but as just another part of the beauty of the natural world. In 'Colibri', also found in *Songs of a Worker*, O'Shaughnessy writes:

> Above it monstrously the trees
> Have stridden, and their crossed limbs are bent
> And locked in the contorted throes
> Of savage strife, while o'er them grows,
> Darkening with cumbersome increase
> The dank black parasite.[130]

Here is a true engagement with the 'struggle for survival' that dominates Darwin's theory, as well as a poetic representation of parasitism in the wild, as a mere fact of nature.[131] This passage is part of a description of a beautiful rainforest, untouched

---

[129]   Cf. Tess Cosslett, *The 'Scientific Movement' and Victorian Literature* (Sussex/New York: The Harvester Press/St. Martin's Press, 1982).

[130]   O'Shaughnessy, 'Colibri', *Songs of a Worker*, p. 141.

[131]   The most oft-mentioned plant in O'Shaughnessy's tropical poetry is the liana, which is also a parasite, growing off of other plants. This parasitic status is acknowledged and accepted, and does nothing to dim the exotic allure of the liana plant. Parasites were of particular interest to evolutionary scholars in terms of the negative side of evolution: degeneration. Both Herbert Spencer, in *Principles of Biology* (1864), and E. Ray Lankester, in *Degeneration: A Chapter in Darwinism* (1880), focus much of their discussion on parasites as living examples of the possibility of degeneration. Parasites and parasitic plants were an aspect of nature that was nearly impossible to assimilate into a progressive view of evolution. As Peter Bowler writes, 'Darwin was tempted to believe that increasing specialization was indeed a form of progress, because it meant that the descendents were better prepared than their ancestors to cope with a particular way of life … He was forced to admit, however, that some kinds of specialization – parasites, for example – result in actual degeneration' (*Evolution*, p. 170).

by man, and its beauty is not diminished by the reality of parasitic plants or the fight for resources that are part of natural selection. O'Shaughnessy is, then, a truly 'Darwinian' poet in Holmes's terms, joining a surprisingly small rank of writers in the nineteenth century who can be seen to face the reality of Darwin's theory in both its positive and negative attributes.

It is clear, then, that the divide between the worlds of art and science that O'Shaughnessy proclaimed in poems such as 'Nostalgie des Cieux' was a fabrication that was impossible to maintain, even within his own poetry. In those early poems, he used 'science' as a blanket term for his own unhappiness at the museum – unhappiness fuelled more by office politics and unpleasant co-workers than the actual science of nature. O'Shaughnessy's poetry declares his frustration with the minute taxonomic work he was called on to perform, and the contrast between living and dead nature, but it also evinces the influence of naturalism, in his desire to 'know' the living, vital natural world. Further, we can see O'Shaughnessy engaging with the 'bigger picture' of scientific theory in several of his poems, evincing the interdependent and interconnected nature of poetic and scientific discourse at this time.

Chapter 2

'I Carve the Marble of Pure Thought': Work and Art in the Poetry of Arthur O'Shaughnessy

In a letter written shortly before his death, published as part of the preface to his posthumous collection *Songs of a Worker*, O'Shaughnessy attempted to define himself in relation to contemporary artistic labels, saying:

> I have been represented as saying with Baudelaire, "Art for Art", and laying myself open to all the unfavourable limitations which that dictum is unjustly supposed to imply. Truly, I think that a little "Art for Art" has already done a great deal of good in England, and that a little more is needed, and would be equally beneficial. But with Victor Hugo I do not say, "Art for Art", but "Art for humanity", and my meaning is that Art is good – is an incalculable gain to man; but art, in itself equally perfect, which grows with humanity and can assist humanity in growing – is still better.[1]

I argue that O'Shaughnessy allied himself with what he perceived as the 'non-work' culture of the anti-bourgeois aesthetic movement as a reaction to his dissatisfaction with his daily working life as a natural historian at the British Museum. However, throughout his verse we can see a pervasive desire for utility in art – 'art for humanity' – that leaves him at odds with aspects of aestheticist theory, creating a source of tension in his early poetry. O'Shaughnessy found himself caught between two simultaneous anti-bourgeois models: the non-productive aristocracy, aped by many of the aesthetes of the Victorian period, and the labouring and productive working class. It is in his final volume, then, that O'Shaughnessy was able to reconcile this conflict through a redefinition of 'work' and 'production' in relation to poetry.

I.

The aesthetic movement of the late Victorian period is often considered to have been 'an engaged protest against Victorian utility, rationality, scientific factuality, and technological progress – in fact, against the whole middle-class drive

---

[1] Preface to *Songs of a Worker* (London: Chatto & Windus, 1881), p. viii. This collection was published only a few months after O'Shaughnessy's death in January 1881. It was assembled by his cousin, Alfred Newport Deacon, but it seems clear that Newport Deacon had little to do in the way of compilation, as the manuscript was left near-complete.

to conform'.[2] That is, an anti-bourgeois movement, associated with the French literary idea of *l'art pour l'art*, made famous by Théophile Gautier.[3] Implied by the phrase 'art for art' is the rejection of art for anything else. Aestheticism, therefore, is traditionally seen as a cultural retreat from social or political engagement, into the ivory tower of art, a continuation of the Romantic ideal of the solitary artist.[4]

By the middle of the nineteenth century, the presumed audience for art had become the consumerist and religious middle class – the newly rich bourgeoisie – which, its critics claimed, feigned shock at all art that could not be 'lisped in the nursery or fingered in the schoolroom'.[5] Members of the middle class wielded considerable new power over the arts at this time, with disposable income to spend and a desire for a culture of their own, independent of the aristocracy. Their patronage of the arts was, in part, shaped by a desire to flaunt their new wealth, but often in a way that made it clear they were different from the dissolute upper classes they saw themselves as supplanting. Rather than following the standards of 'taste' as set by the upper classes, the middle class demanded standards of its own, which were often shaped by decorum and morality more than beauty or skill.[6]

This newly created audience placed a burden on the artist to conform to the market, to create art that met bourgeois demands.[7] One of these demands,

---

[2]   Regenia Gagnier, *Idylls of the Marketplace: Oscar Wilde and the Victorian Public* (Aldershot: Scholar Press, 1987), p. 3. Although scholarship of the 1990s focused on refuting this point, critics continue to portray the Aesthetic movement in this light, with Tim Barringer asserting in 2005, 'Art's active engagement with the world – with labour, with ethics, politics, science, or religion – was foresworn in favour of a quest for beauty alone', in the Aesthetic movement. *Men at Work: Art and Labour in Victorian Britain* (New Haven and London: Yale University Press, 2005), p. 315.

[3]   See Théophile Gautier's 'Preface' to *Mademoiselle de Maupin* (1835), trans. Joanna Richardson (Middlesex and New York: Penguin Books, 1981).

[4]   As Catherine Maxwell describes it, 'In the high Romantic poetry of Keats and Shelley, the idealised figure of the poet is different to other men. A hyper-sensitive solitary ... he lives embowered in his own imagination.' *The Female Sublime from Milton to Swinburne: Bearing Blindness* (Manchester and New York: Manchester University Press, 2001), p. 25.

[5]   Algernon Charles Swinburne, *Notes on Poems and Reviews* (London: John Camden Hotten, 1866), p. 20.

[6]   See Linda Dowling's suggestion that the drive for realism (as promoted by John Ruskin and his 'truth to nature') can be traced to middle-class religious faith, and a conflation of 'truth to nature' and 'truth to God', bringing Christian morality to bear on even degree of representational skill. Dowling, *The Vulgarization of Art: The Victorians and Aesthetic Democracy* (Charlottesville and London: University Press of Virginia, 1996), pp. 28–9.

[7]   As compared to an older system of artistic patronage that relied on personal taste rather than market demand. As Pierre Bourdieu notes, in the 'field of cultural production' being shaped by this market culture, the artwork is created not only by the artist or the patron, but by wider culture in general. 'Thus, as the field is constituted as such, it becomes clear that the "subject" of the production of the art-work – of its value but also of its meaning – is not the producer who actually creates the object in its materiality, but rather the entire set of agents engaged in the field. Among these are the producers of works

'I Carve the Marble of Pure Thought'

indicated by Swinburne's complaint quoted above, was for a standard of morality in art. This demanded a mode of representation – in both literary and pictorial art – that supported and reinforced Victorian middle-class moral values. Beyond that, however, in a utilitarian culture, in a class that had founded itself on values of industry and labour, art that was merely beautiful seemed to have very little 'use'. While philosophers of aesthetics had, for over a century, been arguing for a disconnect between use and beauty, the middle class refused art that had no higher moral or social purpose.[8]

To negate the consumerist culture of art that pandered to middle-class respectability, the aesthetes attempted to render art autonomous, to remove it from the demand for utility by declaring it 'useless'. As Gautier, perhaps the first aesthete, declared, 'Nothing is really beautiful unless it is useless; everything useful is ugly, for it expresses a need, and the needs of man are ignoble and disgusting, like his weak infirm nature. The most useful place in a house is the lavatory.'[9] In these lines Gautier degrades utility to the level of filth, undermining the belief that it could have any connection to art or beauty. He rejects Kant's adherent beauty, suggesting that utility actively negates aesthetics. Attitudes like these culminate in the ultimate aesthete, Oscar Wilde, declaring, 'Art never expresses anything but itself.'[10] In *Idylls of the Marketplace*, Regenia Gagnier suggests that this attitude is merely a posturing of the aesthetes to reject a market culture that was rejecting them in turn.[11] While this may certainly be a factor in the aesthetes'

---

classified as artistic (great or minor, famous or unknown), critics of all persuasions (who themselves are established within the field), collectors, middlemen, curators, etc., in short, all who have ties with art.' Pierre Bourdieu, *The Field of Cultural Production: Essays on Art and Literature*, ed. Randal Johnson (Cambridge: Polity Press, 1993), p. 261.

[8]   See, for example, Kant's distinction between free and adherent beauty, in his *Critique of Judgment* (1790), in which free beauty, that which is not tied to purpose or use, is privileged over adherent beauty, that is, beauty in utility. Immanuel Kant, *Critique of Judgment* (New York: Cosimo Press, 2007), p. 49. For a discussion of Kant within the wider aesthetic/utilitarian debate, see Paul Guyer's *Values of Beauty: Historical Essays in Aesthetics* (Cambridge: Cambridge University Press, 2005).

[9]   Gautier, 'Preface', p. 39.

[10]   Oscar Wilde, 'The Decay of Lying: a Dialogue', *The Nineteenth Century: A Monthly Review* 25 (January–June 1889): 35–56 (p. 51).

[11]   Gagnier, p. 12. The degree to which the Aesthetes actually rejected consumerist culture is a much-argued point. Gagnier suggests that Aesthetes like Oscar Wilde cleverly played the bourgeois consumer class, in creating an aristocratic, dandified persona to sell to them, dismissing public opinion and yet courting it all the while. This is an opinion reiterated by critics such as Linda Dowling in her *The Vulgarization of Art: The Victorians and Aesthetic Democracy* (1996) and David Wayne Thomas in his *Cultivating Victorians: Liberal Culture and the Aesthetic* (2004). However, critics such as Angela Leighton still profess exactly the withdrawal from life that Gagnier argues against (Angela Leighton, *On Form: Poetry, Aestheticism, and the Legacy of a Word* [Oxford: Oxford University Press, 2007]). And Denis Donoghue was willing to proclaim aesthetic culture as forever divided from consumerism and capitalism in his *Speaking of Beauty* (New Haven: Yale University

withdrawal from popular culture, I am more interested in the narrative they created for themselves, styling themselves as an artistic elite, removed from the public and consumerist spheres. This is particularly important for artists on the outskirts of the movement, like O'Shaughnessy, who were not creating these narratives, but merely making use of them.

Gagnier argues that the aesthetes' rejection of utility manifested itself in a glorification of a culture of non-work that would be inaccessible to the middle-class public.[12] Utility, as expressed by Gautier in the quotation above, becomes associated with necessity, the fulfilment of a need. And the ultimate necessity of working- and middle-class life is that of earning a living. Lefebvre posits that a capitalist labour market forces man to renounce work that *itself* satisfies a need in favour of work that is 'a mere *means* to satisfy needs outside itself' – through waged labour.[13] In this 'realm of necessity', human needs are demonized and degraded. 'They represented "the sad necessities of everyday life". People had to eat, drink, find clothes ... and so they had to work. But people whose only reason for working is to keep body and soul together have neither the time nor the inclination for anything else. So they just keep on working, and their lives are spent just staying alive.'[14] Thus, Lebfebvre suggests that the necessity of fulfilling basic human needs – and *only* those basic needs – robs work of its creative possibilities and transforms it into a societal punishment: '[the worker's] labour, which ought to humanize him, becomes something done under duress instead of being a vital and human need, since it is itself nothing more than a means (of "earning a living") rather than a contribution to man's essence, freely imparted.'[15] Lefebvre suggests, then, that base-level work which only fulfils base-level needs is inherently opposed to the creative forces with which the aesthetes of the nineteenth century aligned themselves. This idea is apparent in the aestheticist thinking of the nineteenth century, with Charles Baudelaire insisting that artists must 'possess, to their hearts' content, and to a vast degree, both time and money, without which

---

Press, 2003), saying, 'If a society doesn't labor to be beautiful, it becomes indifferent to smog, litter, what Henry James called "trash triumphant", lurid communications, wretched TV, billboards, strip malls, blatancies of noise and confusion – or it considers these things the price you have to pay to make more money' (p. 3). Joseph Bristow, too, asserts that late Victorian poetry evinced a turn away from politics and mainstream culture, saying, 'in its concentration on individual states of mind, Victorian poetry found itself doing two things at once: first, it demanded greater attention to the uniqueness of human character in opposition to the stultifying forces of the "march of mind" (industrial "Progress" and the utilitarian values underpinning it) and second, it discovered that this focus of interests (on the private self) actually evacuated it from the space it wished to occupy – the *centre* of culture.' Bristow, *The Victorian Poet: Poetics and Persona* (London and New York: Croom Helm, 1987), p. 8.

[12]   Gagnier, p. 10.

[13]   Henri Lefebvre, *Critique of Everyday Life*, 3 vols, trans. John Moore (London: Verso, 1999), vol. 1, p. 59.

[14]   Ibid., p. 173.

[15]   Ibid., p. 166.

'I Carve the Marble of Pure Thought' 65

fantasy, reduced to the state of ephemeral reverie, can scarcely be translated into action'.[16] A man must be 'freed from any profession' in order to 'cultivate the idea of beauty'.[17] The language Baudelaire uses here denies the label of 'profession' to any artistic accomplishments, raising it above the level of utility. The aesthetes adopted a stance outside the productive system of labour and earning, creating the figure of the withdrawn, solitary genius that often characterizes their movement.

I suggest that O'Shaughnessy was particularly drawn to this 'revolution of non-work', as Gagnier describes it, not as a rejection of work or utility in itself, but of his own specific work, and the lack of use he felt in his own career.[18] In the distinction William Morris draws in 1888's *Signs of Change*, O'Shaughnessy's work falls into the category of 'useless toil' in which merely being 'employed' is not enough to define a man as 'useful', because, 'though they work, [they] do not produce'.[19] In Marxian terms, by selling his labour rather than producing for himself, O'Shaughnessy becomes a 'commodity' to be bought and sold in the free-market, a dehumanizing force.[20]

O'Shaughnessy, therefore, appropriated the language and self-aggrandizing narratives of aestheticism as an antidote to the frustrating lack of usefulness that he saw as symptomatic of his own bourgeois existence. As shown in the previous chapter, O'Shaughnessy found little enjoyment in his work at the Museum and his superiors constantly reminded him of his shortcomings. It seems apparent from his way of referring to his work in his correspondence that he would have happily given it up if he had been able to support himself with his poetry alone.

In this sense, his friend and mentor Dante Gabriel Rossetti probably represented O'Shaughnessy's ideal of the figure of the artist. Rossetti was in some ways the ultimate non-worker, a 'marginal within the productive system', in Gagnier's words. Unlike Morris and Swinburne, who were both independently wealthy, and thus had the freedom to pursue their artistic careers, Rossetti had no inherited wealth. This left him at a disadvantage, but also meant that in his artistic life he was situated outside class boundaries, as well as the world of commerce. He published little and nearly always refused to show his paintings. He supported himself almost entirely through private commissions, forging a network of like-minded artists and art connoisseurs, the ultimate artistic aristocracy.[21] This was, in

---

[16] Charles Baudelaire, 'The Painter of Modern Life', *Baudelaire: Selected Writings on Art and Artists*, trans. P.E. Charvet (Cambridge: Cambridge University Press, 1972), p. 419.

[17] Ibid., p. 27. See also Gautier's 'Apres le feuilleton' ('After the Article'), which laments the need to work for a living, thus forcing creative endeavours to wait for the weekend. *Théophile Gautier: Selected Lyrics*, ed. and trans. Norman R. Shapiro (New Haven and London: Yale University Press, 2011), p. 201.

[18] Gagnier, p. 10.

[19] William Morris, 'Useful Work versus Useless Toil [1884]', *Signs of Change* (Bristol, UK: Thoemmes Press, 1994), p. 101.

[20] *Communist Manifesto*, I.

[21] Cf. Lionel Stevenson's *The Pre-Raphaelite Poets* (Chapel Hill: University of North Carolina Press, 1972 and 2011), as well as *The Correspondence of Dante Gabriel Rossetti*, ed. William E. Fredeman, 8 vols (Cambridge: D.S. Brewer, 2002–2009).

66 *Arthur O'Shaughnessy, A Pre-Raphaelite Poet in the British Museum*

many ways, the ideal lifestyle of the aesthete and one for which O'Shaughnessy longed. It is important to remember that none of the men he looked up to in his artistic circle held a 'day job' (largely because of independent wealth). The literary culture on both sides of the channel seemed to scorn the idea of a writer holding a second (or primary) profession; in addition to Baudelaire's comments quoted earlier, Swinburne once wrote to a friend, 'You know there is really no profession one can take up with and go on working. Item – poetry is quite work enough for any one man. Item – who is there that is *anything* besides a poet at this day except Hugo?'[22] I suggest the impact of this cultural attitude was far-reaching in O'Shaughnessy's poetry.

For O'Shaughnessy the job at the Museum was 'work' – his way of earning a living – and so his poetry could never be categorized as such. It was these distinctions – art v. science, poetry v. work – that drew him to the language of the aesthetic movement. His rejection of the ordinary world in his verse is so pervasive that it led F.R. Leavis to specifically name O'Shaughnessy as representative of Victorian poetry that 'admits implicitly that the actual world is alien, recalcitrant and unpoetical, and that no protest is worth making except the protest of withdrawal'.[23]

On the relationship between work and leisure Lefebvre writes:

> Thus the so-called "modern" man expects to find something in leisure which his work and his family or "private" life do not provide. Where is his happiness to be found? He hardly knows, and does not even ask himself. In this way a "world of leisure" tends to come into being entirely outside of the everyday realm, and so purely artificial that it borders on the ideal.[24]

Poetry – O'Shaughnessy's 'leisure' activity – must therefore necessarily be both idealized and completely opposed to 'work'. In his early poems about the nature of art O'Shaughnessy categorizes poetry as an act of spontaneous genius, a moment when an artist gains entry to another world, another plane of being. This access is granted only to a special breed of person – the artist. Here O'Shaughnessy joins with the aesthetes in a revitalization of the language of genius that defined the Romantic period. Thus, O'Shaughnessy wrote in an unpublished note in 1870:

> Do you wonder how I who speak plain & common words to you can have written such great & beautiful ones as you have read as mine? It is not I who speak to you who are capable of those other things; but it is one somewhat greater & higher than myself which one I indeed become in certain rare moments: it is a higher degree of myself into which I am wholly striving to rise.[25]

---

[22]   Letter to Pauline, Lady Trevelyan, dated 19 January 1861. *The Swinburne Letters*, ed. Cecil Y. Lang (New Haven: Yale University Press, 1959), vol. 1, p. 39.

[23]   F.R. Leavis, *New Bearings in English Poetry: A Study of the Contemporary Situation* (London: Chatto & Windus, 1950), p. 15.

[24]   Lefebvre, vol. I, p. 34.

[25]   Unpublished notebook, Queen's University, Belfast, O'Shaughnessy Manuscript Collection, MS 8/22, p. 6, dated 3 January 1870.

This sentiment is reflected throughout his verse:

A thousand thrilling secrets lived in me;
   Fair things last whispered in that land of mine,
   By those who had most magic to divine
The glowing of its roses, and to see
What burning thoughts they cherished inwardly;
Yea, and to know the mystic rhapsody
   Of some who sang at a high hidden shrine,
   With voices ringing pure and crystalline.[26]

Here O'Shaughnessy appropriates the language of the aesthetic movement to privilege the special status of the artist. This language is evident in Baudelaire's 'The Painter of Modern Life', in which he describes the artist as 'a singular man, whose originality is so powerful and clear-cut that it is self-sufficing', who has access to vision greater than the average man and can distil life into something better and more beautiful. '[T]hings seen are born again on the paper, natural and more than natural, beautiful and better than beautiful, strange and endowed with an enthusiastic life, like the soul of their creator.'[27] As Eric Warner and Graham Hough note of Baudelaire, '[he] develops the romantic line of Rousseau by conceiving of the creative process as an entirely subjective matter; art, he claims, is born out of the solitary artist fathoming his own mind and tracing the design of his own thought – which is why every true artist is unique, *sui generis* as he puts it.'[28] O'Shaughnessy appropriates the ideas of both solitude and innate genius so common in aestheticism in order to distance himself from 'ordinary' men, represented in his poetry by his scientific colleagues. By undermining the importance of the everyday world, he undermines the significance of his own failures at the museum. He adopts a stance outside society, not to reject utility or consumerist claims on art, but to downplay his own inability to participate successfully in the productive system. With the rising dominance of the middle class, work and the ability to earn a living became an integral part of a normative – and particularly a masculine – identity. O'Shaughnessy's failures at the Museum were not just failures as a naturalist, but as a man and as a useful member of society. The language of aestheticism transformed these failures into a purposeful protest against the encroachment of the world upon art.

For O'Shaughnessy, then, the idealized world of leisure (non-work) becomes equated with the 'world of art', a notion he returns to throughout his body of work. The first poem in O'Shaughnessy's first volume, *An Epic of Women*, is entitled 'Exile' and reflects the disconnect between work and leisure that Lefebvre theorizes. Lefebvre suggests that an inherent sense of alienation stems from the split consciousness of the work/leisure divide, and we can see an example

---

[26]   Arthur O'Shaughnessy, 'Nostalgie des Cieux', *Music and Moonlight* (London: Chatto & Windus, 1874), p. 151.

[27]   Baudelaire, p. 395, p. 402.

[28]   Warner and Hough, p. 170.

68   *Arthur O'Shaughnessy, A Pre-Raphaelite Poet in the British Museum*

of this in 'Exile' as O'Shaughnessy describes himself as an 'exile' from his true home – the realm of art. The poem begins with an epigraph from Victor Hugo: '*Des voluptés intérieures / Le sourire mystérieux*', which roughly translates to 'the internal pleasures, the mysterious smile'.[29] This epigraph immediately establishes the intriguing spatiality of O'Shaughnessy's conception of the 'realm of art' – it is both internal and external, buried far within the artist, yet also a separate reality that is open and boundless. Thus, he describes it as both 'some far inward zone' and a 'limitless abyss'.[30] The poem opens:

> A common folk I walk among;
>   I speak dull things in their own tongue:
> But all the while within I hear
>   A song I do not sing for fear –
> How sweet, how different a thing![31]

'Exile' comes at the beginning of O'Shaughnessy's career and suggests an awareness that he has not yet staked out his identity as an artist. The central figure of the poem, therefore, is still trapped among the 'common folk', unable to acknowledge, and celebrate, his differences. The poem plays with imagery of disguise, of veils and masks. There is a clear joy to be found in having access to the 'surpassing sphere' of creativity, but the solitude that comes with that access – central to the aesthetes' conception of the artist – is a source of suffering for the speaker. He is 'quite alone', just waiting for his 'sad pilgrimage' to end.

In 1874 O'Shaughnessy returned to the themes explored in 'Exile' in 'Nostalgie des Cieux'. Once again, the speaker is from another world, 'Of wondrous meadows, where strange flowers did grow', in which the 'strange flowers' call to mind the *fleurs du mal* of Baudelaire.[32] Allusions like this help to shape an exotic, enchanted landscape of art, which is contrasted with the dull world of reality the speaker is forced to inhabit. The other world from which the speaker hails is explicitly the world of poetry, as it is described as a place of 'music', 'strange words of joy', 'swift language', and 'mystic rhapsody'.

In 'Exile' the 'dull obscurity' of the 'common' world is juxtaposed with the 'limitless abyss' of the world of art. This contrast is magnified in 'Nostalgie' – thus, the land of art is described as 'shining', 'dazzling', 'glowing', and the land of 'the rising sun', contrasted with the 'sunless folk' and the 'cold wraiths', who are 'soulless, dreamless', in 'deathly darkness'.[33]

---

   [29]   Arthur O'Shaughnessy, *An Epic of Women and Other Poems* (London: John Camden Hotten, 1870), p. 9. This epigraph is taken from Hugo's poem 'Aimons toujours! Aimons encore!' My translation.

   [30]   Ibid., p. 10, p. 11.

   [31]   Ibid., p. 9.

   [32]   *Music and Moonlight*, p. 150.

   [33]   Ibid., p. 157, p. 158.

'I Carve the Marble of Pure Thought' 69

Long time, amazed and dumb, I looked around,
   Seeming a very alien, and alone
   Among a sunless folk I ne'er had known,
Who called themselves my kindred.[34]

Light and dark imagery dominates this poem, illustrating the contrast between the artist and the rest of the world. In O'Shaughnessy's poems about the artist, the world of art both resembles and takes the place of Heaven. In 'Seraphitus' (1870) the artist is an angel-like figure sent down 'from some paradise' to bring beauty to the common world:[35] 'He was some Spirit from a zone/ Of light, and ecstasy and psalm, / Radiant and near about God's throne'.[36] This pseudo-religious imagery is repeated in poems like 'Nostalgie', in which the world of art is equated with the 'upper rooms' of a mansion through which his soul soars, contrasted with the 'lower gloom' of the ordinary world. Heaven and the world of art are so blurred in these passages that many can be mistaken for religious poems. In conflating art with religion, O'Shaughnessy explicates the interior/exterior spatiality of his conception of the special realm of the artist. Like religion, the realm of art is something deeply personal held within each individual, but also the reality of another world to which many people can gain access.

In each of these poems the artist is inherently *different* from the rest of mankind – he is from the Heavenly realm of art. Despite this, the language of these poems makes it clear that O'Shaughnessy is not quite confident in the special status of the artist. Even while he employs this language to distance himself from his everyday life at the museum, the poems suggest that he cannot escape the ordinary world. The verses are haunted by the underlying fear that the ordinary might destroy art and block access to the artistic realm. Recurring throughout 'Nostalgie' are images of sight and blindness; O'Shaughnessy was quite literally being blinded by the work he performed at the Museum, and the poem suggests a figurative blinding to the light of art.[37] He writes:

Then year by year quite joyless I became,
   For no one understood my words' bright way,
   Till lips and eyes were sealed up with dismay.[38]

---

[34]   Ibid., p. 153.

[35]   O'Shaughnessy is here alluding to Honoré de Balzac's 1834 novel *Séraphita*, in which the character of Sîraphitüs is an other-worldly being, an androgynous creature who has transcended the bourgeois ideas of humanity. In O'Shaughnessy's poem, this character becomes the embodiment of art and, like Balzac's, above all human concerns. The poem ends as the novel does, with the character ascending to a pure, spiritual realm.

[36]   'Seraphitus', *An Epic of Women*, p. 26.

[37]   See Chapter 1, detailing O'Shaughnessy's struggles at the Museum due to his poor eyesight.

[38]   *Music & Moonlight*, p. 152.

70 *Arthur O'Shaughnessy, A Pre-Raphaelite Poet in the British Museum*

The poem moves from the dazzling realm of art to the darkened ordinary world, dragging the speaker and the reader along. The central figure feels unable to express himself, but more than that, he worries his artistic vision – the prophetic vision that gives him access to the realm of art – is being taken from him.[39] The contrast between the vision of ordinary people and that of the artist is made explicit as he writes:

> They set themselves to darken the clear sight,
> Unfailing as a star's, wherewith my glance
> Too surely pierced each semblance like a lance
> Of steel; they made me grope with the scarce
>   light
> Of their own self-deception in the night.[40]

O'Shaughnessy's use of enjambment and caesura here interrupts the carefully standard rhyme and metre of this stanza, mirroring the interruption of his artistic vision. The internal rhyme on 'semblance', an unusual technique for O'Shaughnessy, crowds the line leading up to the sharp caesura at 'steel', creating a sensation of stumbling that artfully reflects the blindness and groping in the following line. Here the light/dark imagery overlaps with the sight/blindness to make it clear that to live too long in the dim ordinary world will blind one to the realm of artistic light.

In 'Exile' and 'Nostalgie' the relationship between the ordinary world and the world of art is explicitly antagonistic. These poems attack the ordinary world and, more specifically, the world of science, employed as a foil for art. For O'Shaughnessy science was inextricably linked with the Museum, and the problems he had there. For many, the British Museum was a place of discovery, but for O'Shaughnessy it was an office, with paperwork to file and superiors to appease. Thus, he appropriated aestheticism and its anti-consumer narratives to express the discontent of the petty bourgeois, the lowly worker, the office drone.[41] He glorifies the useless precisely because of the frustrating lack of utility he found in his everyday life.

We can see this attitude summed up in his 1870 sonnet 'A Discord':

---

[39] Catherine Maxwell details the legacy of the blind poet in *The Female Sublime from Milton to Swinburne: Bearing Blindness* (2001). However, the blindness she sees poets such as Shelley, Tennyson, Browning, and Swinburne embracing is a loss of mortal vision, not poetic vision – the loss of the former is compensated with gains in the latter. Maxwell writes, 'This motif of a beauty produced from sacrifice and loss is one that recurs over and over again in the myths that explore the birth and development of poetry and music' (p. 12). In the legacy of Milton, blindness here becomes 'the burden of the poets who would attain the vision of the gods' (p. 9). In contrast, O'Shaughnessy laments a blindness to poetic vision, a loss for which there is no compensation.

[40] Ibid., p. 154.

[41] See Chapter 1, showing that O'Shaughnessy's duties at the Museum were largely clerical.

'I Carve the Marble of Pure Thought'

It came to pass upon a summer's day,
  When from the flowers indeed my soul had
    caught
  Fresh bloom, and turned their richness into thought,
That – having made my footsteps free to stray –
They brought me wandering by some sudden way
  Back to the bloomless city, and athwart
  The doleful streets and many a closed-up court
That prisoned here and there a spent noon-ray.
O how most bitterly upon me broke
The sight of all the summerless lost folk! –
  For verily their music and their gladness
  Could only seem like so much sadness
Beside the inward rhapsody of art
And flowers and *Chopin*-echoes at my heart.[42]

Here O'Shaughnessy employs many of the tropes of Romanticism – the contrast of the urban and the rural for instance – but rather than celebrating a 'pure' nature as Wordsworth or Coleridge do, he uses 'nature' only as a metaphor for the idealized world of art. The sestet of this sonnet eschews the enjambment and caesura that O'Shaughnessy typically favours and which dominates the first eight lines of the poem. This technique draws attention to the rhymed couplets, the standardization of which appears to represent the world of art for O'Shaughnessy. In this sonnet he adopts the posture of the alienated, enlightened artist observing city life, described by Baudelaire as one who is 'at the very centre of the world, and yet … unseen of the world'.[43] He is a 'solitary mortal endowed with an active imagination, always roaming the great desert of men'.[44] Although in O'Shaughnessy's own life he was one of the workers in the 'bloomless city', here he adopts a stance that is both in the midst of, and yet distant from, those workers: observing rather than participating. This conception of the artist as separate from mankind even when in its midst becomes central to O'Shaughnessy's own view of the artist in his early poetry. He is an 'exile' in his own life.

As I have shown, for O'Shaughnessy it was a desire for autonomy from bourgeois working life that caused him to ally himself with the aesthetes and their language of non-work. O'Shaughnessy appears to have taken comfort in his status as poet in the face of his troubles at the museum, relying on the aesthetes' conception of the artist as special and superior to the ordinary man. However, the self-aggrandizing language O'Shaughnessy appropriated from the aesthetes denies art a political or social use – the very use we see O'Shaughnessy searching for in his poetry. Here we find a source of tension in his early verse, as the figure of the alienated artist is at odds with O'Shaughnessy's desire to be a useful part of society. This tension is revealed in the surprising violence of his depictions of that alienation:

---

[42] Arthur O'Shaughnessy, 'A Discord', *An Epic of Women*, p. 174.

[43] Baudelaire, p. 399.

[44] Ibid., p. 402.

> They set themselves to maim frail, unfelt wings,
>> That used to be the fellows of swift will,
>> And bring me softly to each glittering sill
> Of joyful palaces, where my heart clings
> Now faintly, as in mere fond hoverings,
> About a distant dreamwork. Wretched things,
>> Cold wraiths of joy, they chained me to, to kill
>> My soul, yet rich with many a former thrill.[45]

This is a very different conception of the alienated artist from the one found in Baudelaire's 'The Artist, Man of the World, Man of the Crowd, and Child'. Baudelaire described the state of the artist as 'to be away from home and yet to feel at home anywhere'.[46] O'Shaughnessy, on the other hand, sees the artist as an 'exile', forever persecuted for his differences. Rather than an invisible observer of the world, as Baudelaire suggests, O'Shaughnessy's artist is not only visible, he is visibly *different*, and therefore subject to attacks. In the four years between the publication of 'Exile' (1870) and 'Nostalgie des Cieux' (1874), O'Shaughnessy's conception of the place of the artist in society becomes much darker. The central figure of the poet can no longer pass as part of society; rather, he is attacked and alienated for his differences. Unlike Baudelaire, O'Shaughnessy could not easily conceive of an artist who is both separate from, and at the centre of the world. The violent language and imagery of many of O'Shaughnessy's poems about art reflect the impossibility of being different from the rest of the world and yet a part of the greater community. By embracing aestheticism's conception of the artist as a special breed apart, O'Shaughnessy put himself at odds with normative Victorian society, leaving him feeling like an exile.

II.

Within O'Shaughnessy's poetry we can trace anxieties about the personal identity he was shaping by allying himself with aestheticism. As the middle class became dominant in Victorian society, work became an integral part of a normative masculine identity, separating the bourgeoisie from the dissolute aristocracy. Work as an exclusively male sphere served to demarcate the middle from the working class, whose women were by necessity part of the labour force.[47] Thus, Davidoff and Hall assert that the division of the home from ideas of labour and

---

[45] 'Nostalgie des Cieux', *Music and Moonlight*, p. 153. Here, again, we see a reference to O'Shaughnessy's career at the museum: the maiming of wings calls to mind the work of the entomologist, pinning the wings of specimen to be displayed.

[46] Baudelaire, p. 399.

[47] Furthermore, as Lenore Davidoff asserts, mainstream economists 'regarded service as unproductive labour because it added nothing defined as of economic value and was carried on outside a recognized workplace'. *Worlds Between: Historical Perspectives on Gender and Class* (New York: Routledge, 1995), p. 3.

commerce was essential to middle-class identity.[48] Elaine Showalter considers the increasingly gendered spheres of domestic and public life, suggesting that in times of change and unrest, gender boundaries are more strictly policed. She explains, 'If men and women can be fixed in their separate spheres, many hope, apocalypse can be prevented and we can preserve a comforting sense of identity and permanence in the face of that relentless spectre of millennial change.'[49] The Victorian ideal, then, figured middle-class men as the sole breadwinners, leaving women confined to the domestic sphere, consuming rather than producing.[50] Martin Danahay asserts, 'The compulsion to labour was thus made an integral part of normative masculinity', with work serving as the 'basic building block of masculine identity'.[51] Conceived of in these terms, a rejection of work can be seen as an explicit challenge to that identity; this is partially why the work of the aesthetes was coded as sexually immoral and dangerous. The later Victorian figure of the dandy is symptomatic of the rejection of normative masculinity; as a non-working gentleman (or aspiring gentleman), he is rendered effeminate in the hegemonic discourse of the period. Danahay calls the dandy 'the antithesis of the productive male worker', 'a figure who called into question the very definition of masculinity'.[52] The ultimate dandy of Victorian aestheticism was, of course, Oscar Wilde. Gagnier says of the Wilde trial:

> As the prosecutors pushed the connections between the art world and domestic and sexual deviation, aestheticism came to represent a secret, private realm of art and sexuality impervious to middle-class conformity. In other words, aestheticism came to mean the irrational in both productive (art) and reproductive (sexuality) realms: a clear affront to bourgeois utility and rationality in these realms and an apparent indication of the art world's divorce from middle-class life.[53]

Thus, non-work became equated with illicit and possibly deviant sexuality and personal identity.

Even for those artists who did not actively reject work culture, intellectual, and particularly artistic, labour was emasculated in the rhetoric of the Victorian period.

---

[48]   Lenore Davidoff and Catherine Hall, *Family Fortunes: Men and Women of the English Middle Class, 1780–1850* (London: Hutchinson, 1987), p. 17.

[49]   Elaine Showalter, *Sexual Anarchy: Gender and Culture at the Fin de Siècle* (New York and London: Viking Penguin, 1990), p. 4.

[50]   As Davidoff and Hall suggest, the 'purpose' of work for the male middle class was to save the women and children of the family from needing to work. For the middle-class Victorian man, 'business existed to provide for his family. His politics were devoted to ensuring the representation of heads of households like himself ... whose manhood was legitimated through their ability to secure the needs of their dependents.' *Family Fortunes*, p. 17.

[51]   Martin A. Danahay, *Gender at Work in Victorian Culture: Literature, Art and Masculinity* (Aldershot: Ashgate, 2005), p. 7, p. 30.

[52]   Ibid., p. 45.

[53]   Gagnier, p. 11.

In *Gender at Work in Victorian Culture* Danahay explores the phenomenon in which work was typically represented in terms of visible, physical labour that excluded intellectual pursuits. As we have seen, the industrial culture of the day privileged utility and productivity, achievements that are difficult to measure in intellectual terms. Danahay notes, 'The emphasis on "industry" as production skewed Victorian values in favor of material products and visible signs of industrial production.'[54] However, books and paintings were not included in the definition of 'material goods' sanctioned as the products of useful labour.[55] Tim Barringer agrees, noting, 'Such [male] work within the domestic sphere – the sedentary labour of Carlyle in his Chelsea study or Brown in his Hampstead studio – was to become a flashpoint of anxiety, troubling to the theory of the sexual division of labour.'[56] Intellectual labour therefore became aligned with women's work, because it was non-physical and often performed in the home.[57] For those artists and intellectuals unwilling to adopt transgressive gender roles (such as that of the dandy), this was a source of great anxiety. O'Shaughnessy's desire for productive work that was of some use to society can be read as a desire to reassert his masculine identity in the face of emasculating aesthetic influence, in which the revolution of 'nonwork' became associated with leisure, consumption, and femininity.[58]

O'Shaughnessy's anxieties over his masculine selfhood can further be traced to anxieties about his physical body. All accounts of the poet's appearance note that he was a small man, but more than that, he is often described as delicate and almost feminine. Thomas Wright, for example, describes him as 'a thread-paper of a man' and a 'Dresden-china looking figure'.[59] Margaret Russett, in a consideration of De Quincey, a notoriously small man, suggests that during the nineteenth century, 'Diminutiveness signifies, in particular, an imputed lack of creative vitality', and equates a focus on small stature to a status as a minor poet.[60] While this can't be considered universally applicable, in O'Shaughnessy's case his secondary status within the Pre-Raphaelite movement seems to have been mirrored by his diminutiveness next to such robust figures as Dante Gabriel Rossetti and William Morris. In reference to an encounter with Rossetti in which O'Shaughnessy was 'uncompromising', his lover Helen thus says, 'have you never noticed how very ill men receive any sort of self-assertion from men younger

---

[54] Danahay, p. 42.

[55] Ibid., p. 9.

[56] Barringer, p. 53.

[57] Davidoff and Hall assert that at this time, 'The home was strongly associated with a form of femininity', further noting that 'domestic tasks which took place in the private sphere of the home have been unacknowledged as *work*'. *Family Fortunes*, p. 25, p. 33.

[58] Barringer writes, 'Effeminacy and nonwork are thus dialectically opposed to the masculine quality of work, which is strong and effective' (55).

[59] Thomas Wright, *The Life of John Payne* (London: T. Fisher Unwin, 1919), p. 21.

[60] Margaret Russett, *De Quincey's Romanticism: Canonical Minority and the Forms of Transmission* (Cambridge: Cambridge University Press, 1997), p. 224.

than themselves, especially when, like you, they have a slight, frail, Dresden china exterior? A big man, without or with brains, may be uncompromising as he pleases.'[61] Here O'Shaughnessy is figured secondary to Rossetti in age, size, and – it is implied – talent.

O'Shaughnessy's acquaintance Louise Chandler Moulton described the poet, noting his 'noticeably small hands and feet, so well-shod and gloved, in which he took an innocent pride'.[62] These descriptors – small hands and feet, an interest in clothing and ornamentation, and pride in appearance – all figure O'Shaughnessy as effeminate. The unusual smallness of O'Shaughnessy's hands and feet is mentioned in nearly every description of the poet. Although Moulton notes O'Shaughnessy's pride at his gloves and shoes, adorning those delicate extremities, here we find another source of masculine anxiety within the gender constructs of the Victorian age. In a consideration of visual representations of masculine and feminine work, Danahay notes an emphasis on hands:

> [A] writer's hands would be soft and not calloused, whereas the men they idealized would have rough and dirty skin. Their intellectual labor was thus not immediately or obviously "masculine" and as a result they faced difficulties in representing what they did as manly work. Just as women's bodies were "unstable" so were men's when it came to representing work; men's hands, if uncalloused and clean, could appear dangerously close to a woman's hand rather than a worker's hand.[63]

O'Shaughnessy's small, delicate, and well-gloved hands are a far cry from the calloused hands of the kind of manual labourer celebrated as an exemplar of masculinity in images such as Ford Madox Brown's *Work* (1865).[64]

Perhaps stemming from the unsettled masculine identity thrust upon O'Shaughnessy by his rejection of work culture, in his interactions with his lover Helen Snee he is very distinctly gendered feminine and submissive. Throughout their correspondence, Helen praises his 'sweet disposition', 'gentle voice', 'dear little face', and 'pretty, bright eyes', and addresses him as 'O, pretty'.[65] She was a well-off married woman and on one occasion sent him money so that he could 'have good dinners' that week.[66] In another letter she corrects a piece of his writing,

---

[61] *A Pathetic Love Episode in a Poet's Life, being letters from Helen Snee to Arthur W.E. O'Shaughnessy. Also a letter from him containing a dissertation on Love*, ed. Clement King Shorter (London: printed for private circulation, 1916), p. 11.

[62] Louise Chandler Moulton, *Arthur O'Shaughnessy: His Life and Work with Selections from His Poems* (Cambridge and Chicago: Stone & Kimball, 1894), p. 18.

[63] Danahay, p. 14.

[64] Madox Brown was a friend of O'Shaughnessy's – it was at his parties that O'Shaughnessy met all the prominent members of the Pre-Raphaelite movement, as well as Westland Marston, father of his wife, Eleanor Kyme Marston. O'Shaughnessy also formed a close friendship with Madox Brown's son, Oliver.

[65] Cf. Shorter's *A Pathetic Love Episode*.

[66] *A Pathetic Love Episode*, p. 9, letter dated 11 January 1870.

76   *Arthur O'Shaughnessy, A Pre-Raphaelite Poet in the British Museum*

noting, '"Lilliputians" is spelled with two "l's", pretty'.[67] The casual correction of his work is compounded by her attempt to gentle the sting with a feminine epithet, combining to suggest a pervasive emasculation of O'Shaughnessy in their interactions. Thus, while O'Shaughnessy struggled to conceive of himself in terms that would align him with normative Victorian masculinity – namely productivity in his work – his personal life rendered him effeminate. He was not dominant in either his social or his sexual relations, and despite his commitment to earning a living at the Museum, he was not the 'breadwinner' in his romantic relationships until his marriage to Eleanor in 1873.

Many aesthetes embraced dandyism and the effeminacy that came with it, in modes of dress and living.[68] They purposefully challenged the notions of dutiful work as defining Victorian masculinity, and instead attempted to create a new kind of masculinity that rejected work in favour of a celebration of the cultivation of the senses.[69] Danahay suggests that those artists who actively rejected the hegemonic heteronormativity of the period were closer to the feminine and therefore more sympathetic to issues of women's rights.[70] However, many others artists were uncomfortable with the femininity attributed to them and their work, and in them we can see both a longing to construct 'art' as 'work' and reclaim their masculine identity and an attempt to reassert dominance over the feminine in forms of violence and misogyny. Bram Dijkstra suggests that late Victorian misogyny is indicative of a longing in middle-class men 'for a power which escaped them in real life', in a volatile free market.[71] He suggests, 'the middle class therefore became the class of the moved, not that of the movers', and set up the feminine – particularly in the figure of the *femme fatale* – as a sacrificial scapegoat who could be destroyed in order to reassert the 'true masculine'.[72] The *femme fatale* dominates much of O'Shaughnessy's early poetry, particularly his 1870 'An Epic of Women', which drew censure for its depiction of women as lustful beings with no souls. It is in the poetry he did not publish, however, that we find O'Shaughnessy's most shocking fantasies about womankind. In a poem entitled 'Pagan', dated 5 November 1867, the narrator fantasizes about life as a pagan king, an amalgam of god and man that invokes the aesthete's image of the artist, explored earlier in this chapter in poems such as 'Seraphitus'. The poem, like many of O'Shaughnessy's, is decidedly sexual, but it is the desire for the subjugation of woman that sets apart this unpublished work. The narrator imagines buying 'fair women & splendid

---

[67]   *A Pathetic Love Episode*, p. 29.

[68]   As James Eli Adams explains, during this period the epithet 'effeminate' was not yet associated with sexuality, and thus men being labelled as such were being called unmanly, but not necessarily homosexual. *Dandies and Desert Saints: Styles of Victorian Masculinity* (Ithaca and London: Cornell University Press, 1995), p. 4.

[69]   Cf. James Eli Adams, *Dandies and Desert Saints* (1995).

[70]   Danahay, p. 16.

[71]   Dijkstra, *Idols of Perversity: Fantasies of Feminine Evil in Fin-de-Siècle Culture* (New York and Oxford: Oxford University Press, 1986), p. 116.

[72]   Ibid., p. 353, p. 374.

steeds', trading female and horse flesh alike on an open market. He shops for 'the fairest, the ... noblest breeds / All tresses of gold or rich colours of wine / All glories of form that excite'.[73] 'I will choose them indeed for the red of their mouth / And the rose of their limbs', he proclaims.[74] This examination of mouth and limbs mirrors the act of buying a horse, shopping for the 'noblest breed'. The merging of woman and horse is pushed to the furthest extreme as he writes:

> I will take all the women I ever have kissed
> And they shall be harnessed to go before
> To draw my bright car with their locks many tressed
> And all the nations shall bow & adore.[75]

These kinds of misogynistic fantasies of the subjugation and humiliation of women can be seen as symptomatic of O'Shaughnessy's own unstable masculine identity, jeopardized by his unproductive career at the museum, his alliance with the effete decadent movement that eschewed productive labour of all kinds, and his personal relationship with a married woman that placed him in a submissive role. In poems such as 'Pagan', O'Shaughnessy enacts a reassertion of male dominance, which can be read as an attempt to stabilize his identity within the terms of Victorian norms.

III.

O'Shaughnessy's anxieties over his relationship to work manifest in his verse in moments of violence towards woman as well as violence towards the poet figure. However, as early as *Music and Moonlight*, we find him searching for a new way of regarding both art and work that would ease this tension and alleviate his feelings of isolation and exile. O'Shaughnessy was drawn to the language of non-work, but we can see evident in his poetry the desire to be of some use to society, and therefore an inability to fully commit to the idea of 'useless' art. This conflict plays out in his best-known poem, his 'Ode' of 1874. In this poem, O'Shaughnessy's conception of the relationship between the artist and society is very different from the one expressed by the aesthetes. Baudelaire posited the fundamental alienation of the artist from society, an attitude O'Shaughnessy echoed in 'A Discord'. In contrast, the 'Ode' depicts the artist as integral to society, rejecting the central tenet of aestheticism: that art's only responsibility is to itself. In the 'Ode', the artist shapes public opinion and thus guides society to a better future. The alienation that Baudelaire posited has not completely receded; the disconnect between the artist and society is apparent in the language of the 'Ode': '*our* dream' becomes '*their* present', for instance. The artist does not share in this present or this society, but nevertheless should feel a responsibility towards it, a responsibility born of the

---

[73] 'Pagan', Queen's, MS 8/3, p. 93.

[74] Ibid., p. 89.

[75] Ibid., p. 98.

78 *Arthur O'Shaughnessy, A Pre-Raphaelite Poet in the British Museum*

artistic gift he has been given. There is a tension evident here, between a desire for social engagement on the part of the artist, as championed by William Morris or Matthew Arnold, and the alienation of the aesthetes, who believed that art did not answer to society.[76]

The first eight lines of the poem are centred on declarative statements, defining what artists *are*, and seemingly invoking an aestheticist separation from the rest of society: 'We are the music makers, and we are the dreamers of dreams.' The only other verbs that appear in these lines are rather weak – 'wandering' and 'sitting' – and add to the overall picture of the Romantic lonely artist. In the second stanza, however, O'Shaughnessy shifts his focus to action, as he introduces the idea of artists as 'movers and shakers':

> With wonderful deathless ditties
> We build up the world's great cities,
>   And out of a fabulous story
>   We fashion an empire's glory:
> One man with a dream at pleasure,
>   Shall go forth and conquer a crown;
> And three with a new song's measure
>   Can trample a kingdom down.[77]

The verbs in this stanza are all strong and active: 'build', 'fashion', 'conquer', and 'trample'. These verbs are neatly linked with the accompanying nouns of songs and stories, demonstrating that dreaming and working are not opposites, but are instead inherently linked. In this second stanza O'Shaughnessy moves from the Romantic notion of poet as inspired genius, emphasized in the first stanza's conception of what poets *are*, to a discussion of what poets can *do*, which addresses the more immediate concern of the use and impact of literature.

The first half of the second stanza shifts into an aabb rhyme scheme and maintains strict tetrameter, which leaves each line ending feminine. This lends lines 9–12 a sing-song quality that renders them less weighty than lines 13–16, which returns to the abab rhyme scheme with a masculine rhyme falling on lines 14 and 16 (crown/down). The effect of this shift in meter is that the first four lines seem to spiral lightly upward, as befits the miraculous creation of song (build/ fashion), while the second four are weightier to emphasize the power of the poet's words (conquer, trample).

Despite the power promised in these lines, O'Shaughnessy does not suggest that poets function as the leaders of society, but instead suggests the benefits of a pseudo-socialist society in which each person uses their own particular gifts to contribute to the greater good:

> The soldier, the king, and the peasant
>   Are working together in one,

---

[76] Art and arts and crafts formed a central tenet of William Morris's socialist politics. See *Signs of Change* (1888).

[77] O'Shaughnessy, 'Ode', lines 9–16.

'I Carve the Marble of Pure Thought'　　79

> Till our dream shall become their present,
>　　And their work in the world be done.[78]

The 'Ode' ends with a utopian view of society guided and influenced by art, invoking Matthew Arnold's notion of the 'sweetness and light' that would come from a 'Hellenised' world.[79]

> Great hail! we cry to the comers
>　　From the dazzling unknown shore;
> Bring us hither your sun and your summers,
>　　And renew our world as of yore;
> You shall teach us your song's new numbers,
>　　And things that we dreamed not before:
> Yea, in spite of a dreamer who slumbers,
>　　And a singer who sings no more.[80]

Like Arnold's Hellenised society, or Morris's utopian *News from Nowhere*, the Ode is a genuine call for the proliferation of the arts throughout society, in line with Morris's socialist notions of pleasure in work and life, and a uniting of work and leisure.

By suggesting that it is artists who are the 'movers and shakers' of society, the poem lays the groundwork for O'Shaughnessy's theory of 'art for humanity' that would mature and develop over the course of his career. In the 'Ode', then, we can see the beginning of O'Shaughnessy's shift from a false aloofness, spurred by his unhappy career at the museum, towards a new view of art as a useful form of work that could take the place of his museum job.

'Europe', the final poem in *Music & Moonlight* (bookending the volume with the 'Ode' and drawing a natural connection between the two), offers an alternate to the ending of the 'Ode' and serves as a warning to society of what will happen if art, beauty, and pleasure are not embraced as guiding forces. Echoing the criticisms put forth by Matthew Arnold in his *Culture and Anarchy* (1869), O'Shaughnessy conjures a mob of Philistines, deaf to the 'sweetness and light' of poetry.

> Then came upon me the discordant tone
> Of vulgar untuned voices. As I gaze,
> Vile crowds, a populace, your men, your own,
> Polluted France! burst forth with hideous praise
> Responding to your call; the paltry shout
> Of each besotted individual voice;
> The senseless swaying of that rabble rout.[81]

---

[78]　Ibid., lines 29–32.

[79]　Matthew Arnold, *Culture and Anarchy*, first published in 1869 (Cambridge: Cambridge University Press, 1955), p. 37.

[80]　O'Shaughnessy, 'Ode', lines 65–72.

[81]　'Europe', *Music and Moonlight*, p. 200.

In this nightmarish scene, the masses are 'vile', 'hideous', 'polluted', and 'senseless', but more importantly, they are 'discordant' and 'untuned'. These adjectives serve as a contrast to the musical voices of the poets, which are being drowned out by the shouts of the populace. In many ways this poem mirrors the opinion expressed in *Culture and Anarchy*. Arnold famously wrote his treatise after witnessing the Hyde Park Riots of 1866, led by the Reform League. This demonstration led Arnold to the conclusion that England needed to 'Hellenise' – that is, to embrace culture, which he defined as 'sweetness and light' – rather than focusing on strength and material progress. According to Arnold, the only thing that could save the country from anarchy was a love of beauty.

In 'Europe', O'Shaughnessy specifically addresses the political situation in France in the early 1870s, a situation he blames on their poor choice of leaders.[82] According to him, many of the problems of the society were exposed in the exile of their artists and poets.

> No man shall find
> Their names at all with thine in after time,
> Dull tottering Republic. Lone and grand,
> One, from a lifelong exile by the sea
> Returning, lives an exile still in thee,
> His soul for ever in his dream sublime!
> And One is dead – alas! 'tis even He
> Who was the priest of beauty.

These lines most likely refer to Victor Hugo and Théophile Gautier. Hugo took part in the Revolution of 1848, but after the coup d'état which formed the Second Republic in 1851, he fled Paris for Brussels. He remained on the island of Guernsey (an 'exile by the sea') until 1870, and the reconstitution of the republic. Gautier (the 'priest of beauty') died in 1872, two years before the publication of *Music and Moonlight*. 'Europe', then, echoes the 'Ode' in calling for the influence and guidance of artists, as the true 'movers and shakers' of society. It also echoes the views of Arnold and Morris as O'Shaughnessy advocates for education and culture for the working class, in an effort to mould them into conscientious citizens. The 'Ode' and 'Europe' demonstrate the 'use' that O'Shaughnessy was beginning to find for art and poetry, and how he could conceive of the artist as a productive member of society.

---

[82] 'Europe' addresses the political situation in France at the time, namely the fall of the Second French Empire in 1870. An uprising in Paris on September 4, 1870 forced the abdication of Napoleon III, who had ruled since 1852, and ended the Second Empire. Although O'Shaughnessy expresses distress at the mob rule evinced by this uprising, he does not directly engage with the political situation, offering no reasons for his apparent support of Napoleon III and his authoritarian regime. 'Second Empire', *Encyclopædia Britannica*, *Encyclopædia Britannica Online*, Encyclopædia Britannica Inc., 2011, Web, 31 October 2011.

'I Carve the Marble of Pure Thought'   81

These ideas come to fruition in O'Shaughnessy's final volume of poetry.[83] In the titular poem of the collection, 'Song of a Fellow-Worker', O'Shaughnessy reconciles his affiliation with the aesthetic movement with his desire for utility and productivity in his life in a very simple way: redefining art as work.

The division between 'art' and 'work' during this period was so widespread that even William Morris, so invested in the artistry of labour, conceived of them as separate. In *Signs of Change* he classes art as 'leisure', something to be pursued primarily outside the workday.[84] O'Shaughnessy viewed natural history as merely the way he earned a living, and poetry as a part of his essential self. This, according to Lefebvre, leads to the feelings of alienation that we see expressed in O'Shaughnessy's verse: a negative, violent alienation, as compared to the privileged position outside society adopted by the aesthetes. Lefebvre posits that work is external to man when he is not working 'for himself'.[85] In contrast, a man working 'for himself', 'perceives and becomes conscious of his own self. If what he makes comes from him, he in turn comes from what he makes; it is made by him, but it is in these works and by these works that he has made himself.'[86]

O'Shaughnessy is able to reconcile art with work, and therefore, in Lefebvre's terms, reconcile himself with his work, by a focus on 'making', the act of

---

[83]   *Songs of a Worker* was published in 1881 by O'Shaughnessy's cousin Alfred W.N. Deacon. According to W.D. Paden, shortly after O'Shaughnessy's death, Edmund Gosse sent a letter to Deacon in which he 'stated his conviction that O'Shaughnessy had never edited his own verse with sufficient rigour; and to have more than intimated his [Gosse's] willingness to act as editor of a posthumous volume' (Paden, 'Ancestry', p. 443). Just a few days before in his published obituary for O'Shaughnessy, Gosse had asserted that '[O'Shaughnessy's] mind was lacking in that critical sense which is now so common, and which used not to be considered at all a necessary attribute of the poet. But the result of this, so far as O'Shaughnessy was concerned, was that the quality of his work was exceedingly unequal' (Gosse, 'Obituary', p. 99). Deacon therefore rejected Gosse's offer, saying:

> [O'Shaughnessy] had left clear directions among his papers as to this new volume & its contents so that they must be carried out but I quite agree with you as to the value rather of quintessence than bulk & in a collected edition it should be carried out – On which subject let me thank you for your kind offer a very valuable one as coming from one whose critical poetical faculty is so highly and deservedly rated. I shall be glad some day to talk the matter over with you. (Quoted by Paden, 'Ancestry', p. 444)

Songs of a Worker was thus assembled entirely by Deacon, who stated in the Preface that 'of the poems, however, evidently intended for publication, none have been omitted' (*Songs*, p. vi). As this was clearly not the editing tactic that Gosse intended to take, he rather spitefully said of the volume that it 'ought never to have been published' (Edmund Gosse, *Ward's English Poets*, ed. T.H. Ward [New York: Macmillan, 1902], vol. 4, p. 629). While this assessment was probably motivated in part by personal bias, it is true that *Songs of a Worker* was not a success, and the poet quickly dropped out of the public's memory.

[84]   William Morris, 'How We Live and How We Might Live', *Signs of Change*, p. 19.

[85]   Lefebvre, vol. I, p. 39.

[86]   Ibid., p. 163.

82 *Arthur O'Shaughnessy, A Pre-Raphaelite Poet in the British Museum*

production (and, in Lefebvre's terms, the making of himself). In the nineteenth century, 'production' was intrinsically associated with industrial work culture and factory life, which, as Morris argued, was devoid of creativity.[87] However, in the notion of 'being productive', I suggest we can find a dual meaning of 'being useful' and 'making something new'. Again we see O'Shaughnessy's conception of his career as a poet shaped by his career as a naturalist. His work at the Museum was predominantly clerical; even in his scientific work he was not generating new information, but merely reassessing the work of those who came before him. His taxonomic papers largely confirm previous species identification, or record details of specimens of known species. Most frequently, O'Shaughnessy performed organizational or secretarial work for his superiors. In the sense of making or creating, he produced nothing at the Museum. In 1870, Albert Günther, his immediate supervisor, summarized O'Shaughnessy's responsibilities at the Museum: 'to name and enter into the Catalogues those of the recent additions which could be easily determined by comparison with previously named examples; to prepare a list of duplicate specimens and the alphabetical Index to the Catalogue of Fishes; to look over the first proof sheets; & to do other miscellaneous work of the same nature'.[88] We can see from this list that O'Shaughnessy 'produced' very little at the Museum. Furthermore, this work is as abstracted from the kind of masculine manual labour valorised at this time as O'Shaughnessy's artistic pursuits were.

Therefore, it is in the act of creation itself that O'Shaughnessy finds a 'use' for poetry. While the aesthetes and dandies challenged the idea of art as work by returning to the Romantics' language of inspired genius, other artists combated the anxieties inherent in the notion of art as feminized, unproductive non-work by focusing on the labour of art. In his final volume, O'Shaughnessy concentrates on the *physicality* of the act of creation, and is therefore, in nineteenth-century terms of production, able to shift the label of 'work' from his non-productive museum career to that of his poetry. He was finally able to reject the bourgeois culture of the middle class, not by conceiving of himself as a part of an artistic aristocracy, but by aligning himself with the working class, as a physical labourer. Here we see clear similarities with Morris, who also adopted the voice of the working class. However, while Morris was attempting to infuse production with creativity, O'Shaughnessy needed to find the act of production in the creative.

Danahay suggests that artists' romanticization of manual labour as an ideal of virility during this period subverted their own masculinity, generating the anxieties already discussed.[89] However, in 'Song of a Fellow-Worker' O'Shaughnessy explicitly allies manual labour and poetry, equating the effort of stone work with that of writing verse, despite the fact that one is physical labour and the other is 'brain labour'. The unifying symbol of *Songs of a Worker* is stone, as

---

[87] This association is reflected in the language Morris uses in 'How We Live and How We Might Live' in *Signs of Change*.

[88] In a letter to the Principal Librarian of the Museum, assessing O'Shaughnessy's progress in the Natural History Departments, 4 November 1870. BMOP, C.11400.

[89] Danahay, p. 13.

'I Carve the Marble of Pure Thought'   83

O'Shaughnessy couches his artistic theory in the form of the most physical of the visual arts: sculpture. As a sculptor carves stone, the poet carves thought; both craft something new. This act of carving is then equated with the work of the 'lowly' stonemason in 'Song of a Fellow-Worker', as the poet speaks of his 'toil' – 'My toil was fashioning thought and sound, and his was hewing stone'.[90] In their shared labour, the two men are made equal. Here O'Shaughnessy rejects the language of the alienated artist in favour of aligning himself with a community of masculine workers, in which the work they do is different, but it is all performed for the greater good of society.[91]

At the beginning of the poem, the narrator speaks of the 'burden of [his] loneliness'. Alienation dominated O'Shaughnessy's early poetry; this burden is eased by the stoneworker, who demonstrates to the poet that they are both part of a larger fellowship of workers:

> I went forth hastily, and lo! I met a hundred men,
> The worker with the chisel and the worker with the pen –
> The restless toilers after good, who sow and never reap,
> And one who maketh music for their souls that may not sleep.[92]

In this stanza O'Shaughnessy allows the regular rhyme scheme to dominate, highlighting the rhythm of his words and therefore the craft of poetry. Thus, while the stonemason creates the streets all men travel down, the artist creates as well – he crafts beauty and pleasure, soothing the other workers in their toil. For O'Shaughnessy both are equally important and serve a purpose in society. Morris would express a similar 'use' of art several years later in his *Signs of Change*, in which he writes:

> And I may say that as to that leisure, as I should in no case do any harm to any one with it, so I should often do some direct good to the community with it, by practising arts or occupations for my hands or brain which would give pleasure to many of the citizens; in other words, a great deal of the best work done would be done in the leisure time of men.[93]

The 'use' of art is the production of pleasure, and for O'Shaughnessy the 'work' is the careful craft of poetry. Thus, he unites the desire for utility we find in Morris and

---

[90] 'Song of a Fellow-Worker', *Songs of a Worker*, p. 3.

[91] This emphasis on community reflects, again, the theories of Matthew Arnold, who wrote, 'Perfection, as culture conceives it, is not possible while the individual remains isolated. The individual is required, under pain of being stunted and enfeebled in his own development if he disobeys, to carry others along with him in his march towards perfection, to be continually doing all he can to enlarge and increase the volume of the human stream sweeping thitherward.' Here Arnold argues for education for all, rather than just a cultural elite. Arnold, *Culture and Anarchy* (Cambridge: Cambridge University Press, 1955), p. 48.

[92] *Songs*, p. 5.

[93] Morris, *Signs of Change*, p. 19.

other mid-Victorian artists with the craft of poetry, the careful formalism that was a hallmark of the aesthetic movement. Unlike Morris, whose focus on craft meant championing every man as a potential artist, or at least artisan, O'Shaughnessy continued to depict the artist as privileged with access to a kind of divine realm: the world of art. But this privilege no longer separates artists from the rest of mankind. Rather, it is their particular gift, or skill, that they bring to their work, just as the stonemason's strength is the innate skill he brings to his own work. It is this idea of art as skilled labour that separates it from the feminized domestic sphere of non-work, reasserting the masculine in artistic practices.

O'Shaughnessy always conceived of art as beautiful and pleasurable; it is the language of work and production that distinguishes this final volume from his earlier poetry. This linguistic shift can be illustrated by comparing a stanza detailing the act of writing from the 1870 poem 'Seraphitus', with that of 'Song of a Fellow-Worker' (1881):

> But all about that house he set
>   A wondrous flowering thing – his speech,
> That without ceasing did beget
>   Such fair unearthly blossoms, each
> Seemed from some paradise, and wet
>   As with an angel's tears, and each
> Gave forth some long perfume to let
> No man forget.[94]

> I said, O fellow-worker, yea, for I am a worker too,
> The heart nigh fails me many a day, but how is it
>   with you?
> For while I toil great tears of joy will sometimes fill
>   my eyes,
> And when I form my perfect work it lives and never
>   dies.
> I carve the marble of pure thought until the thought
>   takes form,
> Until it gleams before my soul and makes the world
>   grow warm.[95]

The first focuses on the special status of the poet: here he is like a heavenly being, with access to 'unearthly' things. The act of writing poetry is compared to a 'flowering plant' – that is, self-generating. This is the language of inspiration, not work. In the second poem the poet 'toils', 'works', 'carves', and 'forms'. Effort is depicted here, as well as the frustration of potential failure. The former is focused on generation – he 'begets' his poetry – the latter on creation and the act of making. 'Song of a Fellow-Worker' marries the aesthetes' language of the special poetic gift to ideas of work and utility.

---

[94] *Epic*, pp. 28–9.

[95] *Songs*, p. 3.

'I Carve the Marble of Pure Thought'   85

Art as the creation of beauty and pleasure can be contrasted with O'Shaughnessy's work at the Museum, in which he merely catalogued knowledge, creating nothing. These ideas clearly tie in to the changing world of production and business in the latter half of the nineteenth century, when 'work' was no longer about what one made, and business became abstracted from the realities of production or consumption. This was the age of the clerk, the creation of the pencil-pusher, where a man could go to an office every day and create nothing, change nothing, affect nothing. It was this life, that of the ordinary office worker, that O'Shaughnessy tried to combat in his poetry. Here we find the distinction between 'useful work' and 'useless toil' that Morris makes in *Signs of Change* (1888), in which he defines the middle class as 'non-producers', employed uselessly as mere 'wage earners'.[96]

The designation 'worker' had, by the end of O'Shaughnessy's career, become an integral part of his personal identity. Instead of conceptualizing art as 'non-work' in order to distinguish it from his scientific career, he shifted his focus to production and the creation of something new. In this way, he was doing more 'work' as a poet than as a naturalist, and was able to privilege his art as his career. He accepted the fact that he was a 'worker', with its entomological signification of being one of the drones, the lower order, but the fact that he is not a 'mover and a shaker' does not mean that his work is unimportant.[97] In the nineteenth century the definition of 'worker' came to include 'one who is employed for a wage', distinguished from a capitalist or a producer of wealth.[98] O'Shaughnessy, then, rejected this non-productive definition and returned to an older model. In Biblical language, a worker is 'one who makes' and is synonymous with God the Creator.[99] In this act of redefinition, taxonomy, the urban office environment, and poetry all coalesce under one new heading: work and the worker.

In O'Shaughnessy's early poetry, particularly the 'Ode', we can see a longing for communion with his fellow man, but the separatist posturing of the aesthetes, central to his conception of a work/art divide, denied that communion. By turning his back on this language and redefining art as work, O'Shaughnessy was able to join with the rest of humanity and regain the normative masculine identity he had inadvertently cast off by allying himself with the dandified aesthetes. In this way, he finally fulfilled his commitment to 'art for humanity', quoted earlier. This did not come in the form of great ideas, or political or social reform, but in the acknowledgement that every worker makes a minute difference in the world, and that the artist is no different.

> And so we toil together many a day from morn till
>   night,

---

[96]   Morris, 'Useful Work versus Useless Toil', pp. 98–120. Morris defines the middle class as such in 'The Hopes of Civilization', p. 76.

[97]   O'Shaughnessy was initially hired as an entomologist at the British Museum.

[98]   OED. The first use of 'worker' under this definition is attributed to Charles Kingsley in 1848.

[99]   Ibid.

I in the lower depths of life, they on the lovely height;
For though the common stones are mine, and they
    have lofty cares,
Their work begins where this leaves off, and mine is
    part of theirs.

And 'tis not wholly mine or theirs I think of through
    the day,
But the great eternal thing we make together, I and
    they.[100]

'Song of a Fellow-Worker' employs the longest line that O'Shaughnessy ever used, utilizing decapentasyllabic verse, or 'political verse'. This is a Byzantine form of poetry with 15-syllable lines (adding a single syllable to the more common heptameter), which has a long oral tradition and is associated with folk songs.[101] Here 'political' means 'of the people', making this a very deliberate choice for the 'Song of a Fellow-Worker'. The longer lines add more weight than the ballad metre commonly associated with English folk songs, while still drawing the connection of art to the greater community of humanity and deliberately eschewing the 'high art' forms that O'Shaughnessy experimented with in his earlier poetry. Thus, in this final volume O'Shaughnessy not only creates *for* humanity, but *with* humanity. In this way, he comes the closest in his career to unifying the seemingly disparate concepts of 'art for art's sake' and 'art for humanity's sake' into one productive aesthetic theory.

---

[100]   *Songs*, p. 7.

[101]   Political verse is further marked by rhymed distichs and a caesura falling after the eighth syllable of each line, demarcating two distinct thoughts in each line, which we can see apparent in the stanza quoted above. For more on this form, see Peter Mackridge, 'The Metrical Structure of the Oral Decapentasyllable', *Byzantine and Modern Greek Studies* 14 (1990): 200–212, and Vassilios Letsios, 'The Life and Afterlife of Political Verse', *Journal of Modern Greek Studies* 23, no. 2 (October 2005): 281–312.

Chapter 3
'The Purest Parian':
The Formalism of Arthur O'Shaughnessy

As we have seen, O'Shaughnessy turned away from his early insistence on spontaneous generation to depict poetry instead as a form of 'toil'. In order to maintain a contrast with his non-productive labour at the Museum, O'Shaughnessy sought to align poetry with manual labour and production through a focus on the artisanal craft of writing. Even in his earliest work, O'Shaughnessy's verse evinces a commitment to the formal craft of poetry, a commitment that would transform over the course of his career into his theory of poetic *work*, enacted through the metaphor of stone work, or sculpture.

O'Shaughnessy's rejection of the capitalist culture which necessitated his earning a living can be seen to extend to a rejection of consumer culture in general, and consumerism in art specifically. Thus, O'Shaughnessy's artistic production turns to an older, pre-capitalist model in which a man produces for himself, or for his community, rather than to create a product for sale on the free market. As Marx insists in *Capital*, capitalism is when products become commodities, rather than fulfilling the needs of the producer.[1] This rejection of consumerism in art is evident in O'Shaughnessy's refusal to conform to the moral standards in art demanded by bourgeois market forces.

I.

The bourgeoisie of the mid- to late Victorian period exercised new and considerable power over the art world. As art became a commodity to be bought and sold on a free market, it began to pander to the demands of the paying customer – increasingly the Victorian middle class. As suggested in the previous chapter, the newly powerful bourgeoisie demanded art that was 'useful' – and one of the 'uses' they saw for art was moral education.[2] Mark Bevir demonstrates

---

[1] *Capital*, p. 148.

[2] The separation of aesthetics and ethics is usually attributed to philosophers of the eighteenth century, such as Shaftesbury, Hutcheson, and Kant. However, Paul Guyer argues against Kant's role in this break, stating, 'Kant thus undermines the idea that there can or should be a rigid barrier between the aesthetic and the ethical even before it gets off the ground.' Paul Guyer, *Values of Beauty: Historical Essays in Aesthetics* (Cambridge: Cambridge University Press, 2005), p. 191. There can be no denying that, no matter what happened during the Enlightenment, in the Victorian period this association was back full-force. Thus, by 1870 Ruskin could assert, 'the most perfect mental culture possible to men

the inherent ties between Victorian evangelicalism and free trade capitalism, in which laissez-faire economics could be trusted to maintain nineteenth-century morality, because success and failure was the remit of a judging God.[3] As Regenia Gagnier suggests, at this time the perceived 'social function of art' was 'to present the normative values of society, to present the middle class'.[4] Thus, one critic in 1869 asserted, 'if we must be quantitative, one great creative poet probably exerts a nobler, deeper, more permanent ethical influence than a dozen generations of professed moral teachers.'[5] It is the responsibility of the poet, it is suggested, to serve as a moral teacher because of the depth and reach of his influence. In his 'Ode', O'Shaughnessy echoes this assertion of the poet's power and influence, but throughout his corpus he rejects the restriction of art and expression at the hands of bourgeois 'respectability'. Rather, he joins with the aesthetes, in France as well as England, in seeking an art freed from the constraints of a narrow moral imperative.

The infamous attack on the Pre-Raphaelite literary circle by Robert Buchanan – 'The Fleshly School of Poetry', 1871 – illustrates the moral demands being placed on literature at the time. Buchanan attacked D.G. Rossetti and the other Pre-Raphaelites for the 'fleshliness' of their poetry, a preoccupation with the physical that becomes 'unwholesome when there is no moral or intellectual quality to temper and control it'.[6] Without spiritual elements to balance the physical, this poetry is 'simply nasty', according to Buchanan.[7] Buchanan complains that throughout his poetry Rossetti is just 'a fleshly person, with nothing particular to tell or teach us'.[8] Implied, of course, is that the purpose of poetry is to 'tell or teach' the public something, rather than to record personal experiences or feelings, an introspective style Buchanan angrily labels 'trash'. Rossetti and his contemporaries – Buchanan calls out Morris, Swinburne, Payne, and O'Shaughnessy by name – are not merely failing to fulfil their role as moral teachers, however. Their poetry, averring as it does 'that the body is greater than the soul, and sound superior to sense', is a 'disease' that 'can be caught by any young gentleman as easily as the measles'.[9]

---

is founded on their useful energies, and their best arts and brightest happiness are consistent, and consistent only, with their virtue.' John Ruskin, *Lectures on Art: Delivered Before the University of Oxford in Hilary Term, 1870* (New York: John Wiley & Son, 1870), p. 28.

[3] Mark Bevir, *The Making of British Socialism* (Princeton: Princeton University Press, 2011), p. 26.

[4] Regenia Gagnier, *Idylls of the Marketplace: Oscar Wilde and the Victorian Public* (Aldershot: Scolar, 1987), p. 65.

[5] J. Morley, reprinted in *Victorian Scrutinies: Reviews of Poetry 1830–1870*, ed. Isobel Armstrong (London: The Athlone Press, 1972), p. 251.

[6] Robert Buchanan, 'The Fleshly School of Poetry: Mr. D.G. Rossetti', *Contemporary Review* 18 (August/November 1871): 334–50 (p. 335).

[7] Ibid., p. 338.

[8] Ibid., p. 339.

[9] Ibid., p. 335, p. 347.

By failing to temper his depictions of love and sex with the necessary moral lessons, Rossetti, Buchanan declares, 'might be really dangerous to society'.[10]

It was attacks such as these in the public press which led Swinburne to snap back:

> There are pulpits enough for all preachers in prose; the business of verse-writing is hardly to express convictions; and if some poetry, not without merit of its kind, has at times dealt in dogmatic morality, it is all the worse and all the weaker for that. As to subject, it is too much to expect that all schools of poetry are to be for ever subordinate to the one just now so much in request with us, whose scope of sight is bounded by the nursery walls.[11]

As Swinburne says, the artists who rejected this moral imperative did so because they felt the scope of art should not be limited in any way. Central to O'Shaughnessy's conception of the 'realm of art' was freedom of expression, as compared to his restrictive job at the museum, which required restrained prose and restrained attitudes. Thus, throughout his career, O'Shaughnessy does not just write 'fleshly' poetry; he actively uses his verse to reject the demand for morality in art.

One of the ways in which O'Shaughnessy accomplished this was to embrace poetry as craft. A return to form was a return to a celebration of poetry *as* poetry, rather than a mere method of delivering a moral. From the beginning of his career, the formal qualities of O'Shaughnessy's verse were commended by critics and friends alike. *The Academy* praised *An Epic of Women*, writing, 'Of the formal art of poetry he is in many senses quite a master; his metres are not only good, they are his own, and often of an invention most felicitous as well as careful', and it compared his 'technical execution' to that of Gautier and Baudelaire.[12] The *Examiner* said: 'The metrical formation, too, is generally marked by elegance and accuracy, while the rhymes are easy and graceful.'[13] Rossetti, too, praised O'Shaughnessy's technical ability, saying of *An Epic*, 'Your book is a fresh evidence among others lately apparent that the contemporary English school of poetry is becoming far more organized than heretofore in respect of artistic

---

[10] Ibid., p. 338. Although Rossetti initially responded to Buchanan with an article entitled 'The Stealthy School of Criticism', in which he revealed Buchanan to be the true author of the original pseudonymous article, and defended his own poetry on a point-by-point basis, the damage of Buchanan's attack was far-reaching. Soon after the furore over Buchanan's article, Rossetti suffered a nervous breakdown and withdrew from literary society. He continued to suffer nervous attacks for the rest of his life.

[11] Algernon Swinburne, letter to the editor, *The Spectator*, 7 June 1862, written in response to a review of George Meredith's *Modern Love*, published 24 May 1862 in *The Spectator*.

[12] Sidney Colvin, 'An Epic of Women and Other Poems', *The Academy* (15 November 1870): 32–3 (p. 33).

[13] *The Examiner and London Review* (29 October 1870): 694.

style, which seems now at last to be taking its place as a settled and technical quality – a gauge of craftsmanship without which admission into the guild cannot be granted.'[14] In a letter to Alice Boyd, Rossetti further praised O'Shaughnessy's technical achievements in the volume, saying it showed 'a decided advance in the practice of the art as an art in our day – that is I mean they *contribute* to the result which I think is becoming apparent in poetic craftsmanship'.[15]

In this revitalization of the craft of poetry, O'Shaughnessy was seen as a disciple of the French *Romantiques*, particularly Théophile Gautier and Charles Baudelaire, who had begun the revival of formalism in France in the 1830s and 1840s. James K. Robinson dubbed French-influenced formalism in England a 'neglected phase of the aesthetic movement', which he called 'English Parnassianism'.[16] Robinson took this name from the Parnassian movement in France, headed by Stéphane Mallarmé, Catulle Mendès, and François Coppée, and counted O'Shaughnessy as one of its early members. O'Shaughnessy was close friends with the Parnassians and translated many of their works for an English audience, and within his verse we can see the influence of their attempt to revitalize the formal art of poetry.[17] Following the example of Gautier and Baudelaire before them, the Parnassians embraced the early fixed forms of poets such as Ronsard, Marot, Charles d'Orléans, and Villon, in order to profess the primacy of form over content:[18]

> [W]hat we desired to banish from poetry were humanitarian commonplaces ...
> false sentiment of that sickening kind which weeps at everything, and thinks
> it does poetical work in dwelling pathetically on a dead bird, or the dog that
> follows the poor man's funeral. Doubtless and incontestably, pity, tenderness,
> love above all are eternal and sublime sources of inspiration; but in themselves
> they are not enough: they must be expressed, brought into relief by novelties of

---

[14] William E. Fredeman, ed., *The Correspondence of Dante Gabriel Rossetti* (Cambridge and Rochester: D.S. Brewer, 2004), vol. 4, p. 543.

[15] Ibid., p. 554. Alice Boyd was the patroness and muse of the poet William Bell Scott, another peripheral member of the Pre-Raphaelite social circle. She helped to support and promote the works of many of the members of that group.

[16] James K. Robinson, 'A Neglected Phase of the Aesthetic Movement: English Parnassianism', *PMLA* 68, no. 4 (September 1953): 733–54. This return to formalism in England carries on in the tradition of Keats's formalism, and was evident in the works of Tennyson, Rossetti, and Swinburne, as well, although Robinson focuses his article on those who were vocal about their French influences, including O'Shaughnessy, Payne, Lang, Dobson, and Saintsbury.

[17] Included in O'Shaughnessy's *Songs of a Worker* were 27 translations of contemporary French poetry, from Léon Dierx, François Coppée, André Lemoyne, Paul Verlaine, Ernest D'Hervilly, Sully Prudhomme, Henri Cazalis, and Catulle Mendès. *Songs of a Worker*, pp. 169–212.

[18] Pierre de Ronsard (1524–1585), known for his sonnets and odes. Clément Marot (1496–1544), Charles, Duke of Orléans (1394–1465), and François Villon (1431–1463), were all noted for their ballades, rondeaux, and chansons.

'The Purest Parian'   91

treatment, by just and lovely imagery, and finally through the means of a perfect style, rhythm, and rhyme – in one word, Form.[19]

In emphasizing the importance of form the Parnassians hoped not only to reject moralistic claims on art, but to revitalize the craft of poetry, which they saw as having been neglected in recent years. Mendès complains that it was 'a time when linguistic inaccuracy in a sonnet was admitted as a proof of sensibility, when a thirteen-foot alexandrine was complacently tolerated, if it only expressed something like *Tous les hommes sont frères*, or *la terre tourne autour du soleil*, when "spectre" as a rhyme to "sceptre" would pass muster, provided the lines so terminating were devoid of rhythmic harmony!'[20] Here Mendès invokes the long-debated question of the relationship between form and content in art, suggesting that by privileging content, form suffers. In England, Walter Pater addressed this question in his essay 'The School of Giorgione', first published in the *Fortnightly Review* in 1877, and added to the third edition of *The Renaissance* in 1888. Pater quotes Friedrich Schiller's demand for freedom of art in *On the Aesthetic Education of Man*, in which he insists that 'the content always has a restrictive access upon the spirit'. Thus, 'the real artistic secret of the master consists in his annihilating the material by means of the form'.[21] Despite quoting Schiller, Pater actually reimagines his dictum; rather than annihilation, he celebrates a *fusion* of form and content. This celebration leads to one of his oft-quoted lines, that 'all art constantly aspires towards the condition of music'.[22] This is not, as some critics have suggested, because music is pure form – in fact, for Pater 'pure form' was represented by sculpture, which he places at the bottom of the spectrum of the arts – rather, it is in music that he finds the perfect fusion of form and content. 'For while in all other kinds of art it is possible to distinguish the matter from the form, and the understanding can always make this distinction, yet it is the constant effort of art to obliterate it.'[23] Here, he reinterprets Schiller's words; the goal is not to annihilate content, but to obliterate the distinction between form and content. He rejects the critical climate of the day, which considered poems and paintings for the narrative and the moral they contained, with no consideration for the lyrical

---

[19]   Catulle Mendès, 'Recent French Poets', trans. Arthur O'Shaughnessy, *Gentleman's Magazine* 245, no. 1786 (October 1879): 478–504 (p. 491).

[20]   Mendès, p. 490.

[21]   'In a truly beautiful work of art the content should do nothing, the form everything; for the wholeness of man is affected by the form alone, and only individual powers by the content. However sublime and comprehensive it may be, the content always has a restrictive access upon the spirit, and only from the form is true aesthetic freedom to be expected. Therefore, the real artistic secret of the master consists in his annihilating the material by means of the form.' Friedrich Schiller, *On the Aesthetic Education of Man, in a Series of Letters*, ed. and trans. Elizabeth M. Wilkinson and L.A. Willoughby (Oxford: Clarendon, 1967), p. 300.

[22]   Walter Pater, *The Renaissance* (Oxford: Oxford University Press, 1998), p. 86.

[23]   Ibid., p. 86.

structure, or strokes of the brush.[24] Buchanan, for instance, not only privileges content over form, but suggests that 'true' art lies only in content, not form. Thus, he writes, 'reduced to bald English [...] all great poems lose much; but how much do they not retain? They are poems to the very roots and depths of being, poems born and delivered from the soul, and treat them as cruelly as you may, poems they will remain.'[25] Pater counters this kind of argument, explaining, 'Art, then, is thus always striving to be independent of the mere intelligence, to become a matter of pure perception, to get rid of its responsibilities to its subject or material.'[26]

In verse, invoking Schiller's dictum meant a return to the formal craft of poetry, with a focus on metre and rhyme. Fixed forms particularly emphasized the physical shape of a poem, drawing the reader's focus to structure rather than message, and thus the Parnassians sought to revive medieval fixed forms such as rondels, rondeaux, ballades, triolets, villanelles, lais, and virelais.[27] Although O'Shaughnessy was drawn to the poetic practices coming out of France, these specific forms were difficult to translate into English.[28] Instead of attempting English rondels and triolets, O'Shaughnessy adopts aspects of the fixed forms, particularly refrains and burdens, into his verse, signalling an interest in French formalism without making himself slave to prescribed structures. He also plays with the expectations generated by an invocation of French formalism, subversively reinterpreting these newly revived forms, and in turn drawing further attention to the relationship between form and content in his verse. In his papers,

---

[24]   As Denis Donoghue rightly notes, 'The formal properties of the painting are not examined. No attempt is made to separate the seen thing from the mind that has seen it. The seeing gathers to itself everything seen, retains the essence of it, and makes it an extension of the critic's sensibility.' *Speaking of Beauty* (New Haven and London: Yale University Press, 2003), p. 99. Pater is concerned with personal sensation and reaction, which precludes the idea of pure form; as well, as the value and impact of the work of art is based on not just form, but the reaction that the viewer brings to the artwork.

[25]   Buchanan, p. 348.

[26]   Pater, p. 88.

[27]   A *rondel* most often consists of 14 lines, but can be written in 13. It consists of lines of eight or 10 syllables, divided into two quatrains and a sestet. The first two lines of the first stanza serve as a refrain at the end of the second and third stanzas. The *rondeau* is a 13-line poem with two rhymes and the opening line repeated twice as the refrain. A *ballade* repeats the closing line of each stanza, and maintains the same rhyme scheme throughout the poem. A *triolet* is an eight-line poem, most often in iambic tetrameter, in which the first, the fourth, and the seventh line are identical. The *villanelle*, adopted from a form popular in Italy, is a 19-line poem. In its most prescribed form, it is broken down into five tercets and a final quatrain, consisting of seven-syllable lines, using only two rhymes. A *lai* is a short romance written in octosyllabic verse, made famous by Marie de France (see Chapter 5). A *virelai*, like a *rondeau*, has only two rhymes, and the first and last stanzas are identical.

[28]   Swinburne, too, experimented with the newly revived French fixed forms. Facing similar difficulties with translating rhyme patterns between languages, he created his own fixed form, called the 'roundel'. Despite the similarity of the name to the *rondel*, the 'roundel' is actually a variation on the *rondeau*. It is a shorter form than either, at only nine lines.

a draft of the song 'She has gone wandering away' appears, there titled 'Rondel'.[29] Despite the title, this poem is actually a rondeau, of 13 lines with two half-line refrains (repeating a portion of the opening line of the poem – here, 'she hath gone wandering away'). The only change to the standard structure of a rondeau is that O'Shaughnessy's second stanza is rhymed babA (with the A representing the refrain), rather than the standard aabA, merely adding a rhyming pair to the second stanza, where traditionally there is none. While one might assume that O'Shaughnessy simply confused the names of these older fixed forms, mistaking a rondeau for a rondel, we can see a similar disingenuousness in naming throughout his corpus. This is immediately evident in his 1872 volume *Lays of France*. While the poems do reimagine the medieval *lais* of Marie de France, they range from 37 to 103 pages in length, and therefore do not quite fit the description of a 'short narrative poem'.[30] In 1870's 'The Miner: A Ballad', O'Shaughnessy again names a form in his title, and yet does not follow through on the expectations that title creates.[31] Far from employing the standard 'ballad metre' O'Shaughnessy uses elsewhere, here he keeps to no metre at all. There is repetition – a requirement of the ballad form – but refrains do not fall where one would expect, namely the end of each stanza. Rather, the first line and the fourth line of the first stanza are identical, repeated as the first line of the third stanza. He makes use of far more rhymes (10 in total) than are usually permitted in a short ballad, and the rhyme scheme follows no apparent pattern. For all that, O'Shaughnessy chose to title this poem a 'ballad' and thus is purposefully bringing the reader's expectations of a ballad to the poem, only to undermine them at nearly every turn.[32] His subversion of expectations actually draws further attention to the form of the poems, as readers seek the expected structure and encounter something new and different. The structures he does employ are – as his friends and critics noted – crafted with technical care, negating any sense that O'Shaughnessy was merely a sloppy practitioner of fixed forms.

O'Shaughnessy's technical care in verse can be highlighted by an examination of a short poem entitled 'Has Summer Come Without the Rose?' (1872), which the *Examiner* praised as evincing 'grace of diction, and an aërial delicacy of rhythm' and was 'proof of the exquisite musicalness of the poet's endowment'.[33]

---

[29]   'Song', *Music and Moonlight*, pp. 46–7. Song, here called 'Rondel' ('She has gone wandering ...'), London, ca. 1874, MS, 1p. poem, Columbia University, Rare Book & Manuscript Library, MS #0956.

[30]   OED.

[31]   'The Miner: A Ballad', *An Epic of Women*, pp. 211–13.

[32]   In contrast, 1874's 'Fountain of Tears', while not labelled a 'ballad', meets nearly all the criteria of being one. Recounted in octosyllabic verse, this poem employs a very standard rhyme scheme (abbc ddaC, with C representing the refrain), and four of the nine stanzas close with the refrain 'the Fountain of Tears' (with the remaining stanzas deviating but still closing with the word 'tears'). O'Shaughnessy was thus perfectly capable of following the format of a ballad, but chose not to in the one poem entitled 'a ballad'. 'The Fountain of Tears', *An Epic of Women*, pp. 166–9.

[33]   'Review: Music and Moonlight', *The Examiner* (28 March 1874): 320–21 (p. 320).

94   *Arthur O'Shaughnessy, A Pre-Raphaelite Poet in the British Museum*

Has summer come without the rose,
  Or left the bird behind?
Is the blue changed above thee,
  O world? Or am I blind!
Will you change every flower that grows,
  Or only change this spot –
Where she who said, I love thee,
  Now says I love thee not?[34]

In this poem O'Shaughnessy makes use of the ballad metre – quatrains of alternating lines of tetrameter and trimeter – as well as a ballad-like refrain, with slight variations on the line 'love thee not' ending every stanza. The use of a refrain immediately aligns this poem with the fixed forms popular in France. He employs a nearly monosyllabic vocabulary and eschews enjambment, lending the poem an air of simplicity, perhaps even triteness. This is interrupted only by the rhyme scheme, which is not standard throughout the poem. It is in the rhymes, then, that he catches a reader off-guard, interrupting the expectation of a pattern. The first and third stanzas follow the same rhyme scheme (abcb adcd), but the second stanza is completely non-standard, and the fourth begins the same, but then ends with the rhyme scheme inverted (as cdad). In this way he toys with the incredible standardization of the ballad form, with its simple metre – sometimes known as 'common metre' – and its repetition in the refrain. Thus, he both adopts the older form and undermines it to subvert the reader's expectations. This is reflected by the content of the poem, in which the superficial sameness of the summer is acknowledged, but rejected, as the speaker refuses to believe that that world could go on as it was, now that his feelings for his lost love have changed. We understand that the summer continues on as it always was in the background of this poem, yet that standardization is broken apart by the poet and his emotions.

II.

O'Shaughnessy's experimentation with form was both a sign of his dedication to the production of poetry as a craft and also of his attempts to undermine the moral imperative of the bourgeois consumer class by emphasizing form over content. A return to poetic formalism was not the only way O'Shaughnessy and the aesthetes championed the supremacy of form, however. We can also see evident in O'Shaughnessy's corpus a celebration of a kind of artistic synaesthesia, or the intermixing of artistic forms, that emphasized art as an object. The model the aesthetes took for this was Keats's 'Ode on a Grecian Urn'.[35] By writing about an art object, Keats removes the demand for a moral narrative, and is able to

---

[34] 'Has Summer Come Without the Rose?', *Lays of France (Founded on the Lays of Marie)*, 2nd ed. (London: Chatto & Windus, 1874), p. 250.

[35] See Chapter 1 for a discussion of O'Shaughnessy's self-conscious echoing of Keats' poetry in 'A Neglected Harp' (1870).

'The Purest Parian' 95

focus exclusively on form and aesthetics, and thus declare, 'Beauty is truth, truth beauty'.[36] This model was replicated by the late Victorian aesthetes, resulting in a flurry of poems about paintings, sculptures, and other art forms. In *On Form*, Angela Leighton says of this phenomenon that it was 'as if art *about* art could ensure art *for* art, and thus eliminate the question of truth or life outside'.[37] Leighton refers to this process as 'cross-breeding' and notes that it created an ideal 'which could seem to protect artistic integrity by emphasizing the self-enclosed inviolability of art *on* art'.[38]

Despite this, Leighton notes:

> Theories of "art for art", while invoking form as the justification for a merely formal artistry, without political or moral point, also, contradictorily, give it a new and specific sense of bodily presence. Form is, on the one hand, thinned into mere style or manner, and, on the other, fleshed out into beauty's desirable shape.[39]

Leighton therefore contends that 'art for art's sake' is inextricably linked to 'illicit sex'.[40] This link is obvious in Buchanan's attack on the Pre-Raphaelites; although he targets sexually explicit poems like Rossetti's 'Nuptial Sleep' – which he deems 'trash' – he also attacks the 'delight in beautiful forms, hues, and tints', as well as the 'thinness and transparence of design' found throughout Pre-Raphaelite poetry.[41] It does not matter to Buchanan whether a poem is actually addressing love or sexuality; the materialistic focus on the physical inherently conjures the sexual. Therefore, it is in O'Shaughnessy's poetic series most criticized for its shocking sensuality that we see him struggling to combat moral criticisms in a turn to form. 1870's 'An Epic of Women' is made up of seven poems, each depicting a famous *femme fatale* from literature. This series, heavily influenced by

---

[36] Keats, 'Ode on a Grecian Urn', *The Poetical Works of John Keats*, a new edition (London: Edward Moxon, 1847), pp. 211–12.

[37] Angela Leighton, *On Form: Poetry, Aestheticism, and the Legacy of a Word* (Oxford: Oxford University Press, 2007), p. 42. See also Stefano Evangelista's *British Aestheticism and Ancient Greece: Hellenism, Reception, Gods in Exile* (Basingstoke, UK: Palgrave Macmillan, 2009) and Denis Donoghue, *Speaking of Beauty*. Evangelista argues that the 'truth' of Keats's poem is accessed by an appeal *to* history, in the form of the classics, whereas Donoghue argues that the truth is found in a turn *from* history. Thus, he argues, 'the urn is pure form, removed from its first use ... It is as if the urn, now that it has been removed from its historical setting, can speak of a time when Beauty and Truth will be one and the same because they will alike and equally be products of the imagination' (Donoghue, p. 78). I would argue with Donoghue that this artistic synaesthesia is a turn inward, away from all externals, including history and morality, to access a personal truth, rather than a universal one. However, there is clearly an appeal to cultural/historical authority inherent in the selection of a *Grecian* urn for Keats's subject matter.

[38] Leighton, p. 30.

[39] Ibid., p. 9.

[40] Ibid., p. 33.

[41] Buchanan, pp. 336–7.

96 *Arthur O'Shaughnessy, A Pre-Raphaelite Poet in the British Museum*

Gautier and Baudelaire, was criticized for its sexual content as well as its negative portrayal of womankind. Thus, Louise Chandler Moulton describes the series as 'audacious, mystical, sensuous [and] Swinburnean', and the illustrator of the volume, J.T. Nettleship, reports that his sister-in-law read the sequence, saying, 'I suppose it is natural, being a woman, that she enquires with some candor, not to say resentment, "why is woman in these poems represented as only beautiful but utterly soulless, fickle & false, & the steel the only thing to make her true?"'[42]

The central conceit of 'An Epic' is that women have no souls and are therefore driven only by lust and material greed. This notion is laid out in the opening poem, 'Creation', which depicts God's creation of Eve.

> He feasted her with ease and idle food
>   Of gods, and taught her lusts to fill the whole
> Of life; withal He gave her nothing good,
>   And left her as He made her – without soul.
>
> And lo, when he had held her for a season
>   In His own pleasure-palaces above,
> He gave her unto man; this is the reason
>   She is so fair to see, so false to love.[43]

The 'He' in this passage is God himself, having taken the first mortal woman as a lover, teaching her to love only luxury in the kingdom of heaven. After quoting these lines, *The Saturday Review* protested, 'We entirely fail to see what object a man can set before himself in writing this kind of nonsense.'[44] Gosse would later defend the poem, saying, 'if we exclude the cynicism of the last stanza, it is pure Catholic doctrine, and might have been signed by St. Bernard'.[45] This is, of course, false. Catholic doctrine does not hold that women have no souls, nor has any Christian denomination asserted a sexual relationship between God the creator and Eve, as O'Shaughnessy depicts here. Rather than 'pure Catholic doctrine', this is pure decadent doctrine, invoking the type of the *femme fatale* so popular in France at the time.

Critics often point to the *femme fatale* as symptomatic of the deep-seated misogyny prevalent at the time, with her inevitable death serving as a fantasy of the reinstatement of male dominance. Thus, Bram Dijkstra describes, 'The turn-of-the-century male's fascination for, horror of, and hostility towards woman, culminating in an often uncontrollable urge to destroy her, to do violence to that perverse, un-Platonic reflection of the Platonic idea of perfect beauty he was so

---

[42] Louise Chandler Moulton, *Arthur O'Shaughnessy: His Life and Work with Selections from His Poems* (Cambridge and Chicago: Stone & Kimball, 1894), p. 23. Duke University Manuscript Collection, 6th 11:A Box 1, c.1, letter dated December 1870.

[43] 'Creation', *An Epic of Women and Other Poems*, p. 85.

[44] 'Minor Poetry', *The Saturday Review* (4 March 1871): 282–3 (p. 282).

[45] Edmund Gosse, 'Obituary', *The Academy* 457 (5 February 1881): 98–9 (p. 99).

eager to pursue.'[46] A first reading of O'Shaughnessy's 'An Epic' might uphold the opinion of Nettleship's sister-in-law, seeming to reflect Dijkstra's notion of the *femme fatale* as a sacrificial scapegoat for the powerless middle-class man, a potential reaction to the O'Shaughnessy's unsatisfying work at the museum, as we saw in the poem 'Pagan' in the last chapter.[47] The seven poems focus on the inherent cruelty of womankind, attributed to her lack of a soul. As a mere sexual body, she cares nothing for the pain she causes the men who love her. The second poem of the sequence, 'Wife of Hephaestus', recounts the mythical story of Hephaestus and Venus, and focuses on woman's vanity and superficiality.[48] Caring only for what is beautiful, Venus spurns the love of her dutiful husband, the cripple Hephaestus, instead carrying on an adulterous affair with her brother Ares. The third and fourth poems of the series are both entitled 'Cleopatra' and detail what seems to be the inevitable consequence of loving a *femme fatale*: death.

> And he thought how, since the first fate began,
>   The lot of every one hath been so cast:
> One woman bears and brings him up a man,
>   Another woman slays him at the last.[49]

'Daughter of Herodias' also ends in the death of the male hero; here, the crime is compounded by the saintliness of the victim, John the Baptist. The sixth poem takes on the story of Helen of Troy and focuses on the selfishness of womankind, showing Helen in the years after her flight to Troy with Paris. She regrets leaving her husband Menelaus, but only because she knows her husband and the people of her homeland no longer love her. After demonstrating the cruelty, vanity, and selfishness of the *femme fatale*, 'An Epic' turns to the nineteenth century and a modern, adulterous woman. With the lessons learned from the previous poems, her lover takes the only path available; by killing her he ensures that she will never stray again. 'A Troth for Eternity' employs the common decadent end for the *femme fatale*, allowing man to regain his dominance over a cruel woman by killing her.

Although critics at the time focused on the apparent misogyny of 'An Epic' – with one reviewer suggesting it was nothing but a revenge fantasy inspired by 'the jaundice of disappointment' – there is an alternate reading available to us.[50] In a reflection of the artistic synaesthesia embodied in Keats's 'Ode', many aesthetes of the later Victorian period focused on the *femme fatale* as personification of the art object, and thus freed from traditional morality. This kind of depiction

---

[46] Bram Dijkstra, *Idols of Perversity: Fantasies of Feminine Evil in Fin-de-Siècle Culture* (New York and Oxford: Oxford University Press, 1986), p. 149.

[47] Ibid., p. 353.

[48] O'Shaughnessy mixes Greek and Roman names here, where traditionally Hephaestus (the Greek name for the god of fire and metalwork) would be paired with Aphrodite (the Greek goddess of love). The Roman name for the god of fire is Vulcan.

[49] *Epic*, p. 103.

[50] 'Minor Poetry', *The Saturday Review*, p. 282.

of the *femme fatale* took hold in the late 1870s and 1880s, with the works of Stéphane Mallarmé, Joris-Karl Huysmans, and the artist Gustave Moreau.[51] In England, this trend reached its height with Oscar Wilde's play, *Salome* (published in English in 1894). In these works, the *femme fatale* is just as cruel and heartless as in other decadent works, but rather than being a symbol of immorality, she symbolizes the amorality of art. As H.G. Zagona contends, like art the *femme fatale* is 'coldly beautiful, cruel, unrelenting, existing gratuitously, with no need of justification, with no purpose but to be admired'.[52] As an art object she is above the common concerns of life, freed from both morality and utility. Here we see Lefebvre's conception of the nineteenth-century rejection of the everyday which took the form of the idealized, the artificial, and the marvellous, and which strives to 'demote' and 'degrade' the everyday.[53] Thus Salome embodies the decadent/ aesthetic rejection of bourgeois culture and its demand for didactic sentimentality in art – the kind of poetry that Mendès represented the Parnassians as rejecting at the beginning of this chapter.

Charles Bernheimer dates the beginning of what he dubs 'Salomania' – the popularity of the Biblical character of Salome – to 1870, but it is in 1876, with the exhibition of Gustave Moreau's 'Salome Dancing Before Herod' and 'L'Apparition' that she became intimately connected with art for art's sake.[54] It was these works that inspired the Salome of Flaubert's *Herodias*, as well as the chilling passage in Huysmans's *A Rebours*, in which the narrator obsesses over Moreau's work. However, O'Shaughnessy's 1870 'An Epic', which focuses on Salome at the peak of its narrative arc, can be seen to make the same links between the *femme fatale* and 'gratuitous art'. The assertion that women have no souls figures them as nothing more than beautiful objects to be admired, and thus aligns them with the art object. The association of the *femme fatale* with the work of art is established at the very start of 'An Epic.' Although purportedly about Eve, the description of the creation of womankind is far more redolent of the mythology of Ancient Greece than Christianity. The language immediately calls to mind the creation of Venus, and more specifically, the *Birth of Venus* by Botticelli.[55]

---

[51]   Grace Zagona's work on the Aesthetes' use of the Biblical character of Salome traces this incarnation of the character to Heinrich Heine's 1847 *Atta Troll*, popular in translation in France. Zagona contends that it is in Heine's work that the inversion of the *femme fatale* from villain to heroine is cemented, seeing in his depiction of Herodias in *Atta Troll* an Aesthetic manifesto, in which the traditionally evil figure of Herodias is the personification of 'gratuitous art'. Helen Grace Zagona, *The Legend of Salome and the Principle of Art for Art's Sake* (Genève: Libraire e Droz, 1960), p. 26.

[52]   Ibid., p. 22.

[53]   Lefebvre, vol. 1, p. 34.

[54]   *Decadent Subjects: The Idea of Decadence in Art, Literature, Philosophy and Culture of the Fin de Siècle in Europe*, ed. Charles Bernheimer, T. Jefferson Kline, and Naomi Schor (Baltimore and London: The Johns Hopkins University Press, 2002), p. 104.

[55]   While there is no specific evidence of O'Shaughnessy's familiarity with Botticelli, the painter was quite popular within the Pre-Raphaelite and Aesthetic movements in

The coral colour lasted in her veins,
  Made her lips rosy like a sea-shell's rims;
The purple stained her cheeks with splendid stains,
  And the pearl's colour clung upon her limbs.

She took her golden hair between her hands;
  The faded gold and amber of the seas
Dropped from it in a shower upon the sands;
  The crispèd hair enwrapped her like a fleece;
  …
The sun and sea made haloes of a light
  Most soft and glimmering, and wreathed her close
Round all her wondrous shapes, and kept her bright
  In a fair mystery of pearl and rose.

The waves fell fawning all about her there
  Down to her ancles; then, with kissing sweet,
Slackened and waned away in love and fear
  From the bright presence of her new-formed feet.[56]

Sea imagery dominates this poem, and it is only in the last few stanzas that it becomes clear this is the Christian creation of Eve, rather than that of Venus, born out of the foam of the waves. The comparison of the woman to the pearl, twice in these few stanzas, also echoes the image of Venus emerging from the half-shell in Botticelli's work, as does the description of her golden hair, enwrapping her like a fleece.[57] While Gosse tried to defend the poem by showing it to be in line with Catholic doctrine, it would be far more accurate to say that the poem does not represent Christianity at all, but rather classical art. While the implication that the Christian God would take mortal woman as a lover is blasphemous, those types of dalliances were standard in Greco-Roman myth and art.

England, and thus we can assume knowledge of his work in O'Shaughnessy. For more on the popularity of Botticelli with figures such as D.G. Rossetti, Swinburne, and Walter Pater, see Adrian S. Hoch's 'The Art of Alessandro Botticelli through the Eyes of Victorian Aesthetes', *Victorian and Edwardian Responses to the Italian Renaissance*, ed. John Easton Law and Lene Østermark-Johansen (Aldershot: Ashgate, 2005), pp. 55–86. Furthermore, the image of Venus rising from the sea is a common one in the work of Théophile Gautier. See 'Carmen', 'Sur les lagunes' ('On the Lagunes'), and 'La nue' ('The Cloud'), all published in *Emaux et Camées. Théophile Gautier: Selected Lyrics*, ed. and trans. Norman R. Shapiro (New Haven and London: Yale University Press, 2011), p. 31, p. 187, p. 237.

[56] *Epic*, pp. 82–3.

[57] The play on 'golden fleece' in these lines also encourages the reader to consider the connection to Greek mythology, referencing the story of Jason and the Argonauts and the quest for the Golden Fleece, recounted in the *Argonautica* by Apollonius of Rhodes. This story is also told in the more popular *Metamorphoses* of Ovid, book seven. O'Shaughnessy seems quite familiar with mythology – see his take on the story of Helen of Troy – and we know he would, at least, have been familiar with the story through William Morris's *The Life and Death of Jason* published in 1867.

Throughout 'An Epic' O'Shaughnessy describes the women as if he were describing works of art, and the height of their sin is often the most aestheticized moment of the poem. The first description of Cleopatra reads much like the description of a painting:

> She was reclined upon a Tyrian couch
>   Of crimson wools: out of her loosened vest
> Set on one shoulder with a serpent brooch
>   Fell one arm white and half her foamy breast. [58]

The description does not read like that of a living, moving woman, but rather a static art object. Thus, her loosened vest seems to be caught eternally mid-fall down her white arm, rather than being a fleeting disarrangement of clothing. In moments like these, 'An Epic' embraces a kind of Pygmalionism – the blurring of art object and woman, but also the futility of loving her. She is still and beautiful, something to be observed and loved from afar – but incapable of returning the feeling.

While Moulton accused this series of being 'Swinburnian', a comparison of 'An Epic' to Swinburne's most famous *femme fatale* poems highlights the differences between the two. While 'Creation' echoes the sentiment at the heart of Swinburne's 'Faustine' – 'But God, who lost you, left you fair, / We see, Faustine'[59] – the way the poets describe the women is very different. As Kathy Psomiades writes, 'the bodies of *Poems and Ballads* are less seen than felt'.[60] Swinburne's *femmes fatales* are experienced viscerally by the reader – his verse offers tangible sensation, rather than the distanced descriptions O'Shaughnessy provides. As Swinburne himself writes in 'Anactoria', 'Thy body were abolished and consumed'.[61] This is an apt description of his *femmes fatales*; they are consumed by the poetry about them, their bodies lost in the swirl of colour, scent, sound, taste, and touch. Even in Swinburne's most descriptive moments, it is hard to visualize the lover, except hazily, flashes of description emerging from sensation:

> And all the broken kisses salt as brine
> That shuddering lips make moist with waterish wine,
> And eyes the bluer for all those hidden hours
> That pleasure fills with tears and feeds from flowers,
> Fierce at the heart with fire that half comes through,
> But all the flower-like white stained round with blue;
> The fervent underlid, and that above
> Lived with laughter or abashed with love.[62]

---

[58]   'Cleopatra', *An Epic of Women*, p. 93.

[59]   Algernon Charles Swinburne, 'Faustine', *Poems and Ballads* (London: John Camden Hotten, 1866), p. 123.

[60]   Kathy Alexis Psomiades, *Beauty's Body: Femininity and Representation in British Aestheticism* (Stanford: Stanford University Press, 1997), p. 76.

[61]   Swinburne, 'Anactoria', *Poems and Ballads*, p. 69.

[62]   Ibid., p. 66.

'The Purest Parian' 101

The distance that O'Shaughnessy's narration maintains from the *femmes fatales* is completely absent here. Swinburne's descriptions rely on senses other than sight – smell, taste, and touch dominate:

> That with my tongue I felt them, and could taste
> The faint flakes from thy bosom to the waist!
> That I could drink thy veins as wine, and eat
> Thy breasts like honey![63]

Even when Swinburne is describing an art object, rather than a living person, his verse is far more sensual and active than 'An Epic'. Consider, for example, his 'Hermaphroditus', written 'au Musee du Louvre', about the *Sleeping Hermaphrodite*.[64] Describing this poem – along with Shelley's 'Medusa' – Catherine Maxwell writes, 'indeed, rather than documenting the particularity of these artworks the poems become something else – epitomes of poetic vision. Unconcerned with or partially blind to the actual physical details of the artworks, Shelley and Swinburne's speakers are overwhelmed by the uncanny force of the images of Medusa and Hermaphrodite and engage with them in scenes of their own.'[65] Inspired by the art object, Swinburne imagines the emotions and sensations of the dual-sexed character. There is no description of the incredible body at all. Rather, the poem focuses on the 'waste wedlock of a sterile kiss' inherent to the notion of a male-female hybrid.[66]

It is far more apt, therefore, to draw a comparison between O'Shaughnessy's 'An Epic' and the work of Gautier. An obvious influence is 'Le Poème de la femme' ('The Poem of Women'), which describes a woman of renowned beauty posing for various artworks – Venus 'unclad beside the sea', a 'Sultana of the harem', and a famed courtesan.[67] The series of descriptions as she poses for each piece clearly suggest the longer descriptions at the heart of 'An Epic'. However, Gautier's work focuses on the woman in the art, while O'Shaughnessy highlights the art in the women. In fact, while his title seems a purposeful allusion to 'Le Poème de la femme', it is Gautier's descriptions of art objects that most suggest O'Shaughnessy's inspiration. In 'Le château du souvenir' ('The Castle of Memory'), a series of tapestries and portraits, lining a long hall, are described:

> Daphne, her hips in tree-bark trapped,
> Spreads leaf-grown fingers; vainly tries
> To flee, in his rude arms enwrapped
>
> ...
>
> A rosebud, scarcely opened, on

---

[63] Ibid., p. 69.

[64] Swinburne, 'Hermaphroditus', *Poems and Ballads*, pp. 91–3.

[65] Catherine Maxwell, *The Female Sublime from Milton to Swinburne: Bearing Blindness* (Manchester and New York: Manchester University Press, 2001), p. 200.

[66] Swinburne, 'Hermaphroditus', *Poems and Ballads*, p. 91.

[67] Gautier, 'Le Poème de la femme', *Selected Lyrics*, pp. 11–17.

The ribboned bodice round her pressed,
Barely ruffles its lace upon
An azure-veined and snow-white breast.
...
On rouged cheek gold-tinted glints bestow
The arm blush of a crimson hue,
And jet-fringed eyelids let the glow
Of sunshine, beaming, filter through.[68]

It is here, rather than in Swinburne's *femmes fatales*, that we find the kind of static descriptions that dominate 'An Epic' – the women's beauty frozen in a moment.

While 'An Epic' as a whole did not find favour with the critics, it was the final poem – 'A Troth for Eternity' – that drew the most criticism and seemed to validate the accusations of misogyny in the poet. It is in this final poem that woman is slain for her false ways. However, a consideration of the form of the seventh poem highlights the underlying criticism of demands for moral narratives in art, central to the notion of the *femme fatale* as amoral art object. The first six poems of the sequence are told in the third person, with the final poem shifting to first person. It was, perhaps, this narrative shift that led the *Saturday Review* to suggest that this poem expressed the true feelings of the poet. However, the use of first person here does not reveal the inner workings of the poet's mind, but rather suggests a dramatic monologue, reminiscent of the type favoured by Robert Browning. As Maxwell says, 'Victorian critics sometimes had difficulty understanding the relation of the author to the speaker of the dramatic monologue ... the poetry emphasises the poet'.[69]

In 'A Troth', the entirety of the poem is placed in quotation marks, and the lack of the omniscient narrator actually creates more distance between the poet and the content of the poem. The interjections of the voice of the knife with which the crime will be committed heighten the surrealism of the poem, distancing it even further from the rest of the sequence. The tone of this final poem is completely different from that of the previous six poems – hysterical where they were staid – making it clear that this voice is a dramatic persona.

You will be mine; you *are* mine; yes, my Love,
I do believe you now; I may, I can –
(For *that* sings under the pillow; believe Me! –)
I bless and kiss you for them all.

She sleeps.

The Steel is singing to me now; its voice
Creeps through and through; – go on, she cannot
    hear –

---

[68] Gautier, 'Le château du souvenir', *Selected Lyrics*, pp. 211–15.

[69] Maxwell, p. 181.

'The Purest Parian'   103

The things it sings are death and love; ay, love
That death keeps true; – She sleeps, she cannot hear.[70]

The dashes in the lines, the pauses and interruptions, speed up the rhythm of the words, so they pour out upon the reader in a frenzied, feverish manner. The two voices – the man and the knife – crowd upon each other in the same line, increasing the frenetic tone of the poem. Although O'Shaughnessy keeps to a standardized metre, the abandonment of rhyme in these lines undermines the regularity of the metre, aided by the unusual punctuation. All this contributes to the overwrought, melodramatic effect of this final poem.

At the time of its publication 'An Epic of Women' was read as a young poet playing at misogyny because it was in vogue among a certain artistic set, namely that of the 'French Romantiques'.[71] Given the nature of the final poem, however, this sequence can be read as satire of the moral demands being made upon art at the time. As we have seen, it was considered the social duty of the artist to uphold the values of middle-class Victorian society; in 'good' art, then, wicked characters would always be punished. Given this moral imperative, the speaker's conclusion in 'A Troth' is the correct one – his lover must die for her sins. That this was the moral climate at the time of publication is evidenced by one reviewer's reaction to (and misreading of) 'An Epic'. The reviewer complained that 'the absence of a soul in the lover's victim deprives the stabbing, after all, of what very slender moral palliation it might otherwise lay claim to'.[72] As disturbed as he is by the sequence, this anonymous reviewer does not seem to find anything disturbing in his own assertion that if the woman possessed a soul, then the stabbing would in some way offer a moral balm to the whole of the sequence.

In 'A Troth' O'Shaughnessy pushes the requirement for a 'moral palliation' in art to the point of the absurd, and in doing so, draws attention to the absurdity of the requirement in the first place. Throughout the sequence, O'Shaughnessy aestheticizes sin. Like Art, these women are beautiful not despite their lack of morality, but because of it. Employing the richly sensuous language and imagery of decadence, each poem focuses on the aesthetic qualities of the women's crimes: the beauty of Venus even as she is caught in another man's arms; the exotic, wasteful splendor of Cleopatra's court; and the tantalizing, sensual movements of Salome's dance. The physicality associated with the *femmes fatales'* wickedness implies that immorality makes for good art. The narrator of the final poem, however, does not merely appreciate the stories that made up the first six poems as art – he searches for a moral lesson from them. He says:

---

[70]   'A Troth for Eternity', *An Epic of Women*, p. 157.

[71]   Thus, many reviewers suggested a lack of sincerity apparent in this sequence, with the *Academy* writing that it 'reads like a somewhat youthful sort of secondhand, and is at any rate in false taste' (15 November 1870, p. 33) and the *Saturday Review* saying it was cast in a 'false light' (4 March 1871, p. 282).

[72]   'Minor Poetry', *The Saturday Review*, p. 282.

O all ye Messalinas of old time –
Ye Helens, Cleopatras, ye Dalilahs,
Ye Maries, ye Lucrezias, Catherines –
Fair crowned or uncrowned – courtezans alike
Who played with men a calculated game –
Your moves their heart-wounds, deaths and ruins –
                    sure
Of your inconstancy and their soft loves,
Had I been lover in the stead of them,
Methinks the histories of you had been changed,
And some of your worst falsenesses redeemed
By flawless faithfulness to one last love.[73]

The first six poems, which the final poem repeatedly references, retell some of the greatest stories in history: *The Iliad*, Genesis, Antony and Cleopatra, among others. If a moral lesson is to be gleaned from these works, then the narrator's choice is the correct one. The absurdity of the final poem, then, is a strict warning against the confusion of ethics and aesthetics. Art, by definition unreal, has no application in reality, and to try to force it to apply is not only absurd, but dangerous. The reviews suggest, however, that this reading of the poem was lost on most critics, who instead focused on the physicality of the poems, which spoke of forthright sexuality.

III.

O'Shaughnessy returns to the message of 'An Epic' most forcefully in his final (and posthumous) volume of poetry, *Songs of a Worker*. In a sequence of 12 poems entitled 'Thoughts in Marble', he continues his attempt to defend art from the moral demands of the consumer class, but he also undertakes a defense of his own poetic corpus, particularly 'An Epic of Women'. 'Thoughts in Marble' fully embraces the aesthetic synaesthesia of writing about an art object. Each of the 12 poems of the sequence ostensibly takes sculpture as its focus, with artistic cross-breeding evident in the title itself, intermingling the ethereal (thought) with the substantive (marble). O'Shaughnessy's defence of 'Thoughts in Marble' in the Preface to *Songs* reflects the 'self-enclosed' model of art on art as an attempt to negate questions of morality in his work, as discussed earlier in the chapter:

> I wish to provide against the series of poems which I have associated with the art of sculpture being judged from an erroneous point of view. My artistic object is gained if, in them, I have kept strictly within the lines assigned to the sculptor's art, an art in which I have as yet failed to perceive either morality or immorality. They are therefore essentially thoughts in marble, or poems of form, and it would therefore be unjustifiable to look in them for a sense which is not inherent in the purest Parian.[74]

---

[73]   *Epic*, p. 147.
[74]   *Songs of a Worker*, p. vii.

'The Purest Parian' 105

Here O'Shaughnessy returns to the question of the relationship between form and content, particularly that expressed in Pater's 'School of Giorgione'. However, we can see O'Shaughnessy pushing the autonomy inherent to formalism even further than Pater does. Most notably, O'Shaughnessy embraces the art form that Pater considered lowest on the spectrum of the fusion of form and content – sculpture. Pater saw sculpture as being the medium in which it was easiest to separate form and content, and therefore to judge one without the other, the very style of critique he was attempting to eliminate. Thus, earlier in *The Renaissance* (1873), Pater says of sculpture, 'That limitation results from the material, and other necessary conditions, of all sculptured work, and consists in the tendency of such work to a hard realism, a one-sided presentment of mere form.'[75] O'Shaughnessy, however, celebrates sculpture for this very reason. As he noted in his Preface, if an artwork was pure form, there could be no demands for morality or accusations of immorality. 'Thoughts in Marble', then, addresses the same concerns as Pater, but is closer to Schiller's original dictum to annihilate content with form. O'Shaughnessy's more extreme position here evinces the move towards the more radical formalism found in later aesthetic works.

Although in the Preface to this final volume O'Shaughnessy distanced himself from 'art for art', this sequence draws directly on Gautier's manifesto poem 'L'Art' (1859), the '*ars poetica* of the Parnassian "Art for Art's Sake" movement in French poetry'.[76] In this poem, Gautier preaches a turn away from the 'ethereal, often vaporous lyricism of the earlier Romantics' by drawing a comparison between poetry and stone.[77] Gautier writes:

> Yes, fair-wrought verse shuns pliant
> Form; beauty craves the touch
>   Defiant:
> Marble, onyx, and such.[78]

Gautier suggests art in all forms – poetry and painting – should aspire to the fixity of sculpture, to live on for eternity. This idea – the immortality of art – forms the backbone of O'Shaughnessy's sequence.[79]

O'Shaughnessy employs stone as a unifying motif in *Songs of a Worker*, and particularly in 'Thoughts in Marble', chosen not just for its amorality, but also for its timelessness. Within the longer sequence of 'Thoughts' is a smaller sequence, made up of three poems named after locations famous for their stone – 'Pentelicos',

---

[75]   Pater, p. 42. By the time he wrote 'The School of Giorgione' in 1877, Pater's views of sculpture had evolved to admit that 'sculpture aspires out of the hard limitation of pure form towards colour, or its equivalent' (p. 85).

[76]   *Théophile Gautier: Selected Lyrics*, ed. Norman Shapiro, notes, p. 496.

[77]   Ibid.

[78]   Gautier, 'L'Art', *Selected Lyrics*, p. 263.

[79]   O'Shaughnessy references 'L'Art' throughout 'Thoughts in Marble'. He further signals his debt to Gautier in the poem entitled 'A Priest of Beauty' – a title he had previously bestowed upon Gautier in 'Europe' (1874).

106   *Arthur O'Shaughnessy, A Pre-Raphaelite Poet in the British Museum*

'Paros', and 'Carrara'.[80] Embodied in these poems is the aesthetic creed of 'Ars Longa, Vita Brevis', or life is brief, art endures.[81] The sequence inverts the classic story of Pygmalion, privileging art above all else, even human love. In rejecting Pygmalion's wish for statue to become flesh, the poem also rejects accusations of immorality in art, suggesting that it is people, not art, who are immoral and false. Thus, in the first of the poems, 'Pentelicos', the speaker laments the faithlessness of a mortal woman – 'Love's last deceits that loveliest did seem' – and is haunted by the pure type of beauty, represented by a statue of Venus:

> When, sometimes, mid these semblances of love,
>   Pursued with feverish joy or mad despair,
>   There flashes suddenly on my unrest
> Some marble shape of Venus, high above
>   All pain or changing, fair above all fair,
>   Still more and more desired, still unpossest.[82]

Like Pygmalion, the speaker admits desire for the marble form, but he desires it *because* it is stone – it is 'above all pain or changing', unlike a mortal woman. Turning stone to flesh would not allow the artist to finally possess that beauty, but would instead destroy it. In the next poem, 'Paros', the actual act of creation is depicted (and again, we can see O'Shaughnessy's interest in the *physicality* of that creation). Having been visited by 'flashes' of the marble shape in 'Pentelicos', the sculptor takes up clay to create his perfect woman. The allusion to Pygmalion is clear: here, as in the original myth, the act of creation is conflated with the sex act. 'When I took clay – with eager passionate hand / Inspired by love – to mould the yielding curves'.[83] The language directly references the moment of transformation in Ovid: 'Beneath his touch the flesh grew soft, its ivory hardness vanishing, and yielded to his hands.'[84] Yet, unlike Pygmalion, the sculptor doesn't wish for the stone to actually yield to his desiring touch. He is shaping not his perfect woman, but the perfect art object. The mythic transformation is reversed in 'Paros', as the sculptor turns flesh to stone, preserving and improving upon the human form in marble.

---

[80]   Pentelicos, or Pentelicus, is a mountain in Greece historically renowned for its quarries, which now lends its name to a kind of marble. Carrara is a city in Tuscany, Italy, also famed for its marble. The most famous of the three is Paros, an island in Greece, which gave rise to the term 'Parian' to describe a certain quality of marble or china (*Encyclopaedia Britannica*). Carrara and Paros are both mentioned in Gautier's 'L'Art'.

[81]   'Ars longa, vita brevis' are the first two lines of the Latin translation of an aphorism by Hippocrates, and were adopted as a motto for the Aesthetic movement. William Morris had these words emblazoned above his living room fireplace in his Red House in London.

[82]   *Songs*, p. 107.

[83]   Ibid., p. 108.

[84]   Ovid, *Metamorphoses*, trans. A.D. Melville (Oxford: Oxford World Classics, 1998), p. 233.

'*The Purest Parian*' 107

> Then, undismayed, as at a god's command,
>> Laborious, with the obedient tool that serves
>> The sculptor's mighty art and never swerves,
> Beside the crumbling form I carved the grand
> Imperishable marble.[85]

In a surprising reversal of language in these lines, it is the human woman who 'crumbles', unlike the immortal stone. Unlike the tradition of the blazon, which immortalizes the woman in art forever, here it is art that remains, while the woman who inspired it has been supplanted and forgotten. The poem, therefore, condemns Pygmalion's wish as a betrayal of art and beauty, in favour of something false and fleeting. 'Paros' ends:

> Henceforth – seeing
> The glory of her nakedness divine –
>> My heart is raised, I bend the knee and deem her
> Not simply a woman and not merely mine,
>> But goddess, as the future age shall deem her,
> Ideal love of man's eternal being.[86]

In an ironic turn, O'Shaughnessy rejects the accusation of 'fleshliness' that came in 1870 with a turn to pure materialism. He disparages the flesh of mortal women, yet these poems are no less sensuous or physical than his earlier works, despite the claims he makes in his Preface. This is why Louise Chandler Moulton dismissed the sequence out of hand, saying, 'In the group of poems called by a singular misnomer Thoughts in Marble, we certainly find little of the cold chastity of sculpture. The poems are, indeed, oversensuous – going beyond even the not too rigid boundaries the author set for himself in An Epic of Women.'[87] Moulton was correct to draw a comparison between 'An Epic' and 'Thoughts' – both are concerned with the same central issue of the relationship between morality and art; however, 'Thoughts' can also be seen as a response to much of the criticism directed at 'An Epic' at the time of its publication.

In the final poem of the stone sequence, O'Shaughnessy addresses the charge of immorality in form-focused art. 'Carrara' denies the connection between form and sexual desire, focusing instead on the reverse Pygmalionism which rejects flesh in favour of 'pure' art. The artist desired the woman who appeared in 'Pentilicos', leaving him filled with 'feverish joy or mad despair'.[88] But by shaping her into stone he has made her more than flesh, and thereby divorced her form from desire. Thus, 'Carrara', taking on the voice of the statue itself, insists:

---

[85] *Songs*, p. 108.

[86] Ibid.

[87] Moulton, p. 41.

[88] *Songs*, 108.

108 *Arthur O'Shaughnessy, A Pre-Raphaelite Poet in the British Museum*

> I am the body purified by fire;
> A man shall look on me without desire,
> But rather think what miracles of faith
> Made me ...[89]

Again, we see a focus on the act of production; here, the craft that has gone into the statue denies any potential prurience in the viewer. The mediating presence of art purifies, just as in 'An Epic' the association with the art object rejects any notions of morality or immorality in the *femmes fatales*.

In addition to responding to the charges of 'fleshliness' laid against him, in 'Thoughts in Marble' O'Shaughnessy addresses a point of contention in Victorian sculpture, as some art critics considered classical statuary depicting the nude form to be too shocking for public consumption. For example, when a cast of Michaelangelo's *David* arrived at the South Kensington Museum in 1857, gifted to Queen Victoria by the Grand Duke of Tuscany, a plaster fig leaf was added so as to protect the innocence of female viewers – including the Queen herself.[90] This was symptomatic of the whole critical climate of the day, and O'Shaughnessy directly attacks this modest cant in 'A Venus':

> Fallen from ancient Athens to the days
> > When sculpture hides her forms beneath a shroud,
> > I mingle sometimes with the bourgeois crowd
> Of rich church-going serious folk, to gaze
> On each demure-faced Venus who obeys
> > The crabbed daily rule of some purse-proud
> > Merchant or lawyer.[91]

In a cutting attack, O'Shaughnessy conflates the 'respectability' of the bourgeoisie with their mercantile culture. Beauty had become a commodity to be bought and sold, and thus was hidden away, not for morality's sake, but to guard an economic interest. As Theodor Adorno has suggested:

> The bourgeois wants his art luxurious, his life ascetic ... he becomes alienated from [works of art], as he begins to treat them like a commodity belonging to him and yet expropriable at any moment. This raises fears in him. In short, the false attitude towards art is intimately related to anxieties about loss of property; for the fetishistic notion of art as a good which can be owned and, through reflection, destroyed corresponds neatly with the idea of a piece of property in the psychic household.[92]

O'Shaughnessy rejects the hypocrisy of guarding economic interest with claims of moral decency, and in 'Thoughts in Marble' attempts to set Beauty free from

---

[89]   Ibid., 109.

[90]   Victoria and Albert Museum, vam.ac.uk/content/articles/d/davids-fig-leaf/.

[91]   *Songs*, p. 124.

[92]   Theodor Adorno, *Aesthetic Theory*, trans. C. Lenhardt, ed. Gretel Adorno and Rolf Tiedemann (London and New York: Routledge & Kegan Paul, 1986), p. 19.

'The Purest Parian'   109

both shame and economics. His insistence on 'art for humanity', explored in the previous chapter, implies art for everyone, and thus rejects the commodification of art occurring in the period.

In his 1834 preface to *Mademoiselle de Maupin*, Gautier attacked the hypocrisy of much of the moral cant aimed against art, writing, 'If there is any nudity in a picture or a book [virtuous people] go straight to it, like a pig to filth, and pay no heed to the flowers in bloom, or the luscious golden fruit that is hanging from every bough.'[93] In 'Carrara' O'Shaughnessy also attacks the hypocritical culture that takes a prurient view of artistic expression. The statue in this poem is a composite of many women, depicting martyrs, Queens, priestesses, and saints; any sin or pain that wracked the body of the actual person has been burned away by the act of creation and the art form is left pure and unburdened. Thus, 'I arose / Changed from those beds of pain, and shriven at last / From the whole shameful history of the past'.[94] O'Shaughnessy rejects claims of immorality even when immoral figures are depicted, because the mediating presence of art cleanses the subject matter, so that it can be appreciated for its form alone. This assertion can be seen as an attempt to redeem 'An Epic', as well, referencing the sequence's representation of literature's most wicked women. Thus, in 'Carrara' he writes:

> Raised now amid the hosts
> Of living men, my effigy is grown
> Passionless, speechless through the postured stone
> That holds one changeless meaning in its pose;
> The murmuring myriads pass, and each man knows
> And sees me with a cold thought at his heart;
> For I am that from which the soul must part.[95]

She is flesh incarnate, but also removed from the sins of the flesh and therefore cannot be judged by mortal standards. The repetition of the suffix 'less' in 'passionless', 'speechless', 'changeless', reduces the complex entity of the women depicted down to the bare form, stripping away everything that is not the mere shape of stone.

The celebration of the eternal quality of art was a hallmark of the aesthetes. Thus, Arthur Symons notes that Théophile Gautier:

> [L]oved imperishable things: the body, as generation after generation refashions it, the world, as it is restored and rebuilt, and then gems, and hewn stone, and carved ivory, and woven tapestry. He loved verse for its solid, strictly limited, resistant form, which, while prose melts and drifts about it, remains unalterable, indestructible.[96]

---

[93] Théophile Gautier, *Mademoiselle de Maupin*, trans. Joanna Richardson (Harmondsworth and New York: Penguin Books, 1981).

[94] *Songs*, p. 109.

[95] Ibid., p. 111.

[96] Arthur Symons, *The Symbolist Movement in Literature* (New York: E.P. Dutton & Co., 1919), p. 99.

The mid- to late Victorian period can be somewhat defined by a loss of religious faith and so the aesthetes, faced with their own mortality, sought to replace Heaven with art, to construct an afterlife out of form. As seen in poems such as 'Nostalgie des Cieux' and 'Seraphitus' discussed in the previous chapter, O'Shaughnessy conflated the realm of art with that of Heaven, as both a place of freedom and a substitute for eternity. Thus, while Pygmalion made art human, in his stone sequence O'Shaughnessy makes it divine. The statue he depicts is 'not simply woman' but a goddess for future ages. Here, again, O'Shaughnessy reflects the idea at the heart of Gautier's 'L'Art':

> The gods themselves die; still,
> Princely, poems shall reign
>   And will
> Stronger than brass remain.[97]

In 'The Line of Beauty', O'Shaughnessy invokes William Hogarth's theory of aesthetics from his 1753 *Analysis of Beauty*. Hogarth suggested that the serpentine 'line of beauty' suggested liveliness, whereas straight lines signified stagnation or death. O'Shaughnessy's line of beauty goes beyond this; it is not just lively, but ever-living, eternal.

> What is eternal? What escapes decay?
>   A certain faultless, matchless, deathless line,
>   Curving consummate. Death, Eternity,
> Add nought to it, from it take nought away;
>   'Twas all God's gift and all man's mastery,
>   God become human and man grown divine.[98]

The categories of God, man, and art become conflated and inseparable in this world-view. Again we have the repetition of 'less' in these lines, as these poems are an act of reduction, rejecting from art anything but pure beauty.

In *The Renaissance* Walter Pater reacted to human mortality by insisting on living for the moment, rejecting habit to maximize the experiences of life. Thus, his famous lines:

> Not the fruit of experience, but experience itself, is the end. A counted number of pulses only is given to us of a variegated, dramatic life. How may we see in them all that is to be seen in them by the finest senses? How shall we pass most swiftly from point to point, and be present always at the focus where the greatest number of vital forces unite in their purest energy? To burn always with this hard, gem-like flame, to maintain this ecstasy, is success in life.[99]

---

[97] Gautier, 'L'Art', p. 267.

[98] *Songs*, p. 106.

[99] Pater, p. 152.

Leighton says of Pater's famous Conclusion: 'He undermines, long before twentieth-century theory does, the timeless transcendence supposed to inhere in the art object. Far from being in a timeless preserve, art belongs precisely to "the moment", and the moment snatched, by passionate attention, from universal flux and disintegration.'[100] Pater certainly advocates the pleasure of art in 'the moment', but I disagree with Leighton in thinking he undermines the timelessness of art.[101] The art objects he considers in *The Renaissance* are just as modern, just as relevant to him, as when they were created centuries before. Pater writes his conclusion from the spectator's perspective, but this perspective requires artists who shape the eternal objects that can fill men like Pater with this ecstasy for ages to come.

The classicism apparent in the work of both Pater and O'Shaughnessy, as well as that of other aesthetes, was another way of protesting the moral strictures the middle-class attempted to place upon art. The very timelessness of these ancient art works served as proof for the aesthetes that aesthetics were universal in a way that social and moral codes were not. Pater's *Renaissance* offers a reason why so many artists turned to the classical period for inspiration:

> One of the strongest characteristics of that outbreak of the reason and the imagination, of that assertion of the liberty of the heart, in the middle age, which I have termed a medieval Renaissance, was its antinomianism, its spirit of rebellion and revolt against the moral and religious ideas of the time. In their search after the pleasures of the senses and the imagination, in their care for beauty, in their worship of the body, people were impelled beyond the bounds of the Christian ideal.[102]

Pater conceives of the Middle Ages as a parallel to his own age, and with Matthew Arnold he insists that the nineteenth century needs to Hellenize – to embrace the 'pleasures of the senses and the imagination'. Arnold saw his own age as being dominated by 'Hebraism' and suggested, 'As Hellenism speaks of thinking clearly, seeing things in their essence and beauty, as a grand and precious feat for man to achieve, so Hebraism speaks of becoming conscious of sin, of awakening to a sense of sin, as a feat of this kind.'[103] Many aesthetes considered Greek culture to be 'modern' in a way that the middle ages were not; where the medieval period had been steeped in superstition and asceticism, the ancient Greeks were seen as 'the spiritual contemporaries of modern Englishmen', in ideas of democracy,

---

[100]   Leighton, p. 80.

[101]   Evangelista also counters this idea, emphasizing the modernity that Pater found in ancient art: 'The critic's personal investment, in the form of the pleasure derived from the experience of art, interacts with the art object, taking it out of its remote past and reasserting its very concrete present as object of the senses' (p. 29).

[102]   Pater, p. 16.

[103]   Matthew Arnold, *Culture and Anarchy* (Cambridge: Cambridge University Press, 1955), p. 135.

humanism, science, and commerce.[104] Thus, by the time Wilde wrote 'The Critic as Artist' (1891), he could claim, 'Whatever, in fact, is modern in our life we owe to the Greeks. Whatever is an anachronism is due to mediævalism.'[105] For Pater and Arnold, along with the other aesthetes, knowledge of ancient Greece provided artists with a cultural vantage point from which to criticize the bourgeois values of the Victorian period. The study of Greek and Latin was still a fundamental part of an Oxford or Cambridge degree, and therefore this knowledge provided the aesthetes with the cultural capital necessary to attack all aspects of modern culture – even Christianity.[106] This turn to Greek subject matter, then, was explicitly a turn away from the dominant values of the period, particularly the demand for morality in art.

In looking at O'Shaughnessy's poetic career, we could trace a similar trajectory from medievalism to classicism, as he moved from *Lays of France* in 1872 to 'Thoughts in Marble' in 1881. However, I suggest that O'Shaughnessy employs medievalism and classicism identically in his poetry, as an outside vantage point from which to criticize his own age and its shortcomings. By turning either to ancient Greece or medieval France, as he did in *Lays of France*, O'Shaughnessy was able to step outside the Victorian period in order to explore taboo subjects while evading contemporary demands for morality.[107]

O'Shaughnessy employs the ancient as a critique of the modern to the fullest in his 'Dialogue between Two Venuses'. This poem explicitly sets the ancient and modern at odds, pitting a classical Athenian Venus against its mid-Victorian counterpart. Specifically, the two statues represented are the Aphrodite of Cnidus, the first life-sized statue of Venus, sculpted in the fourth century B.C. by Praxiteles of Athens, and the 'Tinted Venus' by the British sculptor John Gibson, 1850. They are similar statues, both with bared breasts, but the Victorian Venus holds her drapery close to her body, cascading over and concealing her groin, where the ancient Venus merely holds a hand in front of her genitals, just barely shielding them from the viewer's gaze. In O'Shaughnessy's dialogue the two Venuses argue the morality of Beauty. The Victorian Venus argues for the virtue of her age, and the overturning of the ancient sin that the First Venus represents. 'Long since men put away / The ancient in thou symbolest, and broke / Love's altars, and beat down

---

[104] Evangelista, p. 9.

[105] Oscar Wilde, 'The Critic as Artist', *Intentions*, 13th ed. (London: Methuen & Co., 1919), p. 119.

[106] Evangelista, p. 24, p. 125.

[107] In his consideration of Swinburne's poetry, Antony Harrison also rejects the traditional critical claim that the medieval and classical were universally opposed in the Victorian period, stating, 'That Arthurian and Trojan themes are two of the central sources of subject matter for medieval romanceurs reveals how natural the connection between them is, but it was one seldom made during the nineteenth century. However, Swinburne, conscious in his usual scholarly fashion of his place in literary tradition, revives the historical association between Greek and Arthurian mythology.' Antony Harrison, *Swinburne's Medievalism: A Study in Victorian Love Poetry* (Baton Rouge and London: Louisiana State University Press, 1988), p. 141.

'The Purest Parian'   113

his flower yoke'.[108] The First Venus rejects this moral cant as a 'Gothic lie'.[109] She argues instead for a religion of Beauty, the one unchanging aspect of the world. The extremes of modern morality are depicted in the argument of the Second Venus, in which mankind's very existence in the world is a sin and a source of shame:

> Henceforth the daily thought of heaven or hell,
> Chastened man's life; almost he feared to dwell
> His perilous time of travail on the earth,
> Full of pollutions, knowing first his birth
> A shame done when the face of God was turned
> Away in wrath or pity.[110]

The unhappy asceticism of Victorian respectability is highlighted in the modern Venus's words, as she claims that beauty is the 'sister of the serpent-temptress'. O'Shaughnessy gives the last word in this dialogue to the ancient Venus, who insists that Beauty purifies and so its appreciation cannot be a sin. As in 'Carrara' – 'the body purified by fire' – the statue is beauty and form alone, and therefore completely devoid of morality or immorality.

In 'Thoughts in Marble', O'Shaughnessy combines many of the aesthetic attempts to combat the moral imperative of the bourgeois art world; he champions Schiller's annihilation of content by form by embracing the self-enclosed model of artistic synaesthesia and heralds the timelessness of the aesthetic in an invocation of the classicism of ancient Greece. Coming at the mid-point between Pater and Wilde, these 12 poems illustrate the trajectory of aesthetic theory in the later nineteenth century, as art struggled to free itself from the demands of the mercantile bourgeois middle-class. Throughout O'Shaughnessy's body of work, however, we can trace the beginnings of these aestheticist leanings, from the sensual physicality of 'An Epic of Women' that demands that art be freed from limiting moral strictures, to his adoption and adaptation of French fixed forms which seek to create a self-enclosed model of art as craft. O'Shaughnessy was on the forefront of the importation of formalism and aestheticism from France, foreshadowing the English decadence that would take root in the 1890s.

---

[108] *Songs*, p. 114.

[109] The use of the word 'gothic' seems a direct attack on Ruskin's view of morality in art.

[110] *Songs*, p. 119.

Chapter 4
'Those too sanguine singers':
Arthur O'Shaughnessy's French Influences

I.

In the Preface to *Songs of a Worker*, O'Shaughnessy discussed his poetic career in terms of the work of Victor Hugo and Charles Baudelaire, rather than any of his English contemporaries. That O'Shaughnessy privileged the literature of France over that of England is evident throughout his correspondence and his private writings. While he greatly admired the English Pre-Raphaelites and sought their friendships, his strongest influence was the poetry of France.

In his unpublished notebooks, O'Shaughnessy explicitly states the superiority of French literature. In a brief essay entitled 'Comparison between general characteristics of English & of French writers', written in 1870, O'Shaughnessy suggests that while the 'nucleus' of poetry is the same in all men – 'affections which are common to the whole of humanity'– the 'product' of poetry is greatly shaped by nationality.[1] He compares the literature of France and England, noting that the 'spirit which informs the work' of England is 'modern conditions of related social existence: – or circumstances – acted upon individual natures', while in France's poetry 'individual nature [is] traced to [the] absolute development of all its concomitant elements – in harmony with & antagonism to surroundings of circumstance'.[2] The poetic practice of France is, according to O'Shaughnessy, 'evidently the highest & most comprehensive in its relation to individual nature as it admits of the entire study & delineation of the same throughout all its phases', while that of England 'speaks only such portions of nature as come to the surface through the rub of surrounding influences'.[3] Or, to put it more simply, England's poetry 'takes an *outside* cast of the personality, rather than a portrait of the full inward spiritual nature'.[4]

Here we see reflected many of the arguments discussed in the previous chapter: O'Shaughnessy feels that English poetry is inhibited by 'modern ... moral tendencies' and a demand for poetry that expresses the modern condition, rather than personal feelings. It is this poetry of personality that Buchanan criticizes Rossetti for in 'The Fleshly School of Poetry' when he complains, 'In

---

[1]   Belfast, Queen's University, O'Shaughnessy Manuscript Collection, MS 8/22, dated June 1870, pp. 8–12 (p. 10).

[2]   Ibid., p. 11.

[3]   Ibid.

[4]   Ibid.

116   *Arthur O'Shaughnessy, A Pre-Raphaelite Poet in the British Museum*

petticoats or pantaloons, in modern times or in the middle ages, he is just Mr. Rossetti.'[5] Although O'Shaughnessy suggests that France is free from inhibiting modern 'moral tendencies', it is more accurate to say that French poets engaged in more fervent counterattacks against the bourgeois moral imperative. While Rossetti defended his poetry by claiming that Buchanan had merely misread it, the French 'Parnassians' with whom O'Shaughnessy socialized in Paris openly disregarded any moral claims upon their art.[6] Thus, Catulle Mendès sneers at 'dismal didactic pieces' of poetry, insisting that the only concern of the poet was 'to write verse correctly'.[7]

O'Shaughnessy pursued friendships within Parisian literary circles with the same determination as he approached the Pre-Raphaelites in England, sending volumes to well-known members of the movement and awaiting an introduction. A letter from his wife Eleanor written in 1875 provides evidence that O'Shaughnessy strived for literary connections in France with the same vigour as he did in England. She writes:

> I felt while I read [O'Shaughnessy's letters] quite transported from this atmosphere of this sick room into that beautiful artistic one I love to think you are breathing, and that will brace up your intellectual lungs for the winter. It is good to me to think of my pearl of great price being for a time so fitly set. I told you what a sensation you would make.[8]

She closes the letter by sending love from O'Shaughnessy's mother and noting 'she is so glad to think of the recognition you have met with'.[9] It seems evident that O'Shaughnessy took this solitary trip to Paris in order to infiltrate the French literary scene. He took frequent holidays of this nature and was introduced to literary giants such as Victor Hugo, but it was among the younger poets of the day, the so-called Parnassians, that O'Shaughnessy formed the majority of his friendships.[10]

---

[5]   Robert Buchanan, 'The Fleshly School of Poetry: Mr. D.G. Rossetti', *Contemporary Review* 18 (August/November 1871): 334–50 (p. 339).

[6]   Rossetti answered Buchanan's attack in an article entitled 'The Stealthy School of Criticism', published in the *Athenaeum* (December 1871). In it, Rossetti does not maintain that the poet should be allowed to write about all aspects of human life, including sex, but rather that lines from 'Willowwood' were quoted out of context to make them sound more salacious than he intended.

[7]   Catulle Mendès, 'Recent French Poets', trans. Arthur O'Shaughnessy, *Gentleman's Magazine* 245, no. 1786 (October 1879): 478–504 (p. 484, p. 490).

[8]   Columbia University, Rare Book & Manuscript Library, MS #0956, letter dated 1875.

[9]   Ibid.

[10]   Edmund Gosse, *Silhouettes*, Essay Index Reprint Series (Freeport, NY: Books for Libraries Press, 1971), p. 177.

'Those too sanguine singers' 117

This group of young poets – alternately known as the *'fantaisistes'*, the *'impassibles'*, and the 'Parnassians'[11] – took as their inspiration Gautier, Baudelaire, de Banville, de Lisle, Hugo, and Ronsard, and declared that their goal was to 'make an end of the detestable poetical system reinstated in France ... We proclaimed that the subject of a poem is not everything; that emotion or utility is no irrefutable proof of beauty; that to weep or to teach are not enough to make a great poet.'[12] *'Impassible'* was used pejoratively towards the group, but its translation – 'impassive' or 'emotionless' – highlights the Parnassians' central goal of divorcing their poetry from the kind of melodramatic sentimentality they felt overran literature of the day. 'What? we were not satisfied to shed our tears over a family grave! It was not enough for us to see a little child blow its nose as it went to school, to be seized at once with a delicate inspiration!'[13]

These lines appeared in *Gentleman's Magazine* in 1879, in an article suggested, promoted, and translated by O'Shaughnessy. Originally approached by the magazine to provide a study of recent French poets, O'Shaughnessy writes, 'I feel that in enabling my friend, M. Catulle Mendès, to become the collective voice of the entire fraternity which he represents, I have obtained what is far more interesting than any English writing on the subject could be.'[14] In addition to importing the views of these radical French aesthetes directly to the English public, O'Shaughnessy translated contemporary French poetry for an English audience and reviewed French works in the English press whenever possible.[15] Thus, E. Souffrin described O'Shaughnessy as a 'friend and devotee' of Stéphane Mallarmé, reporting that O'Shaughnessy 'tried to make Mallarmé known' 'in his articles in the Athenaeum, the Morning Post, the Saturday Review, etc.'[16] Edmund Gosse writes, 'there was small communication between literary Paris and London in the days immediately preceding the war of 1870. Arthur O'Shaughnessy

---

[11]   Mendès reports that the group first earned the name *fantaisistes* after the publication *Le revue fantaisiste*, founded by Mendès in 1861. They were then given the derogatory name of *impassibles* after 'Louis Xavier de Ricard having let fall, in a published letter, the sentiment that Art should be "impassible", this word was seized upon, repeated and twisted in many different senses, and made to serve as a new byword for the school which was forming' (Mendès, p. 488). The name 'Parnassians' – which has stood the test of time – was taken from the publication *Le Parnasse contemporain*, begun in 1866.

[12]   Ibid., p. 490.

[13]   Ibid., p. 491.

[14]   Editorial footnote in 'Recent French Poets', p. 478.

[15]   This article was accompanied by several translations of the work of the Parnassians by O'Shaughnessy, which were later reprinted in his final collection of poetry, *Songs of a Worker* (1881). O'Shaughnessy reviewed François Coppée's *L'Exile: Poésies* in the *Athenaeum* on 9 June 1877.

[16]   E. Souffrin, 'Coup d'oeil sur la bibliothèque anglaise de Mallarmé', *Revue de Literature comparée* 32 (1958): 390–97 (p. 395). My translation. 'Arthur O'Shaughnessy, un des amis les plus dévoués, qui s'efforçait de faire connaître Mallarmé en lui consacrant des articles dans l'*Athenaeum*, le *Morning Post*, la *Saturday Review*, etc.'

118   *Arthur O'Shaughnessy, A Pre-Raphaelite Poet in the British Museum*

used to go over to France for his holidays and he was the first to bring us back authentic news of the Parnassians.'[17] Gosse here gives O'Shaughnessy primacy in the movement towards the French decadent or Parnassian aesthetic in English literature. Traditionally, Swinburne's *Poems and Ballads* of 1866 is credited with being the first volume to introduce this decadent aesthetic to England. While O'Shaughnessy's own first and most decadent volume was not published until 1870, he took frequent trips to France throughout his youth, and notebooks dated as early as 1864 evince a clear influence by poets such as Baudelaire.[18] It seems Swinburne and O'Shaughnessy came to an appreciation of French aesthetics independently – they did not meet until after the publication of *An Epic of Women* in 1870 – and we can therefore place O'Shaughnessy at the forefront of this literary movement.

O'Shaughnessy's efforts to import French literature into England helped to shape the aesthetic and decadent movements that would flower in the 1880s and 1890s in England, in the works of writers like Oscar Wilde and Arthur Symons. However, the path of influence was not entirely one-sided between France and England, as Jennifer Birkett notes:

> The vigour that resurfaces in French writing in the late eighties owes much to the force of internal politics – the rise of anarchism – but much, too, to influences from across the channel. Ideas which in the first place had come from France were now returned in new, invigorating form.[19]

O'Shaughnessy helped to make a French literary aesthetic both accessible and acceptable in England, paving the way for the aesthetes who would follow, and helping to shape the literary aesthetic that would then be reincorporated into French literature in the decade following his death. His primacy in the revitalization of characters such as Salome in his 'Daughter of Herodias' suggests the path of his influence, since Mallarmé appropriated the same subject in his *Herodiade* (1898), as did Wilde in 1891 in *Salome*.[20] Charles Bernheimer calculates that over 1,000 versions of Salome (written or painted) were produced between 1870 and 1920 – a

---

[17]   Gosse, *Silhouettes*, p. 176.

[18]   See, e.g., Queen's, MS 8/17, 'Ina's Tale', clean copy dated 18 February 1864. The descriptions of the magical Prince's palace in this tale are very reminiscent of the descriptions of Herod's palace in 1870's 'Daughter of Herodias'.

[19]   Jennifer Birkett, *The Sins of the Fathers: Decadence in France, 1870–1914* (London and New York: Quartet Books, 1986), p. 35.

[20]   Several of Mallarmé's later works either consciously or unconsciously revisit O'Shaughnessy's earlier poetry. In his 1889 'Le Cantonnier', Mallarmé compares himself to a road worker, in order to make the point that intellectual work is a kind of labour; in doing so, Mallarmé aligns himself with the proletariat, united against the influence of the bourgeoisie. This is nearly identical in subject matter and intent to O'Shaughnessy's 1881 'Song of a Fellow-Worker', a poem that was written during the period of his correspondence with Mallarmé. See my discussion of 'Song of a Fellow-Worker' in Chapter 2.

phenomenon he dubs 'Salomania'.[21] O'Shaughnessy was one of the first writers of the period to adopt this character as the embodiment of artistic decadence.

O'Shaughnessy's interest in France began at an early age. Louise Chandler Moulton writes that he 'was half a Frenchman in his love for and mastery of the French language; and many of his closest affiliations were with the younger school of French poets'.[22] Although O'Shaughnessy's education by tutor was completed by the time he began work at the British Museum at the age of 17, he was already fluent in French and well read in the language.[23] One unpublished notebook records O'Shaughnessy's reading from June to August of 1870 and reveals that most of his research was conducted in French. Thus, when he wanted to know about the Jewish faith, he read *La kabbale: ou, la philosophie religieuse des Hébreux*, by Adolphe Franck.[24] His interest in Italian literature manifested in his reading of *Histoire de la littérature italienne contemporaine* by Amédée Roux. To find out about Oriental art, he turned to Noel des Vergers's *L'Étrurie et les étrusques*.[25] In fiction and poetry, as well, O'Shaughnessy primarily read French works, many of which were not available in English translations. His correspondence with his lover Helen Snee is often dominated by literary discussion, and of the 14 works mentioned between 1869 and 1871, nine of them are French (with French-influenced works such as Swinburne's *Poems and Ballads* and John Payne's *Masque of Shadows* among the number in English). Helen and O'Shaughnessy read and discussed works by Baudelaire, Gautier, Dumas, Flaubert, and Balzac. Helen writes, 'I am delighted at your selection of Gautier's charming stories', and later calls him 'our dear Théophile'.[26] Later she writes of Balzac's *Eugénie Grandet* (1833), 'May I

---

[21] *Decadent Subjects: The Idea of Decadence in Art, Literature, Philosophy and Culture of the Fin de Siècle in Europe*, ed. Charles Bernheimer, T. Jefferson Kline, and Naomi Schor (Baltimore and London: The Johns Hopkins University Press, 2002), p. 104.

[22] Louise Chandler Moulton, *Arthur O'Shaughnessy: His Life and Work with Selections from His Poems* (Cambridge and Chicago: Stone & Kimball, 1894), p. 18. Vernon Lee offers a more cutting portrayal of O'Shaughnessy's overwhelming passion for all things French in her character Cosmo Chough. She writes, 'he spoke of French things with an affectation of throaty accent and allusions to his "real country" which greatly puzzled Anne'. *Miss Brown* (Edinburgh and London: William Blackwood and Sons, 1884), vol. 1, p. 282.

[23] It seems O'Shaughnessy had a gift for languages, as he reports translating several articles from the original Swedish and Danish for his superiors at the British Museum. BMOP C.11997.

[24] O'Shaughnessy published an article on the Kabbalah faith in 1879 – referred to in a letter from May Doyle of October 24, 1879. Duke University, Manuscript Collection, 6th 11:A Box 1, c.1.

[25] *L'Étrurie et les étrusques: ou Dix ans de fouilles dans les Maremmes toscanes*, published in 1864.

[26] *A Pathetic Love Episode in a Poet's Life, being letters from Helen Snee to Arthur W.E. O'Shaughnessy. Also a letter from him containing a dissertation on Love*, ed. Clement King Shorter (London: printed for private circulation, 1916), p. 18.

be pardoned for having ever spoken disrespectfully of Balzac? It is a wonderful work, and to me perfect.'[27] O'Shaughnessy cultivated a taste for French literature in his lovers, and a decade later in his courtship of May Doyle, he encouraged the girl towards similar works.[28] He sent her a list of recommendations that included Hugo and Baudelaire, as well as his Parnassian friends: François Coppée, Catulle Mendès, and Sully Prudhomme.

That O'Shaughnessy's literary taste was unusual for an Englishman even in 1879 is evinced by the difficulty May faced in finding any of the books O'Shaughnessy recommended to her. She reports to O'Shaughnessy that the local libraries in Cheltenham carried none of the books he recommended, and even when she wrote to Mudie's in London, she was unable to procure the works of any of the Parnassians, or Baudelaire.[29] A search of the review sections of the *Athenaeum* or *The Saturday Review* reveals similar results. Few reviews or articles appear on even such well-regarded poets as Stéphane Mallarmé until well into the 1880s, and sometimes not even until the 1890s, when interest in these French poets reached its height in England's own flourishing decadent movement.

Shortly before his death in 1881, O'Shaughnessy was appointed English correspondent for *Le Livre* in Paris, continuing his lifelong passion of encouraging literary communion between England and France. Although frequently overshadowed by Swinburne in this regard, O'Shaughnessy is noteworthy for his early attempts to import a French aesthetic to England, during a period that was notoriously resistant to influence from the Continent.[30]

II.

Like the Parnassians he socialized with on his visits to Paris, O'Shaughnessy was heavily influenced in his early poetry by the work of French decadents such as Charles Baudelaire and Théophile Gautier. This was noted in early reviews of O'Shaughnessy's *An Epic of Women*, with the *Academy* writing, 'The influences to which we should be inclined chiefly to refer it are those of a section of the French *Romantiques*, Baudelaire and Gautier at their head.'[31] It is from the *Romantiques* that O'Shaughnessy learned his decadent aesthetic. Decadence was particularly known for its more disturbing or perverse elements, but it was the desire for

---

[27]   Shorter, p. 21.

[28]   Following the death of O'Shaughnessy's wife, Eleanor, he became engaged to the 21-year-old May Doyle, with whom he carried on a significant correspondence in 1879 and 1880. However, O'Shaughnessy's sudden death in January of 1881 meant that the marriage never took place.

[29]   Duke, letters dated 17 September, 27 November, and 4 December 1879.

[30]   Thus so eminent a figure in the English literary scene as Tennyson complained of 'art with poisonous honey stol'n from France'. 'An Epilogue to the Queen', 1872.

[31]   'Review: An Epic of Women and other Poems', *The Academy* (15 November 1870): 32–3 (p. 33).

literature that could explore all aspects of human nature, without the interference of modern morality, that drew writers to this aesthetic. R.K.R. Thornton writes:

> It is not the love of corruption for itself which lies behind this [decadence], however, but a desire to use to the full the tremendous powers of the mature language in describing new and hitherto uncharted areas of experience, claiming as its study everything that is part of life, including those new horrors that come with civilization and its movement away from nature into artifice.[32]

As with his embrace of formalism considered earlier, the desire to divorce art from restrictive standards of Victorian morality can be seen as one of the driving forces of O'Shaughnessy's corpus.

In his writing on Baudelaire, Gautier defines decadence by its 'delicate tints and refinements, gathering all the delicacies of speech, borrowing from technical vocabularies, taking colour from every palette, tones from all musical instruments, forcing itself to the expression of the most elusive thoughts, contours vague and fleeting, listening to translate subtle confidences, confessions of depraved passions and the odd hallucinations of a fixed idea turning to madness'.[33] For Gautier decadence is tonal and atmospheric, reflective of a certain attitude of the writer. In *An Epic of Women*, however, O'Shaughnessy approached French decadence as a highly imitable *genre* of literature, defined by certain easily identified tropes and markers: sensory/sensual details of colour, texture, and odour; the prevalence of imperishable objects of beauty, such as gold and jewels; and Eastern settings peopled by dark-skinned women, all couched in terms of the exotic and erotic. This reductive approach to decadence is particularly evident in an overuse of words such as 'perfume', and an overwrought colour vocabulary – 'amber' is chosen over 'yellow', and 'azure' over blue.

We can see each of these tropes evident in a poem like Gautier's 'Cærulei Oculi', which can be considered stereotypically 'decadent'. It begins 'A woman of dark mystery, / Of sense-distressing beauty', and continues on to describe her: 'Her eyes blend with the bitter blue / Of azure skies – wet with a glint's / Sequin-like twinkle – a dullish hue / Of glaucous ocean's sea-green tints'.[34] Here we already have a prevalence of colour words, a dark-skinned beauty, and a comparison of a woman to a 'paillette' (sequin). The poem, about a Siren, references rare treasures lying at the bottom of the sea: 'the goblet rare of Thule's king', 'Cleopatra's other pearl', 'Solomon's ring', and 'the crown in Schiller's ballad sung'.[35] The Siren acts as a typical *femme fatale*, seducing the narrator, only to drown him:

---

[32] R.K.R. Thornton, *The Decadent Dilemma* (London: Edward Arnold, 1983), p. 19.

[33] *Charles Baudelaire: His Life*, trans. Guy Thorne (London: Greening and Co., 1915), p. 20.

[34] Théophile Gautier, 'Cærulei Oculi', *Théophile Gautier: Selected Lyrics*, ed. and trans. Norman R. Shapiro (New Haven and London: Yale University Press, 2011), p. 67.

[35] Ibid., pp. 67–9.

122   *Arthur O'Shaughnessy, A Pre-Raphaelite Poet in the British Museum*

Come to my pearled couch! Round your waist
My sea-arms shall enlace your hips;
The waves will lose their acrid taste
And flow like honey on your lips.[36]

It is in poems such as this one that we find O'Shaughnessy's inspiration for much of his early decadent verse. It was 'An Epic of Women' that drew the most comparisons to the *Romantiques*, and within this sequence we can see examples of all of the tropes and markers outlined above. For example, the court of Cleopatra is described as follows in 'An Epic of Women' (1870):

More jewelries than one could name or know,
    Set in a thousand trinkets or in crowns
Each one a sovereignty, in glittering row
    Numbered the suppliant lands and all her thrones.

And fairest handmaidens in gracious rank;
    Their captive arms enchained with links of gold,
Knelt and poured forth the purple wine she drank,
    Or served her these in postures manifold.

And beaded women of a yellow Ind
    Stood at the couch, with bended hand to ply
Great silver feathered fans wherein the wind
    Gat all the choicest fumes of Araby.[37]

In a mere 12 lines O'Shaughnessy manages four colour words (gold, silver, purple, and yellow), jewels and other ornaments, Indian women, and Arabic odours. The prevalence of colour words is particularly indicative of stylistic decadence in O'Shaughnessy's work – he employs 62 colour words in 'An Epic of Women'. The setting of 'Cleopatra' further embraces decadent tropes; although it takes place in the open-air on a boat, there is nothing natural about this scene. Decadence favoured close interior scenes, and in 'Cleopatra' we find an entirely artificial world focused exclusively on the human body and its adornment.

Critics have long debated the 'reasons' for the decadent movement, drawing causal links to the French Revolution, the industrial revolution, natural sciences, the violence of the Second Empire, and other points of instability in the nineteenth century. However, Brian Stableford suggests that all decadent writing in England 'divorce[d] the Decadent style from its typical subject matter', treating the literary movement as nothing but 'interesting mannerisms'.[38] For Stableford, this means that 'what passed for Decadence in England was but a pale shadow of

---

[36]   Ibid., p. 71.

[37]   Arthur O'Shaughnessy, 'Cleopatra', *An Epic of Women and Other Poems* (London: John Camden Hotten, 1870), p. 96.

[38]   Brian Stableford, *Glorious Perversity: The Decline and Fall of Literary Decadence* (San Bernardino, CA: The Borgo Press, 1998), p. 124.

'Those too sanguine singers' 123

French Decadence'.[39] In O'Shaughnessy's early works, decadence does have the appearance of an adopted mannerism, shadowing or reflecting the French works that he admired. For example, O'Shaughnessy describes Salome's dance of the seven veils in 'Daughter of Herodias':

> The veils fell round her like thin coiling mists
> Shot through by topaz suns, and amethysts,
>   And rubies she had on;
> And out of them her jewelled body came,
> And seemed to all quite like a slender flame
> That curled and glided, and that burnt and shone
>   Most fair to look upon.[40]

The jewels conflate with the exotic female body, transforming it from perishable to imperishable, and therefore worthy of worship. This imagery immediately calls to mind Baudelaire's 'Les Bijoux' ('The Jewels'):

> Knowing my heart, my dearest one was nude,
> Her resonating jewellery all she wore,
> Which rich array gave her the attitude
> Of darling in the harem of a Moor.
>
> When dancing, ringing out its mockeries,
> This radiating world of gold and stones
> Ravishes me to lovers' ecstasies
> Over the interplay of light and tones.[41]

Again, naked flesh mingles with cold, imperishable jewels and stones, and an Oriental girl dances in the light. The emphasis on the light and tone of the scene – 'the slender flame' in O'Shaughnessy's poem – further echoes Baudelaire's work.

The allusive nature of 'An Epic' was not lost on its readers, and the echoes of Baudelaire, Gautier, and other French decadents raised questions of O'Shaughnessy's sincerity in writing these poems. Thus, the *Academy* said 'An Epic' 'reads like a somewhat youthful sort of second-hand, and is at any rate in false taste' and the *Saturday Review* said it was cast in a 'false light'.[42] Even Rossetti noted, 'I certainly think the "Epic" less in the author's true vein as a whole than the rest. There is something like an affection of cynicism (or perhaps rather an undue indulgence of such morbid mood) which doesn't please me.'[43] There is a sense

---

[39]   Ibid., p. 108.

[40]   O'Shaughnessy, *Epic*, p. 119.

[41]   Charles Baudelaire, 'The Jewels', *The Flowers of Evil*, trans. James McGowan (Oxford: Oxford University Press, 2008), p. 47.

[42]   *The Academy* (15 November 1870), p. 33. *The Saturday Review* (4 March 1871), p. 282.

[43]   *Correspondence of Dante Gabriel Rossetti*, ed. William E. Fredeman (Cambridge and Rochester: D.S. Brewer, 2004), vol. 4, p. 550.

124 *Arthur O'Shaughnessy, A Pre-Raphaelite Poet in the British Museum*

here that the author of poems like 'Fountain of Tears' (a favourite of the critics) could not be genuine in the sentiments expressed in 'An Epic', indicating perhaps a problematic tonal inconsistency in this volume, in which 'An Epic' stands out as quite different from the rest of the poems. This notion of merely playing at decadence is highlighted in Vernon Lee's portrayal of the aesthetic poets, centring on O'Shaughnessy's stand-in, Cosmo Chough:

> Poets, especially the inexhaustible Chough, would recite their compositions, perched on the arms of sofas or stretching on the hearth-rug; while the ladies went to sleep, or pretended to do so, over the descriptions of the kisses of cruel, blossom-mouthed women, who sucked out their lovers' hearts, bit their lips, and strewed their apartments with coral-like drops of blood. Most of these poets, as Anne speedily discovered, were young men of harmless lives, and altogether unacquainted with the beautiful, baleful ladies they represented as sucking at their vitals; and none was more utterly harmless than Cosmo Chough.[44]

By the time Gosse reviewed O'Shaughnessy's third volume, *Music and Moonlight*, after noting that, 'In Mr. O'Shaughnessy's earliest book, attentive eyes saw beneath the high tone of general colouring an outline of individuality that had little in common with the sensuousness of surface', he celebrates the fact that O'Shaughnessy 'no longer has much fellowship with the French Romanticists'.[45] Here Gosse recognizes that in 'An Epic', O'Shaughnessy employed decadence merely as a kind of gilding, a surface sensuousness. As Gosse's words suggest, accusations of insincerity did not persist after *An Epic*.

I suggest, however, that O'Shaughnessy's use of decadence as an imitable aesthetic stems not from insincerity, but from a failure to integrate the realities of his life in the unreality of his decadent art. Rather than merely 'playing' at decadence, I suggest that O'Shaughnessy was particularly drawn to the aesthetic because it intimated a break from the everyday, a revolutionary rejection of the bourgeois reality of his life at the museum. The timing of O'Shaughnessy's first attempts at decadent verse is crucial; in 1869, he was facing the reality of a potentially long service at the Natural History Departments of the British Museum, with very little room for promotion or improvement. Six years into his career as a taxonomist, O'Shaughnessy had realized that he was unsuited for the work, both physically – because of his poor vision – and temperamentally. He had already suffered the embarrassment of the misidentified species and the ensuing conflict with a foreign expert, detailed in Chapter 1. His working conditions were unpleasant and his salary was poor – following a promotion to Senior Assistant in 1866, O'Shaughnessy still earned only £210 per annum.[46] He would, in 1870,

---

[44] Vernon Lee, *Miss Brown* (Edinburgh and London: William Blackwood and Sons, 1884), vol. 2, p. 24.

[45] Gosse, *The Academy* (4 April 1874): 359–60.

[46] BMSCM, Report from the Subcommittee on Finance, 12 January 1861, C.9868–4. This promotion granted O'Shaughnessy a raise from a salary of £150 per annum; he would

'Those too sanguine singers'
125

spend a full £94.2 on the publication of *An Epic of Women* – nearly half his yearly salary. He hoped that his poetry would release him from the necessity of his employment at the museum, but the poems included in *An Epic*, such as 'Exile', do not suggest he was optimistic about the possibility.

At the same time, France was facing the violence and instability of the Second Empire, under Napoleon III. The defeat of Austria by Prussia in 1866 created a new power in Europe, which would eventually culminate in the Franco-Prussian War and the end of the Empire at the hands of the Third Republic. As Debarati Sanyal suggests, much of Baudelaire's aesthetic of detached irony can be read as a mode of 'counter-violence' to the violence of the Second Empire.[47] We can thus read O'Shaughnessy's attraction to the aesthetics of decadence as evidence of his repressed longing for revolution within his own working life. He embraced Baudelaire and the other French decadents of the period as revolutionaries, who could perhaps demonstrate the way to break with the mundanity of everyday life.

Jennifer Birkett notes that among the decadents 'some people had jobs in the despised establishment', and thus, 'economically and politically, this was a generation conscious of its dependence, and it is this dependence that fills its work with those morbid, vengeful images of frustrated adolescent eroticism'.[48] Thus, the necessity of engaging with bourgeois reality produces decadence. O'Shaughnessy's decadence enacts a protest against the bourgeois working life – something Lefebvre suggests when he says, 'Under the banner of the marvellous, nineteenth-century literature mounted a sustained attack on everyday life':[49]

> Everything – life, science, both the ideal and the idea of love, not to mention that arch-sorcerer of the Western world, money – conspires to instil in the sensitive, lucid, cultivated young man with a gift for "belles-lettres" a feeling of unease and dissatisfaction which can only be assuaged by something strange, bizarre or extraordinary.[50]

The marvellous is therefore seen as a counter to the mundanity of working life, producing decadence as a form of escape, not just from the everyday, but from the alarming instability of the nineteenth-century world. Similarly, Birkett suggests that decadence is an attempt to 'substitute fiction for history'.[51] This fiction presents an artificial, heightened reality which 'incorporated all the terrors of the real world and made them safe, creating a territory that simultaneously was and

---

have the opportunity to increase his salary by £20 per year, up to a maximum of £310 – however, his subsequent probation beginning in 1870 froze his salary.

[47] Debarati Sanyal, *The Violence of Modernity: Baudelaire, Irony, and the Politics of Form* (Baltimore: The Johns Hopkins University Press, 2006).

[48] Birkett, p. 14, p. 15.

[49] Henri Lefebvre, *Critique of Everyday Life*, trans. John Moore (London: Verso, 1991), vol. 1, p. 105.

[50] Ibid., p. 121.

[51] Birkett, p. 3.

126 *Arthur O'Shaughnessy, A Pre-Raphaelite Poet in the British Museum*

was not history, populated by figures who seemed vividly real but were totally controlled by their maker's imagination'.[52]

It is in the desire for poetry that is 'entirely outside of the everyday realm, and so purely artificial that it borders on the ideal', in Lefebvrian terms, that creates the uneasy tension in *An Epic* which suggested insincerity and artificiality to critics.[53] As Lefebvre asks, 'how can this pure artificiality be created without permanent reference to ordinary life, without the constantly renewed contrast that will embody this reference?'[54] Lefebvre suggests that the nineteenth century is defined by the 'theme of the marvellous' which is eternally tied to 'the theme of duality', or the division of life into separate spheres of reality, as well as the 'theme of failure and defeat', because, as Lefebvre insists, it is impossible to escape the everyday. Rather, leisure, in its attempted rejection of work, is forever *reflecting* work, in its absence.[55] Here, again, we are presented with the notion of negative space – the outline of what is absent is as dominant a form as that which is present. Lefebvre points to Baudelaire as one of the few men of *belles-lettres* in the nineteenth century who was successful in his presentation of the marvellous, precisely because he did not reject the everyday, but rather integrated it into the 'bizarre' and 'strange' world of his poetry:

> With Baudelaire, and with him alone, the marvellous takes on a life and intensity which were totally original: this is because he abandons the metaphysical and moral plane to immerse himself in the everyday, which form that moment on he will deprecate, corrode and attack, but *on its own level* and as if from within.[56]

Gosse is incorrect, then, that in O'Shaughnessy's later volumes he rejects the influence of the *Romantiques*. Rather, we can see him following Baudelaire's model to shape a decadence that is not merely an artificial aesthetic, lacking a referent in O'Shaughnessy's real life, but is instead a reflection of that reality, a discursive protest from within reality. It is here, Lefebvre says, that true creativity flourishes:

> No so-called "elevated" activity can be reduced to [the everyday], nor can it be separated from it. Its activities are born, they grow and emerge; once they have left the nourishing earth of their native land, not one of them can be formed and fulfilled on its own account. In this earth they are born. If they emerge, it is because they have grown and prospered. It is at the heart of the everyday that projects become works of creativity.[57]

The shift to a marvellous born out of the everyday is apparent in O'Shaughnessy's 'Chaitivel', included in 1872's *Lays of France*, which forms a fascinating contrast

---

[52] Ibid., p. 67.

[53] Lefebvre, vol. 1, p. 34.

[54] Ibid.

[55] Ibid., p. 30.

[56] Ibid., p. 106.

[57] Ibid., vol. 2, p. 41.

'Those too sanguine singers' 127

to 'An Epic', particularly in its critical reception.[58] This poem embraces many of the same decadent markers employed in 'An Epic' and echoes several of the themes of that earlier sequence. Like 'An Epic', 'Chaitivel' is centred on a *femme fatale* figure; the name O'Shaughnessy gives her, Sarrazine, immediately evokes an Eastern descent.[59] Rather than a sincere engagement with a foreign culture, Eastern settings are often used in decadent texts to evoke the distance between the 'real' bourgeois world and the idealized world of art. Thematically, 'Chaitivel' is quite similar to 'An Epic'. The poem introduces the topic of false women, saying, 'Some ages ago, Love's splendid lures / Through the enchanted world made fair / Each woman's soft enamouring snare'.[60] These lines self-consciously echo the sentiment at the heart of 'An Epic' – that women are made 'so fair to see, so false to love'.[61] Later, the poem repeats the notion that women are responsible for bringing men into the world and taking them out of it, in the form of cruel death at the hands of a *femme fatale*. In 'Cleopatra' O'Shaughnessy writes, 'One woman bears and brings him up a man, / Another woman slays him at the last'.[62] 'Chaitivel' says of mothers, 'And, having loved indeed and known / His heart, she left him to the doom / Another woman's love should make: – / Alas, for her down in the tomb!'[63] Thus, 'Chaitivel' echoes the two central conceits of 'An Epic' that were most criticized by the press – 'nonsense', as the *Saturday Review* called them.[64]

The supernatural landscapes of 'Chaitivel' are populated with 'redolent snakelike flowers', 'poisonous fruit', and 'strange-leaved trees' with wafting perfumes.[65] On several occasions the *femme fatale* is conflated with the tempting serpent, a favourite trope of the decadents and one O'Shaughnessy employed in 'Daughter of Herodias' two years earlier. The poem also contains what is arguably one of the most decadent scenes in O'Shaughnessy's body of work. One of Sarrazine's dead lovers, buried with a lock of her golden hair, wakes again to reclaim her love:

> Not merely barren did he feel
>> Death's prison and the silent gloom
>> Around him; but, within, the tomb
> Was opulent with glimmering gold;
>> For the slim tress that once was hid

---

[58]   O'Shaughnessy, 'Chaitivel; or, the Lay of Love's Unfortunate', *Lays of France (Founded on the Lays of Marie)*, 2nd ed. (London: Chatto & Windus, 1874), pp. 89–144.

[59]   'Sarrasins' is a French medieval name for Muslims. There is also a port in Algeria called Sarrazine. This name, which is not included in Marie de France's *lai*, could also reference Balzac's 1830 novel *Sarrasine*, although the titular character there is a man.

[60]   'Chaitivel', p. 92.

[61]   'Creation', *Epic*, p. 85.

[62]   *Epic*, p. 103.

[63]   *Lays*, p. 114.

[64]   'Minor Poetry', *The Saturday Review* (4 March 1871): 282–3 (p. 282).

[65]   *Lays*, p. 96, p. 107, p. 104.

128   *Arthur O'Shaughnessy, A Pre-Raphaelite Poet in the British Museum*

Upon his heart, was grown to fold
On fold that many times had rolled
   About him; and he lay amid
The splendours of it, and thought well
That he should have her soul for hell
   Or heaven.[66]

In this stanza O'Shaughnessy employs one of the common tropes of decadence: the aestheticization of death. An example of this can be seen in Gautier's 1836 tale of the vampire, 'La morte amoureuse' ('Clarimonde' in English translations), in which a death-bed scene is described:

> That chamber bore no semblance to a chamber of death. In lieu of the odours which I had been accustomed to breathe during such funereal vigils, a languorous vapour of Oriental perfume – I know not what amorous odour of woman – softly floated through the tepid air. That pale light seemed rather a twilight gloom contrived for voluptuous pleasure, than a substitute for the yellow-flickering watch-tapers which shine by the side of corpses.[67]

Here Gautier commingles the death chamber with the bridal chamber and salaciously hints at the potential for necrophilia. The aestheticization of death is taken to its extreme in the works of Baudelaire; several poems in *Les fleurs du mal* contain lurid scenes of decay and putrefaction, but always couched in terms of sensual colour and tone. Thus, Swinburne wrote of the volume, 'even of the loathsomest bodily putrescence and decay he can make some noble use; pluck out its meaning and secret, even its beauty, in a certain way, from actual carrion.'[68] In the stanza quoted above, O'Shaughnessy comingles death and decay – the long-dead body of the lover – with beauty and life – the still-growing lock of hair. Decay is both aestheticized and eroticized, and love is conflated with pain and suffering, even after death.

In tone and content, Chaitivel is highly reminiscent of Gautier's more gothic verse, particularly 'Le château du souvenir' ('The Castle of Memory'). Gautier writes:

> Now is the route made clear, and I
> Perceive the sun unveiled, and see
> The distant castle's tower rise high
> Above the forest canopy.

---

[66]   Ibid., p. 107. Published in 1872, this scene may have been inspired by the rumours of Elizabeth Siddal's exhumation in 1869, where it was said that her red hair – considered by the art world, and her husband, to be her best feature – had continued growing after her death and filled the whole of her coffin.

[67]   Théophile Gautier, 'Clarimonde', *Tales from Gautier*, trans. Lafcadio Hearn (London: Eveleigh Nash & Grayson, 1927), p. 41.

[68]   A.C. Swinburne, 'Charles Baudelaire: Les fleurs du mal', *The Spectator*, no. 1784 (6 September 1862): 998–1000 (p. 998). Swinburne references Baudelaire's 'A Martyr', in which the rotting corpse of a woman is shockingly sexualized.

'Those too sanguine singers' 129

Beneath the vaults where light turns shade,
Falling in leaf-swept interlacing,
The old path, on the moss-strewn glade,
Ribbons once more its narrow tracing.[69]

This description is echoed in 'Chaitivel':

The slow cloud found it sweet to rest
    Over each shadow-haunted tower
Of her lone castle, and to remain
Low brooding over that domain
Of deep autumnal wood and plain.[70]

Both poems centre on a manse, haunted by the infidelities of the woman of the house. Both employ typical gothic descriptors, and each poem relies on a muted palette of green, gray, and blue. O'Shaughnessy's inspiration for 'Chaitivel' is clearly modern French decadence as much as the medieval French tale on which it is allegedly based.

In many ways 'Chaitivel' is more decadent than 'An Epic'. Here we find the 'depraved passions and the odd hallucinations of a fixed idea turning to madness' that Gautier suggests define the movement. The poem contains morbid scenes of decaying bodies rising from the dead, implications of necrophilia, and a languid, dreamy tone of supernaturalism. Despite this, 'Chaitivel' has never been called 'decadent' or even 'oversensuous', a complaint so often attached to O'Shaughnessy's work.[71] Nor is there any suggestion from the critics that the poem is mere affectation or imitation. In fact, Moulton praises the 'originality of its conception', even though the poem is couched as a reinterpretation of the tale of the same name by Marie de France, and goes on to say that in 'Chaitivel' O'Shaughnessy reaches his 'high-water mark of inspiration'.[72] Another critic commends the 'fierce imagination' evinced in the poem.[73]

Comparing these remarks to the reviews of 'An Epic', it appears that, at least in part, reviewers and editors did not focus on 'Chaitivel's' decadent tone because they thought the poem was good. The *Athenaeum* picks it out as the best of *Lays*, stating that it was 'managed with artistic force and delicacy'.[74] The *Examiner* calls

---

[69]   Gautier, 'Le château du souvenir', *Selected Lyrics*, pp. 205–7.

[70]   *Lays*, p. 95.

[71]   For example, the *Athenaeum*, which calls 'Chaitivel' the 'finest poem' in the volume, writes, 'Yet the supernatural element is treated with such daring but subtle art, that the spiritual terror excited is natural and unforced.' 'Subtle' and 'natural' are not words normally used to describe decadent literature. *Athenaeum*, no. 2306 (6 January 1872): 8–9.

[72]   Moulton, p. 37, p. 28. For a discussion of 'Chaitivel' as a translation or adaptation of Marie de France's work, see Chapter 5.

[73]   Oliver Elton, *A Survey of English Literature: 1830–1880* (New York: The Macmillan Co., 1920), vol. 4, p. 112.

[74]   'Lays of France', *Athenaeum*, no. 2306 (6 January 1872), p. 9.

130 *Arthur O'Shaughnessy, A Pre-Raphaelite Poet in the British Museum*

it 'better than anything else Mr. O'Shaughnessy has written', and even at the time of O'Shaughnessy's death, Gosse picks 'Chaitivel' out as one of his best poems.[75] As most critics contend, the term 'decadence' was used pejoratively during this period. Elaine Showalter suggests, 'it was the pejorative label applied by the bourgeoisie to everything that seemed unnatural, artificial, and perverse'.[76] More recently Gowan Dawson has shown how 'decadence' was a term used negatively in the press to suggest any kind of moral decay or degeneration. 'Aestheticism was widely connected with various forms of societal and sexual transgression', Dawson argues.[77] The incorporation of decadent tone and markers into 'Chaitivel', then, was perhaps overlooked by the critical press because the poem was deemed too 'good' to be burdened with the negative label of 'decadent'. However, it is also clear that O'Shaughnessy's use of decadence was transforming into something more organic to his personal style of poetry, which was more melancholy and romantic than that of Baudelaire. It is this naturalization of the aesthetic that lends 'Chaitivel' a feeling of sincerity and reality that was lacking in 'An Epic'.

III.

In 'An Epic' O'Shaughnessy treats decadence as a formal quality of verse, a predilection for a certain vocabulary and tone, and thus its manifestation is largely superficial. Decadence, therefore, was originally treated as an escape from O'Shaughnessy's working life; in his later work, however, we can see the ways in which his job at the museum produces his decadence as a reflection, not a rejection, of his position as a natural historian – much as his fantasies of escape often took the form of the South American tropics, as discussed in Chapter 1. As a pejorative term, decadence was often linked to materialism, atheism, and Darwinism. In *Darwin, Literature and Victorian Respectability*, Gowan Dawson explores how the popular press attacked Darwinism and decadence in similar, overlapping terms. He shows that Darwinism was attacked for being immoral like decadence, and decadence was pathologized in Darwinian terms.[78] Dawson writes:

---

[75]   'Mr. O'Shaughnessy's Lays of France', *The Examiner* (24 February 1872), p. 211, and 'Obituary: Arthur O'Shaughnessy', *Academy*, no. 457 (5 February 1881), p. 99.

[76]   Elaine Showalter, *Sexual Anarchy: Gender and Culture at the Fin de Siècle* (New York and London: Viking Penguin, 1990), p. 169.

[77]   Gowan Dawson, *Darwin, Literature and Victorian Respectability* (Cambridge: Cambridge University Press, 2007), p. 16.

[78]   Thus Dawson writes, 'it was regularly avowed that the growing licentiousness of modern culture, and the alleged excesses of aestheticism especially, actually gave warning of the repulsive direction in which society was being taken by the increasingly influential doctrines of Darwinism' (*Victorian Respectability*, p. 5). Despite this, Darwinian terms were often employed to diagnose the 'disease' of decadence. 'Several theorists of degeneration, as historians have long recognized, viewed even literature in similarly diagnostic terms, interpreting certain forms of deviation from conventional artistic standards as evidence of the pathological condition of many modern artists' (p. 207).

'Those too sanguine singers'   131

The 1870s and 1880s, however, mark a particular point of crisis in the social shift from a largely clerical to a secular and scientific cultural elite ... and in this period of intellectual and institutional transition the contemporaneous disputes over the immorality of contemporary literature and the materialism of modern science can be seen to overlap and interact with each other.[79]

Thus, from an external, critical perspective, decadence and Darwinism were believed to stem from the same atheistic, materialistic source. Dawson contends that, 'aesthetic poetry and scientific naturalism were seen as conjoint manifestations of an amoral secularism'.[80] *Victorian Respectability* shows how natural historians attempted to distance themselves from any connection with aesthetic literature in an effort to preserve the respectability of their profession. However, as someone who saw himself as a writer first and a scientist second, the connection being drawn between decadent art and scientific naturalism may have appealed to O'Shaughnessy.

The relationship between decadence and Darwinism from a literary perspective is more complicated. There is a long critical tradition of reading decadence as a rejection of modern science and Darwinian theory. Thus, Silke-Maria Weineck declares, 'we might think of these conflicts as a confrontation between a Darwinian perspective that would sit judgment on healthy and unhealthy developments and an aestheticism that undermines the very premises of organicist thinking in its rejection of nature as the privileged matrix for ethical and aesthetic judgments'.[81] Decadent literature has long been understood to be a reaction to the pre-eminence of literary naturalism as a movement. The rejection of all that is natural in favour of an artificial, heightened reality has been extended by some critics in order to read decadence as a rejection of the whole of the natural world, and the science that studied it. However, we can see many of the ideas and tropes central to decadent literature as rooted in the changing face of natural science. Thus, Elaine Showalter defines decadence as necessarily a 'post-Darwinian aesthetic movement'.[82]

Decadence can be read as a reaction to a radical reinterpretation of man's place in the natural world, revealed by advances in the natural sciences. O'Shaughnessy's proximity to Darwinian theory in his career as a naturalist may explain why he was drawn to this aesthetic before so many of his English contemporaries. His scientific employment meant that he was exposed to the realities of Darwinism – rather than the more optimistic fiction embraced by the public – before many of his literary contemporaries. As we saw in his depiction of the werewolf in 'Bisclavaret',

---

[79] Gowan Dawson, 'Intrinsic Earthliness: Science, Materialism, and the Fleshly School of Poetry', *Victorian Poetry* 41, no. 1 (Spring 2003): 113–29 (p. 115).

[80] Ibid., p. 126.

[81] Silke-Maria Weineck, 'Loss of Outline: Decadence as the Crisis of Negation', *Pacific Coast Philology* 29, no. 1 (September 1994): 37–50 (p. 38). See also Jan B. Gordon's '"Decadent Spaces": Notes for a Phenomenology of the Fin de Siècle', *Decadence and the 1890s*, ed. Ian Fletcher (London: Edward Arnold, 1979).

[82] Showalter, p. 169.

132   *Arthur O'Shaughnessy, A Pre-Raphaelite Poet in the British Museum*

considered in Chapter 1, O'Shaughnessy's writing was underpinned by Darwinian ideas from fairly early on, as he explored the crueller and more dangerous human nature highlighted by the idea of the struggle for survival. Decadence has been seen as a reaction to Darwinism, both as a fantasy of the artificial triumphing over the natural and as a way of making sense of the new world order by exploring degeneration and decay in lurid detail. Bernheimer suggests that decadence reclaims death from nature, putting it back under man's control as a creative force generating literature, rather than a mere biological inevitability.[83] Here decadence enacts the 'creation of imaginary solutions to real problems', as Birkett words it, in fantasies of death reclaimed from nature, as in Gautier's tale of the vampire, quoted above, or Dorian Gray's subversion of the natural process of age and decay.[84] Decadent texts aestheticize inevitable death and decay as evinced in the selections from 'Chaitivel', above. More than this, however, decadent works evince an acceptance of the cruelty inherent to the natural world. Thus, Baudelaire finds justification for de Sade's views of humanity, and asserts:

> Crime, which the human animal took a fancy to in his mother's womb, is by origin natural. Virtue, on the other hand, is *artificial*, supernatural, since in every age and nation gods and prophets have been necessary to teach it to bestialized humanity, and since man by himself would have been powerless to discover it.[85]

In this passage Baudelaire not only inverts the traditional Romantic assumption that humans are born innocent, but plays with the language of decadence's critics, who saw decadence as being the height of unnatural artificiality, based on the presumption that what is 'natural' is inherently good. In reaction, Baudelaire embraces nature's struggle for survival and shows that violence (or death) is natural, and the rejection of such is what is truly artificial; in doing so he justifies his poetic focus on the more perverse and grotesque aspects of the world. Thus, rather than seeing decadence as a rejection of science, critics such as Thornton assert that the decadents employed the scientific method in their approach to the world, considering everything that passed before their eyes, beautiful and ugly alike.[86]

Even the basic markers of decadent literature discussed at the beginning of this chapter can be seen to be in line with scientific thought during this period. The invocation of the senses so prevalent in decadent texts tends to focus on brilliant colours, strong odours or perfumes, and beautiful music. This sensual focus is highly erotic, emphasizing the connection between an aesthetic sense and

---

[83]   Bernheimer, p. 57.

[84]   Birkett, p. 4.

[85]   Charles Baudelaire, 'The Painter of Modern Life', *Baudelaire: Selected Writings on Art and Artists*, trans. P.E. Charvet (Cambridge: Cambridge University Press, 1972), p. 425. Baudelaire wrote these lines just a year after the publication of Darwin's *On the Origin of Species*.

[86]   Thornton, p. 191.

'Those too sanguine singers' 133

the natural drive to reproduce. Darwin's theory of sexual selection, hinted at in *Origin* and fully articulated in *Descent of Man* (1871), highlights the fact that aesthetic appreciation, far from being either artificial or unique to mankind, is entirely natural and common to both man and the lower animals. Of the bird, which Darwin calls 'the most aesthetic' of all animals, he writes:

> They charm the females by vocal or instrumental music of the most varied kinds. They are ornamented by all sorts of combs, wattles, protuberances, horns, air-distended sacs, topknots, naked shafts, plumes and lengthened feathers gracefully springing from all parts of the body. The beak and naked skin about the head, and the feathers are often gorgeously coloured. The males sometimes pay their court by dancing, or by fantastic antics performed either on the ground or in the air. In one instance, at least, the male emits a musky odour which we may suppose serves to charm or excite the female.[87]

Decadent texts particularly emphasize the odour of sexual attraction, with an almost obsessive cataloguing of scents and perfumes. While pheromones were not named until 1959, Darwin's work reveals that science was beginning to understand what art had long known – the power of scent to sexual attraction. Darwin writes, 'there can be no doubt that [scent-producing glands] stand in close relation with the reproductive functions', as '[i]n most cases, when during the breeding-season the male alone emits a strong odour, this probably serves to excite or allure the female'.[88] The highly saturated hues for which decadent texts are famous evoke the plumage of birds, particularly the peacock, developed and displayed purely for sexual purposes. The colours and odours of decadence and the eroticism they invoke, far from being a rejection of the natural world, suggest nothing more than the animalistic drive to reproduce. This overlap between the sciences and arts is mirrored in O'Shaughnessy's own life, and perhaps suggests why he was so drawn to decadent images and themes.

The triumph of the artificial over the natural is often considered to be a hallmark of decadent aestheticism, as evidenced in the later English aestheticism of writers like Arthur Symons, who wrote: 'is there any "reason in nature" why we should write exclusively about the natural blush, if the delicately acquired blush of rouge has any attraction for us? Both exist; both, I think, are charming in their way; and the latter, as a subject, has, at all events, more novelty.'[89] In his particular brand of decadence, however, O'Shaughnessy maintains his Romantic roots, privileging the natural over the artificial. Of Hephaestus, one of the few truly sympathetic characters in 'An Epic', he writes:

> But he was rugged-seeming; all his brows
>   Were changed and smeared with the great human
>   toil;
> His limbs all gnarled and knotted as the boughs

---

[87]   *Descent of Man*, vol. 2, p. 38.

[88]   Ibid., p. 281.

[89]   Arthur Symons, *Silhouettes*, 2nd ed. (London: Leonard Smithers, 1896), p. xiv.

134 *Arthur O'Shaughnessy, A Pre-Raphaelite Poet in the British Museum*

And limbs of mighty oaks are: many a soil
Was on his skin, coarse-coloured as a bark;
   Yea, he was shorn of beauty from the birth;
But strong, and of a mighty soul to work.[90]

The language O'Shaughnessy uses to describe Hephaestus is strikingly earthy. His limbs are like the boughs of an oak tree, his flesh is the colour of bark, and the dirt on his skin indicates his status as a manual labourer. All of this marks him out as different from – and better than – the more traditionally decadent characters in 'Wife of Hephaestus'. Throughout the sequence O'Shaughnessy replicates decadence's emphasis on interior scenes of manmade beauty; however, those interiors are often compared to the beauty of the natural world and found wanting. In 'Daughter of Herodias', Herod's palace is contrasted with the forest in which John the Baptist communed with God:

He never had beheld so many thrones,
As those of ivory and precious stones
   Whereon the noble company was raised
About the king: – he never had seen gems
   So costly, nor so wonderful as blazed
Upon their many crowns and diadems,
And trailed upon their garments' trodden hems:

But he had seen in mighty Lebanon
The cedars no man's axe hath lit upon;
   And he had often worshipped, falling down
In dazzling temples opened straight to him,
   Where One who had great lightnings for His crown
Was suddenly made present, vast and dim
Through crowded pinions of the Cherubim![91]

The palace of Herod is described entirely in negatives – John has 'never beheld' and 'never seen'. This device negates the splendour that is being described, the language subtly turning the reader against the scene, so that we may embrace the reality of the natural world, which is 'made present' by the positive assertions of the stanza – 'he had seen'. The natural world entirely takes precedence.

Unlike most of the French and English decadents, over the course of his career O'Shaughnessy's fetishized exotic becomes the untouched world of nature, rather than the artificial splendour of harems of the East. Thus, in one of the last poems he wrote, 'Colibri', O'Shaughnessy contrasts the decadent civilization of England with the pure and natural world of the jungles of South America. The poem is presented in three cantos. In the first, the untouched, unperverted splendour of the natural world is described, embodied in the purity of a native Brazilian girl.

---

[90] *Epic*, p. 86.
[91] Ibid., p. 115.

'Those too sanguine singers'

Canto 2 sets up a harsh contrast to the first, describing European civilization as beautiful on the outside but rotten at its core:

> I understood each man
> In his consummate coldness, and the lying
> Of every woman's love and jewelled smile
> Was bare to me in secret. I saw dying
> In agonizing bonds, beneath the vile
> Enamelled falsehood of triumphant fashion,
> All lonely loveliness of truth and passion,
> Stung to a poisoned death by one small asp,
> The deathless fiend, Mistrust.[92]

The former love is a stereotypical *femme fatale*, with the 'the soul of Cleopatra'. The love the narrator found with her is, at its heart, nothing more than passionate hate – again, typical of *femme fatale* narratives:

> that love, half hate,
> The rest despair and lust, that woe – that fate –
> That evil I perceive, no one man's doom,
> But a great death in a decorous tomb
> Called Europe.[93]

The beauty and desire of decadent trappings are rejected in this poem. The 'coldness' of the people is reflected in the sterility of the stones and metals they surrounded themselves with. In contrast, the forests of Brazil are warm and alive. Canto 3 details the love of the narrator and the girl – Colibri – whose pure heart distances her so much from 'civilized' people that she is described as more like an animal than a human: 'And they had called her Colibri, / Thinking her brother was the bird / Whose sister was the passion-flower'.[94] This preference for the natural was evident even in his earliest poetry, but becomes one of the dominant strands of O'Shaughnessy's corpus in later volumes.

Recent criticism has overturned the traditional definition of decadence as a rejection of nature in a fantasy of escape to an artificial world, in order to focus on the intersections between literary naturalism and decadence.[95] Bernheimer, for instance, focuses on decadence's roots in the naturalistic works of novelists like Émile Zola, saying, 'Most naturalist texts include, or perhaps I should say produce, decadent moments, whereas the sense of natural process that subtends

---

[92] O'Shaughnessy, 'Colibri', *Songs of a Worker* (London: Chatto & Windus, 1881), p. 147.

[93] *Songs*, p. 146.

[94] Ibid., p. 134.

[95] In the 1950s, A.E. Carter asserted that in decadence, 'The cult of Nature was replaced by the cult of artificiality.' A.E. Carter, *The Idea of Decadence in French Literature, 1830–1900* (Toronto: University of Toronto Press, 1958), p. 29.

most decadent texts is entirely naturalistic in character.'[96] This recalls Dawson's point that decadence was popularly seen by its critics to be stemming from the new and controversial natural sciences, united in their materialism and secularism.[97] He writes of the 'intrinsic earthliness' of aestheticist poetry, in a focus on the physical reality of the material world, or the 'fleshliness' of which Robert Buchanan complained: 'The acute attention to specific tangible details which is a leading characteristic of Rossetti's verse advances, albeit indirectly, a sensuous materialist epistemology which holds that the physical world provides the only reality which can be known indubitably.'[98] This is a proposition commonly attributed to the sciences. In practice and technique, there are many similarities between the artist and the natural historian; they are both focused on recording the minute details of the physical world. Thus, in *Descent of Man*, Darwin reports that, 'The celebrated sculptor, Mr. Woolner, informs me of one little peculiarity in the external ear, which he has often observed both in men and women, and of which he perceived the full signification.'[99] Here the observational powers of Thomas Woolner (1825–1892) – a member of the original Pre-Raphaelite Brotherhood and an aesthete of the day – are identical to that of the natural historian and used to the same end. He 'perceived the full signification' of the peculiarity of the human ear, namely that it was a remnant of humanity's simian past.

Decadence and natural history share a way of viewing the world, an emphasis on minute sensory detail. But even further, in their descriptions of these details, we can see that far from being inherently opposed, decadence and natural history writing have a shared imagery and vocabulary. In fact, popular natural history writing can be seen to employ all of the same superficial tropes that were defined as 'decadent' at the beginning of this chapter. This point can be illustrated by an overview of Philip Gosse's immensely popular 1859 *Evenings at the Microscope,* an amateur natural history text.[100] As explored earlier, Eastern settings were a staple of decadent art. Gosse's text was designed to couch science in terms that made it accessible to the average English person, and yet within his text he invokes the exoticism of the East. He says of the microscope: 'Like the work of some mighty genie of Oriental fable, the brazen tube is the key which unlocks a world of

---

[96] Bernheimer, p. 58.

[97] Dawson, 'Intrinsic Earthliness', p. 126.

[98] Ibid., 117.

[99] *Descent of Man*, vol. 1, p. 22.

[100] In his own scientific career, O'Shaughnessy aspired to a more popular form of natural history. As W.D. Paden reports, 'As we know from documents written by both O'Shaughnessy and Owen, the young man was to look forward to the more suitable task of delivering lectures upon the zoological collections to the general public, gathered in a spacious auditorium at South Kensington.' W.D. Paden, 'Arthur O'Shaughnessy in the British Museum: or, the case of the misplaced fusees and the reluctant zoologist', *Victorian Studies* 8, no. 1 (September 1964): 7–30 (p. 28). However, this was never to be: O'Shaughnessy died at the beginning of 1881, the year the new museum opened.

'Those too sanguine singers' 137

wonder and beauty before invisible.'[101] Here Gosse uses the popularity of Eastern narratives to bring a sense of wonder and mystery to the microscopic world.

As we have seen, an overabundance of colour words is a marker of decadent literature, employed to create both an exotic and sensual mood. However, the use of richly evocative colour words is evident in Gosse's naturalist text, as well, as when he describes some specimens of seaweed:

> Here are exquisitely delicate crimson leaves, as thin or thinner than the thinnest tissue paper, with solid ribs and sinuous edges. Here is a tall and elegant dark red feather, quite regularly pinnated. Here is a tuft of purple filaments as "fine as silkworm's thread". And here is a broad irregular expanse of the richest emerald green, crumpled and folded, yet as glossy as if varnished.[102]

This passage goes beyond a mere recording of detail, choosing 'crimson' where 'dark red' would do, and 'richest emerald green' rather than something more mundane such as 'deep green'. Furthermore, the colour words are specifically used to link the natural fronds of seaweed to luxurious objects of ornamentation. Thus, the red fronds are like a 'feather', and the purple filaments are suggestive of silk. He invokes jewels in his description of the green frond, and in saying that it is 'glossy as if varnished' suggests the artificiality of the man-made. O'Shaughnessy's use of colour words throughout 'An Epic', then, is in line with popular natural history writing just as much as the work of the French decadents to which it was attributed.

Decadent texts are replete with gemstones, symbols of cold, uncompromising beauty and the superiority of the artificial. Despite this, natural history writing is full of similar imagery. Gosse's book is purely focused on the organic minutiae of life, and yet he returns to images of gems repeatedly in *Evenings at the Microscope*. He describes the eyes of insects, saying:

> But as we peer among these slender threads, our attention is riveted by some tiny points that are seated near their bases, which glitter like brilliant gems. They are seen only in those rows of tentacles which spring from the angles of the veils, and not in those which fringe their edges. Even the unassisted sight can detect the gleam and glitter of these little specks; but it is only when we bring the lens to bear upon them that we see all their beauty. Then they look like diamonds or emeralds, each set in a broad ring of dark red substance, which greatly enhances their beauty.[103]

The writings of decadence and natural history, then, are not as divided as the practitioners or subsequent critics have suggested. Instead, they share a materialist

---

[101] Philip Henry Gosse, *Evenings at the Microscope: or, Researches Among the Minuter Organs and Forms of Animal Life* (London: Society for Promoting Christian Knowledge, 1884), p. iii. Philip Henry Gosse was the father of critic Edmund Gosse.

[102] Ibid., p. 59.

[103] Ibid., p. 51.

138   *Arthur O'Shaughnessy, A Pre-Raphaelite Poet in the British Museum*

sensuality that privileged tone and colour, which suggests why O'Shaughnessy the natural historian was drawn to this particularly French aesthetic.

In his later works, O'Shaughnessy turns away from generic decadence, which had drawn criticisms of insincerity and unoriginality, in favour of incorporating elements of decadent style into work that was uniquely his own. We can see evidence of this in a poem from 1881's *Songs of a Worker*, 'Prophetic Spring'. This poem would never be called decadent, and yet within it we can see elements that define O'Shaughnessy's decadent style:

> Awhile beneath the hawthorn sweet
> Our o'erstrained quickening hearts will beat,
> Our purple thirsting mouths will meet
>   And revel in their kiss.
>
> But when pink May becomes red June,
> And summer sounds a glorious tune,
> Under some lordlier tree aswoon
>   Together we shall lie.[104]

O'Shaughnessy again makes use of the evocative colour words that so dominated his earlier decadent work. The effect of these words – the purple mouths and pink May becoming red June – is the same as in his earlier works; they create a voluptuous tone through an invocation of the senses. Written for his young fiancée, May Doyle, the pun on the word 'May' especially adds to the eroticism of the poem, as the young 'pink' girl will ripen into the 'red' June as they lie together.[105] Unlike the strictly artificial splendour of 'An Epic', 'Prophetic Spring' can be seen to invoke both the natural world and a decadent sensibility.

This blending of decadence and natural history is most apparent in 'Colibri'. This poem is yet another example of a fantasy of escape from civilized society to the untouched world of nature. Yet, even in Cantos 1 and 3, set in the natural world, the poem is marked by all the generic decadent tropes considered earlier in this chapter.

> But when all lovely she reposed
> In dense, sweet places where days long
> No foot drew near and no eye saw;
> Where purple-scented stillness grew,
> And red trees had not stirred, for awe
> Of the eternal thing they knew;

---

[104]   'Prophetic Spring', *Songs of a Worker*, pp. 74–5.

[105]   Again, this poem echoes an earlier work of Gautier, 'Lied'. In this poem, Gautier also describes the passage of spring into summer in highly sexualized terms. He writes, 'In April days the earth is pink / As youth and love: a virgin', which we can see O'Shaughnessy echoing in his reference to 'pink May'. Gautier continues, 'In August, drunken maenad, she / Offers lush breasts to Autumn's use, / As, tiger-striped, cavorting free, / She bleeds grapes of their trellis-juice' (*Selected Lyrics*, p. 135).

'Those too sanguine singers' 139

> Strange richness of thought undivulged
> Would roll upon her heart, and dreams,
> In whose remote joy she indulged
> Until the warm day's yellowing beams
> Fell vaguely on her dazzled cheek.[106]

This passage is highly sensual, from the supine woman at the centre of it, to the evocative colour words throughout. Also evident is decadent synaesthesia, or the intermingling of senses, in 'purple-scented stillness.'

In the third canto, the unfettered sexuality of the natural world is made clear:

> In some delicious spot where slowly wind
> The weakened currents round soft oases,
> Linked by their joining flowers, allures us soon
> So overwhelmingly with perfumed breeze,
> And purple glow and wonderful appeal
> Of supernatural colours that reveal
> Strange speechless yearnings of the heart.[107]

The lovemaking of the couple is projected onto the natural world, the description of which is overwhelmed by the senses. This passage builds to a clear moment of sexual climax – again, with nature employed as a metonymical stand-in.

> Nothing said
> Around, beneath, or answered overhead,
> Yet all one soul in one effusion seem
> The opulent odours, the transcendent gleam,
> The radiant heights of verdure – the cool gloom,
> The flowering orgies of unwonted bloom,
> The love, the thought – one soul, one dream, one
> doom![108]

These lines recall the decadent descriptions of 'An Epic', with the emphasis on colour and tone, the inclusion of perfume, and the eroticism of the scene, but transplanted to a natural setting. The exoticism of the Orient that dominates the decadent aesthetic becomes the exotic natural world of the Americas in O'Shaughnessy's verse, bridging the gap between the work he performed as a taxonomist and his poetry. Contrary to Gosse's suggestion, O'Shaughnessy never turned away from the influence of the French *Romantiques*. Rather, in his more mature poetry, O'Shaughnessy breaks down the elements of decadence that attracted him into two parallel branches of his poetry. As shown in the previous chapter, O'Shaughnessy was drawn to the decadents' rejection of a bourgeois

---

[106] *Songs*, p. 134.

[107] Ibid., p. 156.

[108] Ibid., p. 157.

moral imperative in art. To express the realm of autonomous art, he turns to art itself, culminating in his poetic sequence 'Thoughts in Marble'.[109] The impulse is the same in this sequence as in 'An Epic' – the rejection of the demand for morality in art, by embracing the amoral quality of beauty. But he does away with the metaphor of the woman as art object to turn directly to the art object itself, and therefore shield himself from criticism. The colours, odours, and tones of decadence – the atmospheric quality to which Gautier referred, quoted early in this chapter – were incorporated into O'Shaughnessy's nature poetry, uniting the influence of the English Romantics with that of the French decadents. The profusion of life and inevitability of death so apparent in the natural world provide the ideal milieu for O'Shaughnessy's more mature decadent verses, no longer imitative but entirely his own.

O'Shaughnessy progressed from treating decadence as a mere surface gilding to internalizing the aesthetic, incorporating it into his naturalistic verse in a way that bespoke the sincerity critics found lacking in 'An Epic'. Although his later work was not as obviously 'decadent' as his first volume, O'Shaughnessy's final, posthumous volume is, perhaps, the most influenced by the poetry of France. It contains his aestheticist manifesto, 'Thoughts in Marble', as well as a section of translations of modern French verse, the work of his Parnassian friends. It was in the final years of his life that O'Shaughnessy put the most effort into establishing literary ties between England and France, publishing his translations of French works and taking on the position of English correspondent for *Le Livre* magazine in Paris. O'Shaughnessy's lifelong efforts to import French works and a French literary aesthetic into England helped to shape the aestheticism and decadence that would take hold in England in the 1880s and '90s, producing such celebrated writers as Oscar Wilde. He was, therefore, instrumental in bridging the gap between the Pre-Raphaelitism practised by poets such as D.G. Rossetti and William Morris in the 1870s and the aestheticism of the 1890s.

---

[109] See my discussion in Chapter 3.

Chapter 5
'Love's Splendid Lures':
Arthur O'Shaughnessy's Medievalism

The nineteenth century saw a resurgence of interest in the medieval period and its art, literature, and social structures.[1] During the mid-century, Tennyson, Arnold, Morris, Swinburne, Rossetti, and the Pre-Raphaelite Brotherhood all incorporated medieval settings and stories into their verse and visual arts.[2] In 1872, Arthur O'Shaughnessy joined in this medieval revival with his *Lays of France (Founded on the Lays of Marie)*. Appearing as it did fairly late in this revival, O'Shaughnessy's *Lays* faced accusations of unoriginality and imitation, much as 'An Epic of Women' had before it. However, unlike his contemporaries, O'Shaughnessy avoided the Arthurian tales, carving out a unique niche for himself within this popular literary and artistic movement through his appropriation of the *lais* of Marie de France.

I.

In an obituary-review for the *Academy*, George Saintsbury complains of O'Shaughnessy's *Lays* that 'they were very like, or strove to be very like, one of the least imitable of contemporary poets, Mr. William Morris, of whose admirable work they were in some respects almost a caricature'.[3] Here, Saintsbury strongly implies that O'Shaughnessy intended to copy or even parody Morris's *Defence of Guenevere* (1858). However, contrary to Saintsbury's claim that the *Lays* are 'very like' Morris's medieval poetry, the two share little more than their medieval setting.[4] Whereas Morris adapted Arthurian legends, focusing especially on the sin

---

[1] Mark Girouard dates the revival from approximately 1815 to 1880. Girouard, *The Return to Camelot: Chivalry and the English Gentleman* (New Haven and London: Yale University Press, 1981).

[2] For example, Tennyson's *Idylls of the King* (1856–1885), or 'The Lady of Shalott' (1842); Arnold's *Tristram and Iseult* (1852); Morris's *Defence of Guenevere* (1858), the *Earthly Paradise* (1868–1870), and *A Dream of John Ball* (1888), among others; and Swinburne's *Tristram of Lyonesse* (1882). Dante Gabriel Rossetti treated medieval subjects time and again, e.g., the Pre-Raphaelite murals painted in the Oxford Union from 1857–1859, depicting scenes from Arthurian tales.

[3] George Saintsbury, 'Review: *Songs of a Worker*', *The Academy* 483 (1881): 100–101 (p. 100).

[4] Which is not to say that O'Shaughnessy was not familiar with Morris's work. In a letter dated 5 February 1870, O'Shaughnessy's lover, Helen Snee, writes, 'I have found all manner of curious rhymes in Morris; you need be in no apprehension of making any falser than some of his in this last part of the "Earthly Paradise". What do you think of this –

142   *Arthur O'Shaughnessy, A Pre-Raphaelite Poet in the British Museum*

at the heart of the relationship between Guenevere and Launcelot, O'Shaughnessy turned to Brittany and the *lais* of Marie, presenting adulterous love in a positive light. Heavy in dialogue, the *Defence of Guenevere* poems reflect Morris's dramatic style, whereas O'Shaughnessy's lays, with few moments of spoken words, are dominated by lush, dreamy imagery and his usual verbosity. Morris's volume usually employs pentameter, in tercets and quatrains, whereas O'Shaughnessy makes use of iambic tetrameter, often considered a 'medieval metre' (as in Tennyson's 'Lady of Shalott'[5]) with no discernable pattern to his lengthy stanzas. As the poets who participated in the nineteenth-century medieval revival were all working from a similar set of texts, some similarities are to be expected – such as Morris's tetrameter in 'Haystacks in the Floods' and its irregular rhythms. Medieval revival texts also share a propensity for monosyllabic words, archaic vocabulary, frequent repetition and short lines, giving the works a primitive, balladic feel intended to replicate the cadences of medieval literature. Any of these superficial similarities should not be grounds to call a work a 'caricature'. It would be just as easy, and just as inaccurate, to accuse Swinburne of copying O'Shaughnessy in his 1882 *Tristram of Lyonesse,* a work far more similar in theme to O'Shaughnessy's *Lays* than the *Lays* are to Morris's *Defence.* Thus, rather than looking for points of intersection, it is far more useful to consider instead how O'Shaughnessy's medieval verse departs from that of his contemporaries.

Saintsbury's dismissal of O'Shaughnessy's work as a passing fancy or throw-away imitation is unfair to the poet, whose interest in the art and literature of the medieval period was sustained over many years. O'Shaughnessy's first experiment with reinterpretations of medieval texts came in his 1870 *An Epic of Women,* which included 'Bisclavaret', taken from Marie de France's *lai* of the same name. Even earlier, we find in O'Shaughnessy's unpublished notebooks evidence of the breadth of his interest in the medieval period. He attempted several poems on medieval subjects not covered by Marie, including 'Walther of Aquitain', 'Roland', and 'Siward'.[6] Additionally, one notebook, a chronicle of his reading from June to August of 1870, hints at his research on the subject. This included Jules Labarte's 1855 *Handbook of the Arts of the Middle Ages and Renaissance,* Francisque Michel's 1834 The *Roman de la Violette: ou, De Gerard*

"Whose dusty leaves, well thinned and yellowing now, / But little hid the bright bloomed vine bunches. / There daylong 'neath the shadows of the trees", etc. Further on "higher" is rhymed with "sire", which ought to answer Mr. Payne's "lure", "was" and "pass", "are" and "care", "man" and "wan", "upbear" and "gear". ... there are some far worse, but I cannot stay to look for them now.' Morris's work, then, was used not as a measure of achievement, but of what O'Shaughnessy could 'get away with' in verse. *A Pathetic Love Episode in a Poet's Life, being letters from Helen Snee to Arthur W.E. O'Shaughnessy. Also a letter from him containing a dissertation on Love*, ed. Clement King Shorter (London: printed for private circulation, 1916), p. 12.

    [5]   Antony H. Harrison, *Swinburne's Medievalism: A Study in Victorian Love Poetry* (Baton Rouge and London: Louisiana State University Press, 1988), p. 137.

    [6]   Queen's, MS 8/3, MS 8/12, MS 8/20, MS 8/26.

de Nevers, G.L. Way's 1815 translation of Le Grand's *Fabliaux or tales, abridged from French manuscripts of the XIIth and XIIIth centuries*, among many others, some in translation, some in modern French, and some in the original Old French.[7]

Each entry in this 1870 notebook also includes its shelfmark at the British Museum, allowing a fascinating insight into O'Shaughnessy's relationship with his place of work. While he disliked the zoological work he performed in the Natural History Departments of the British Museum, it was a great benefit to him as a poet that in 1863–1881 these departments were still housed under the same roof as the library. During his lunch hour and after work, he had ready access to texts unavailable anywhere else.

There is only one extant notebook of this kind, recording a mere three months of reading and research, and thus we are left with only a fractional record of what we can assume to be his more extensive reading on the subject. But we can see from these unpublished manuscripts and notebooks that medievalism was a dominant influence on O'Shaughnessy's poetic voice throughout the late 1860s and early 1870s, culminating in the *Lays of France*, five long poems founded on the *lais* of the twelfth-century poet Marie de France.

The medieval revival has often been considered a conservative reaction to the changing times of the nineteenth century. In her influential 1971 *A Dream of Order*, Alice Chandler asserts that the nineteenth century was reacting to a chaotic modern world by idealizing the past and engaging in widespread nostalgia for a simpler time.[8] This idealization was a reaction to the industrial revolution and the restructuring of society that many felt left the working class uncared for. As Chandler says:

> Throughout the nineteenth century medievalists expressed horror over the degraded and impoverished condition of the industrial proletariat, working an eighty-four-hour week in lint-choked factories and living in sickness-breeding, filthy hovels. They believed that by comparison to the modern wage slave, even a thirteenth-century serf was fortunate ... In contrast to the alienated and divisive atmosphere of an increasingly urbanized and industrialized society, the Middle Ages were seen as familiar and patriarchal. The feudal society was said to give each man his place in society and, despite many tyrannous and cruel exceptions among its leaders, to have provided men with responsible masters.[9]

This paternalistic focus on positive class divisions, in which the wealthy would care for the poor, is evidenced in the thinking of nineteenth-century men like Thomas Carlyle:

> It was something other than money that the high then expected from the low, and could not live without getting from the low. Not as buyer and seller alone,

---

[7]   Ibid., MS 8/8. The *Roman de la Violette* is a thirteenth-century poem by the troubadour Gerbert de Montreuil.

[8]   Alice Chandler, *A Dream of Order: The Medieval Ideal in Nineteenth-Century English Literature* (London: Routledge & Kegan Paul, 1971), p. 1.

[9]   Ibid., p. 3.

144   *Arthur O'Shaughnessy, A Pre-Raphaelite Poet in the British Museum*

> of land or what else it might be, but in many senses still as soldier and captain, as clansman and head, as loyal subject and guiding king, was the low related to the high.[10]

Carlyle continues, 'Surely of all "rights of man", this right of the ignorant man to be guided by the wiser, to be, gently or forcibly, held in the true course by him, is the indisputablest.'[11] Thus, many critics view Victorian medievalism as an attempted retreat back to feudalism and a stronger aristocracy.[12]

Other critics, such as Charles Delheim, Stephanie Barczewski, and Inga Bryden, argue that medievalism is not a retreat from the present, but rather a direct celebration of the more conservative elements of the nineteenth century, particularly the emerging notion of 'Christian masculinity'.[13] Thus, Bryden suggests that King Arthur 'came to typify, indeed embody, the components of manliness, honour, heroic leadership and liberty which comprised the Teutonic notion of Englishness'. As the archetype of the 'modern gentleman', then, Arthur evinced a masculinity which encompassed 'the military, the spiritual and the domestic'.[14]

Still other critics, like Florence Boos and Chris Waters, point to works like Morris's to signal medievalism as a radical movement, directly challenging the status quo of the nineteenth century.[15] In the reverence for the past, and particularly an emphasis on the previously exalted status of the workman or artisan in the

---

[10]   Thomas Carlyle, *Chartism* (London: James Fraser, 1840), p. 58. Marx asserts that 'The bourgeoisie, wherever it has got the upper hand, has put an end to all feudal, patriarchal, idyllic relations. It has pitilessly torn asunder the motley feudal ties that bound man to his "natural superiors", and has left remaining no other nexus between man and man than naked self-interest, than callous "cash payment"' (*Communist Manifesto*, p. 15).

[11]   Ibid., p. 52.

[12]   For example, Mark Girouard's equally influential *The Return to Camelot: Chivalry and the English Gentleman* (New Haven and London: Yale University Press, 1981), in which he argues for the conservative uses of medievalism and the national myth of chivalry to be constructed out of it. This argument is reiterated in Loretta M. Holloway and Jennifer A. Palmgren's more recent *Beyond Arthurian Romances: The Reach of Victorian Medievalism* (New York: Palgrave Macmillan, 2005).

[13]   See Charles Delheim's 'Interpreting Victorian Medievalism', *History and Community: Essays in Victorian Medievalism*, ed. Florence S. Boos (New York and London: Garland Publishing, Inc., 1992), pp. 39–58. More recent works focusing on the particularly English stories of King Arthur agree with Delheim. See, for example, Stephanie Barczewski's *Myth and National Identity in Nineteenth Century Britain: The Legends of King Arthur and Robin Hood* (Oxford: Oxford University Press, 2000), or Inga Bryden's *Reinventing King Arthur: The Arthurian Legends in Victorian Culture* (Aldershot: Ashgate, 2005).

[14]   Bryden, p. 34.

[15]   Florence S. Boos focuses on the more radical social reform possible in these narratives, in her 'Alternative Victorian Futures: "Historicism", *Past and Present* and *A Dream of John Ball*', in *History and Community*, as does Chris Waters in his 'Marxism, Medievalism and Popular Culture' in the same collection.

Middle Ages, this kind of radicalism falls into the category that Marx defines as 'petty-bourgeois socialism', which:

> [A]spires either to restoring the old means of production and of exchange, and with them the old property relations, and the old society, or to cramping the modern means of production and of exchange, within the framework of the old property relations that have been, and were bound to be, exploded by those means. In either case, it is both reactionary and Utopian.[16]

Marx rejects this kind of middle-class socialism, but we can see it flourishing in the later part of the Victorian period. Mark Bevir goes so far as to assert that British socialism was, in fact, a middle-class movement.[17] Although in many ways O'Shaughnessy's political views may be seen to conform to 'petty-bourgeois socialism', as defined by Marx, particularly in his emphasis on community and craft, his use of the medieval is very different from that of Morris. Morris's *Defence of Guenevere* focuses on how morality can affect a society, through the lens of Guenevere's adulterous love for Launcelot, and further explores what Morris sees as the decline of England following the Hundred Years' War. O'Shaughnessy, on the other hand, avoids the larger issues of society in general, thus eschewing many of the 'reasons' for medievalism so far explored.

In actuality, medievalism was so widespread during the nineteenth century that no one ideology or motivation can be assigned to it, either as an artistic or a social imperative. Medievalism was used by Morris to encourage a socialist uprising in *A Dream of John Ball* (1888), while at the same time Benjamin Disraeli employed it to spearhead the Young England Movement, an aristocratic faction of the Tory Party.[18] What medievalism provided the many different people and movements that employed it was a perspective outside the modern day, through which elements of the nineteenth century that were taken for granted could be highlighted or questioned. Furthermore, as many critics argue, the invocation of a historical period could lend cultural authority to a work or movement.[19] In this sense, medievalism becomes a 'language' that can be employed to discuss a multitude of subjects.

---

[16]   *Communist Manifesto*, p. 47.

[17]   Mark Bevir, *The Making of British Socialism* (Princeton: Princeton University Press, 2011), p. 46.

[18]   The Young England Movement was a splinter group of young, aristocratic Tories. According to Delheim, they sought to undermine the upwardly mobile middle class by turning back to a medieval model of government, attempting to show 'the people' that life had been better under a noble lord, who ate with the men who worked his land, rather than the middle-class factory owners, who didn't know the names or faces of their lower-class workers: 'They reasserted the feudal ideals of social hierarchy and communal responsibility, calling for an alliance of the aristocracy and the people. Genuinely concerned as they may have been with the plight of the working class in industrial cities, they used this issue to discredit the industrial middle class and bolster their own power' (Delheim, *History and Community*, p. 45).

[19]   Ibid., p. 46.

146   *Arthur O'Shaughnessy, A Pre-Raphaelite Poet in the British Museum*

As Holloway and Palmgren assert, 'These individual responses became part of a larger societal conversation in which the Middle Ages provided the Victorians with a common imagery that they used in everything that could be argued about, bought, or sold.'[20] Thus, Chris Waters speculates that Morris made use of this 'language' of medievalism *because* it was so popular and widespread by the time he wrote his most socialist works. '[B]ecause socialists were reformulating a discourse that already exerted a major influence in Victorian society, they were able to articulate their concerns in a language that was recognizable and popular.'[21]

Viewing Victorian medievalism, then, as a language that lends cultural authority to a reassessment of the modern day, I would like to turn back to O'Shaughnessy's use of that 'language.' Charles Delheim has asserted, 'What unites the diverse uses of medieval symbols is that they may all be seen as part of a quest for identity.'[22] If this is true, it seems clear that O'Shaughnessy was attempting to forge a different identity from many of his contemporaries, including Morris. The majority of poets and artists employing a medieval setting in their work turned to the tales of King Arthur and his court at Camelot as source material. As Barczewksi and Bryden note, the stories of King Arthur can be read as an attempt at stabilization in the rapidly changing nineteenth century by crafting a myth of heroic national identity. But O'Shaughnessy subverts this effort by turning away from King Arthur, and England in its entirety, to focus on medieval France in the insular *lais* of Marie.[23]

At first glance, the choice of Marie de France for O'Shaughnessy's subject matter seems a strange one, as evinced by the reception of his 1870 poem 'Bisclavaret', also based on one of Marie's 12 *lais*. While 'Bisclavaret' was almost universally praised, critics and friends of the poet alike were unfamiliar with the source material and therefore at a loss as to the meaning of the poem. In order to understand that the poem is about the release of man's animal nature, one must know that 'Bisclavaret' is the name of the werewolf in Marie's *lai*. Without this information, the poem is much more difficult to unravel. O'Shaughnessy cannot be accused of being deliberately obscure in choosing his source material for 'Bisclavaret', since, in addition to the title, he included an epigraph from Marie's *lai* identifying the medieval author. However, in 1870 the *lais* were not readily available to the reading public, as they had not yet been translated into English. In fact, the *lais* as we know them had only been attributed to Marie at the end of the eighteenth century by Thomas Tyrwhitt.[24] A French edition of the *lais*, edited by J.B.B. de Roquefort, wasn't published until 1820 and even then it proved

---

20   Holloway and Palmgren, p. 2.

21   Waters, *History and Community*, p. 148.

22   Delheim, *History and Community*, p. 54.

23   Unlike the stories of Chrétien de Troyes, or other French medieval writers, the *lais* of Marie do not tell the stories of Camelot.

24   Karen K. Jambeck, 'Warton, Tyrwhitt, & de la Rue: Marie de France in the Eighteenth Century', *The Reception and Transmission of the Works of Marie de France, 1774–1974*, ed. Chantel Maréchal (Lewiston: The Edwin Mellen Press, 2003), pp. 31–90 (p. 51).

'Love's Splendid Lures' 147

unpopular, selling poorly.[25] The first complete English edition of Marie's *lais* was not published until 1944.[26] In contrast, the majority of Victorian medieval poetry – including Tennyson's and some of Morris's – was based on Malory's fifteenth-century *Morte D'Arthur*, made available in a very popular translation by Robert Southey in 1817.[27] In fact, the only reason O'Shaughnessy had access to Marie's *lais* is that they happened to be contained in the Harleian manuscript collection housed in the British Museum.[28]

The obscurity of the *lais* clearly presented a challenge to O'Shaughnessy's readers. When Dante Gabriel Rossetti complained in a letter about his troubles with 'Bisclavaret' – 'after 2 careful readings it still remains obscure to me', and 'I can only half make out the meaning & not at all the application of its motto & title'[29] – O'Shaughnessy was forced to explain the poem to his friend, after which Rossetti replied:

> I have now read Bisclavaret again, and of course after your word of enlightenment, light it is. But I must confess to have been unacquainted hitherto with the Werewolf nomenclature ... When one understands it clearly, the poem is, of course, all the finer for it, but I think it is a pity you did not somehow introduce the word Werewolf somewhere to help the reader.[30]

Of course, not all readers had the benefit of a personal letter from the author to explain the poem to them. Thus, the reviewer for the *Athenaeum* recognized that

---

[25] Mary B. Speer, 'J.B.B. de Roquefort (1777–1834): The First Modern Editor of Marie de France', in *Reception and Transmission*, pp. 225–40 (p. 229). R. Howard Bloch speculates that this was because Marie's *lais* were too feminine for the nineteenth century, as compared to the Arthurian tales written exclusively by men. 'Gaston Paris (1839–1903): Paris France: Marie on the Margin', *Reception and Transmission*, p. 96. De Roquefort's translation was further troubled by the fact that the editor was relying on other people's notes, rather than the manuscript itself, in order to make his translation. *Reception and Transmission*, p. 231.

[26] Glyn S. Burgess, 'Alfred Ewert (1891–1969): The First English Edition of the Lais', *Reception and Transmission*, pp. 251–60 (p. 253).

[27] James P. Carley, ed., *Arthurian Poets: A.C. Swinburne* (Suffolk: The Boydell Press, 1990), p. 1.

[28] The Harleian collection was the private collection of Robert Harley, first earl of Oxford, and Edward Harley, second earl of Oxford, and contained 6,000 manuscripts. Jambeck, *Reception and Transmission*, p. 37.

[29] In a letter dated 15 October 1870, *The Correspondence of Dante Gabriel Rossetti*, ed. William E. Fredeman (Cambridge and Rochester: D.S. Brewer, 2004), vol. 4, p. 543.

[30] In a letter dated 18 October 1870 (*Correspondence*, p. 544). It is evident that O'Shaughnessy also sent a word of explanation to Joseph Knight, as he writes to O'Shaughnessy on 19 October 1870: 'I have not yet availed myself of your letter further than to reread Bisclavaret – the significance of which had I own quite escaped me. I now see its many and most subtle beauties' (Duke University Manuscript Collection, 6th 11:A Box 1, c.1, letter dated 19 October 1870).

148 *Arthur O'Shaughnessy, A Pre-Raphaelite Poet in the British Museum*

he was among the few familiar with Marie's work: 'Many readers of 'Bisclaverit' [sic] will reach the last line without discovering that Mr. O'Shaughnessy has been alluding to the werewolf.'[31] Yet, O'Shaughnessy steadfastly devoted one-quarter of his entire poetic output to these unfamiliar *lais* of Marie.

As discussed earlier, one of the 'reasons' for nineteenth-century medievalism often proffered by critics is the cultural authority lent to a text by historical source material. However, the 'obscurity' of Marie's work would seem to undercut any authority lent by the invocation of a medieval text. Such authority is further undercut by how O'Shaughnessy chose to interpret the original stories. Again he departs from his contemporaries: while they often streamlined the interweaving stories of Malory, on the whole, they remained faithful to the source. Thus, Arnold's rather small deviation in 'Tristram and Iseult' in which Iseult of the White Hands has two children by Tristram, is quite a notable change, and draws much critical attention.[32] In contrast, O'Shaughnessy at times deviates quite radically from Marie – so much so that these changes have formed one of the few points of discussion of O'Shaughnessy's *Lays of France*. Edmund Gosse describes the stories as 'paraphrased very freely from Marie de France'.[33] Taking a more negative tone, Oliver Elton complains, 'O'Shaughnessy often treats the incidents as a mere canvas, and sometimes manages to spoil them', while George K. Anderson notes, 'There is no gainsaying the fact that O'Shaughnessy took the grossest liberties with the *lais* of Marie.'[34] Anderson's entire article is, in fact, an examination of the alterations O'Shaughnessy made to Marie's text, but he is so obsessed with finding instances of Victorian moralization/bowdlerization – which I argue are not there to find – that he overlooks some of the more perplexing changes O'Shaughnessy makes. *Lays of France* consists of five stories based on Marie's *lais*. Three of the lays – 'Laustic; or the Lay of the Nightingale', 'The Lay of Two Lovers', and 'The Lay of Yvenec' – follow her plots quite closely, while 'The Lay of Eliduc' is given an entirely new ending, and 'Chaitivel; or, the Lay of Love's Unfortunate' bears only a passing resemblance to Marie's story of the same name.

---

[31] 'Review: Two Young Poets', *Athenaeum* 2245 (1870): 585–6 (p. 585).

[32] For a discussion of Swinburne's fidelity to his medieval source material, see Antony Harrison's *Swinburne's Medievalism: A Study in Victorian Love Poetry* (1988). For a discussion of Tennyson's moralization of the Arthur stories, see Rebecca Cochran's 'Tennyson's Hierarchy of Women in *Idylls of the King*' in *History and Community* (1992). For a general discussion of the interpretation of these stories by the major poets of the mid- to late Victorian period, including Arnold's deviations from the medieval plot, see Laura and Robert Lambdin's *Camelot in the Nineteenth Century: Arthurian Characters in the Poems of Tennyson, Arnold, Morris and Swinburne* (Westport, CT: Greenwood Press, 2000).

[33] Edmund Gosse, 'Obituary: Arthur O'Shaughnessy', *The Academy* 457 (5 February 1881): 98–9 (p. 99).

[34] George K. Anderson, 'Marie de France and Arthur O'Shaughnessy: A Study in Victorian Adaptation', *Studies in Philology* 36 (1939): 529–49 (p. 533). Oliver Elton, *A Survey of English Literature: 1830–1880* (New York: The Macmillan Co., 1920), vol. 4, p. 112.

'Love's Splendid Lures' 149

In his article, Anderson notes O'Shaughnessy's interest in France, along with his desire to 'dabble' in the Pre-Raphaelite craze for medievalism, concluding, 'A combination of the two influences, the French and the medieval, is obvious in his choice of the lais of Marie de France.'[35] This is clearly an over simplification of O'Shaughnessy's choices. While it might explain why he was drawn to French medievalism rather than the Middle Ages in England, it does not explain his specific choice of Marie. After all, we know that he read extensively in French medieval literature. Edmund Gosse attempts a more thoughtful explanation of this choice, by stating: 'Marie is of all mediæval writers the most like O'Shaughnessy himself, with her artful ease of narrative and her lax, melodious amorosity.'[36] For Gosse, the similarity between Marie's style and O'Shaughnessy's created a natural affinity between the two poets. Here Gosse may have been correct. Criticism of Marie's *lais* is strangely reminiscent of criticism of O'Shaughnessy's poetry. For instance, Ernest Hoepffner says of Marie, 'More modest in her proportions, less brilliant in her qualities of language and style, using a psychology that is less profound and less penetrating, Marie gives off a discrete and rare poetic charm that one hardly finds anywhere else.'[37] The assessment of Marie as being secondary to her contemporaries and yet possessing a unique style that makes her work worth reading is very similar to the critical accounts of O'Shaughnessy's own verse. Gosse himself said of the poet:

> [T]he quality of his work was exceedingly unequal … for there is a great deal of chaff among the wheat. But, when all that is trivial has been winnowed away, there will remain … a residuum of exquisite poetry, full of odour and melody, all in one key, and all essentially unlike the work of anybody else.[38]

Gosse's assessment that Marie is 'like O'Shaughnessy' is largely tonal, focusing on a 'lax, melodious amorosity'. This remains, however, a curious comparison, because stylistically Marie is most known for her amazing brevity, while O'Shaughnessy is often criticized for his verbosity. In their discussions of O'Shaughnessy's adaptations, both S. Foster Damon and Anderson note Marie's 'economy', compared to O'Shaughnessy's trademark excess. For example, Damon notes that O'Shaughnessy's 'Chaitivel' is 1,206 lines, while Marie's is a mere 240.[39] The languidness that Gosse suggests is far more accurate of O'Shaughnessy's lengthy tales than of Marie's brief and dexterous *lais*.

---

[35]   Anderson, p. 530.

[36]   Edmund Gosse, *Silhouettes*, Essay Index Reprint Series (Freeport, NY: Books for Libraries Press, 1971), p. 176.

[37]   *The Anonymous Marie de France*, trans. R. Howard Bloch (Chicago: The University of Chicago Press, 2003), p. 15. Hoepffner's was the third edition of Marie's *lais* to be published. Ernest Hoepffner, ed., *Les Lais*, 2 vols (Strasbourg: Heitz, 1921).

[38]   Gosse, 'Obituary', p. 99.

[39]   S. Foster Damon, 'Marie de France: Psychologist of Courtly Love', *PMLA* 44, no. 4 (1929): 968–96 (p. 974).

150 *Arthur O'Shaughnessy, A Pre-Raphaelite Poet in the British Museum*

Even in the three lays that adhere to the source material quite closely, O'Shaughnessy changes the plot in ways that radically shift the focus and tone of each story. For example, in Marie's 'Yonec' (translated as 'Yvenec' by O'Shaughnessy), a young woman is imprisoned in a tower by her elderly, jealous husband. Her prayers for deliverance are answered in the form of a shape-shifting knight who can take on the guise of a large bird and with whom she begins an affair. Their love is soon discovered, however, and her husband sets a trap for the knight/bird at the window of the tower. He is horribly maimed but manages to tell the girl that she is pregnant with their child, and that when the child comes of age, he will avenge both of them. After the wounded knight flies away, the girl climbs out the tower window and follows the trail of blood in order to find his castle. She tells him she can't return home because her husband, knowing of the affair, will kill her. The knight gives her a ring to make her husband forget everything that has happened, and a sword to give to their son when he comes of age. He tells her that she and the child should visit his tomb, where the son will hear the story of how the knight died. The girl should then present the son with his father's sword and tell him the noble knight is his father, so that he may exact their revenge. This all passes as the knight predicted, and the *lai* ends with Yonec slaying the jealous husband in order to avenge his father's death.[40]

The most important elements of Marie's story, then, are prophecy and fate. The story is named not for the knight or the girl, but the prophesied son, Yonec, as the culmination of the story is his successful avenging of his father's death. In his translation, O'Shaughnessy remains quite faithful to much of the story, but chooses to remove the elements of prophecy and revenge. After the lovers' affair is discovered and the knight is mortally wounded, he does not regain his human shape, and therefore does not deliver the news that the girl is pregnant. Rather, he remains a hawk, and dies, silent, in her arms. Then, compelled by some unseen force – 'then a hand / Was laid upon her heart and wielded / Mysteriously her will; she planned / Nor purposed any course, but yielded / Meekly as in a dream' – the girl exits the tower, not by the window, but by the doors, which are all mysteriously unlocked and unguarded.[41] The same force draws her to the knight's castle, where she finds his human body, still alive. This in and of itself is a confusing alteration to the story, and one O'Shaughnessy doesn't fully explore. Is the knight a shape-shifter, or does he have two bodies? The hawk has died and been left behind in the tower, and yet his human body is in the castle, alive, but also wounded and also dying. One suspects that O'Shaughnessy merely wanted an excuse to write two wrenching death scenes, revelling in the girl's grief. Rather than delivering a prophecy about the future of their son, or giving the girl the ring and sword, the knight merely tells her that she can never stop loving him, or it will destroy his peace in the grave. He then dies again, and she returns to her husband.

---

[40]   Marie de France, 'Yonec', *The Lais of Marie de France*, trans. Glyn S. Burgess and Keith Busby, 2nd ed. (London: Penguin Books, 2003), pp. 86–93.

[41]   Arthur O'Shaughnessy, *Lays of France (Founded on the Lays of Marie)* (London: Chatto & Windus, 1872), p. 283.

'Love's Splendid Lures'   151

O'Shaughnessy provides no moment where the girl – quite rightly – expresses concern that she will be held accountable for her affair. There is no ring to make her husband forget that she had a lover. She merely returns to her tower, now pregnant. O'Shaughnessy's only explanation of her husband's leniency is that 'such great mystery did cling / Upon her face, that seemed to keep / Knowledge of some most holy thing, / No man found ways to try her more / With base reproof or questioning'.[42] Although it would be obvious, in the light of her affair, that the child was not her husband's, no one questions his paternity. He is born and named 'Yvenec, the Deliverer', yet she is not delivered from her husband, nor does he deliver the vengeance required of the story. It merely ends with her seemingly content to live with the man who keeps her imprisoned and murdered her lover and raise her child believing that same man in his father.

At first glance, O'Shaughnessy's changes to Marie's *lai* seem quite odd. Although most of the plot elements are the same, O'Shaughnessy has effectively neutered Marie's tale by removing its central purpose. In fact, the changes O'Shaughnessy makes to Marie's stories – whether small or vast – often serve to undermine or negate the 'point', or moral, of the medieval tale. It is clear, then, that it was not the plots of Marie's *lais* that drew O'Shaughnessy to them. Rather, it is the undercurrent of the tragic nature of love which led O'Shaughnessy to choose this source material. The changes O'Shaughnessy makes to 'Yonec' shift the focus away from the driving hand of fate onto the hopelessness of the love affair. The destiny at the heart of O'Shaughnessy's story is not the prophesied revenge of the son, but the inevitable tragic end of the affair.

In the end, O'Shaughnessy is not offering a translation of Marie, nor even a paraphrase. At his most faithful, he provides an interpretation of the medieval stories, with his own emphasis and interest shifting the focus of the tale. And in the case of 'Chaitivel', it is clear that he was merely inspired by Marie's story to write his own, completely original tale.[43] It was the atmosphere of Marie's tales, more than the actual plots or even characters, which drew O'Shaughnessy's interest. Marie's stories feature far more supernatural elements than Malory's, with shape-shifters and magic potions being par for the course. Furthermore, unlike the stories of the Round Table, Marie's narratives are narrowly domestic. Often confined to a single room – the narrative never ventures outside a single bedroom in 'Laustic' and most of the action of 'Yonec' takes place in the girl's tower – Marie's stories are not concerned with wider social issues, or the implications of these relationships outside the domestic sphere. Malory's ill-fated lovers are destined to bring down whole kingdoms, but Marie is more concerned with the psychological effects of a doomed love affair on the participants. As Bloch asserts, 'Unlike, say, the

---

[42]   *Lays*, p. 292.

[43]   This is the argument Oskar Brönner makes, noting that 'O'Shaughnessy's goal in creating the Lays was not intentionally archaic poetry, but – one may reasonably argue – a grand, individualistic oeuvre, inspired in parts by the amateur poetry of Marie de France' (my translation). Oskar Brönner, *Das Leben Arthur O'Shaughnessy's*, Würzburger Beiträge zur englischen Literaturgeschichte, no. 5, Heidelberg, 1933.

romances of Chrétien or the *Tristran* poets, unlike even the *Fables*, where much attention is paid to government and community ... the couple is the operative social unit within the *Lais*.'[44] Thus, the impact of 'Laustic' is contained in a tiny coffin, holding the body of a dead nightingale, symbolic of lost love. These domestic stories of love evade the wider social or political issues that attracted conservative writers like Tennyson and radical writers like Morris to the medieval period.

It is not merely the focus on love, but the way Marie presents love, that drew O'Shaughnessy's interest. As Damon notes, '[Marie] did not judge (whether to praise or condemn) her characters ... She was a Realist, not a Moralist ... Real love interested her above all things; true lovers had her sympathy.'[45] It is this quality – observation rather than judgment of love affairs – that led O'Shaughnessy to choose these narratives as the basis for his own medieval tales. After all, four of the five *lais* that O'Shaughnessy selected for his volume are centred on adultery, yet the characters are highly sympathetic. If the use of a medieval setting offered artists an outsider's perspective to their own age, the use of Marie's medieval texts allowed O'Shaughnessy to evade contemporary taboos in his treatment of adulterous love affairs. In his consideration of Swinburne's translations of medieval French poetry, Nick Freeman notes, 'by translating a historic text, Swinburne is able to smuggle disreputable content into English homes under the guise of high art.'[46] Tennyson may have punished his Arthurian characters under the moral codes of the nineteenth century, but by relying on the objectivity of the source material, it was also possible to present these affairs without moralizing or condemning the characters.[47] Marie was non-judgmental of her characters, and thus O'Shaughnessy could also present adultery without comment.

Rather than following in his contemporaries' footsteps and translating Malory's Arthurian tales, O'Shaughnessy chose the *lais* of Marie de France partly because of their narrow focus on love, without judgment or condemnation.[48] The stories of Marie make a virtue of forbidden love, elevating it even when it leads to the

---

[44]   Bloch, p. 52.

[45]   Damon, p. 968.

[46]   Nick Freeman, 'The Gallows Nightingale: Swinburne's Translations of Villon', in *Beyond Arthurian Romances*, pp. 133–46 (p. 140).

[47]   See, for example, Rebecca Cochran's 'Tennyson's Hierarchy of Women in *Idylls of the King*' in *History and Community*, or *Camelot in the Nineteenth Century: Arthurian Characters in the Poems of Tennyson, Arnold, Morris and Swinburne*, by Laura Cooner Lambdin and Robert Thomas Lambdin (Westport, CT: Greenwood Press, 2000).

[48]   The Lambdins note that in his rendering of the Arthurian stories, Malory actually eliminated much of the courtly love narrative, instead writing a nationalistic, heroic tale: 'Malory was a knight himself, but apparently not one interested in outmoded concepts of courtly love; possibly for this reason he eliminated many of the love scenes between Launcelot and Gwenyvere, while concentrating on Launcelot as a Christian warrior. Chrétien's *Lancelot* portrays this knight as the Queen's willing pawn who is often made to look foolish for his love. Malory removed from Launcelot's character most aspects of the fawning courtly lover and substituted a warrior of great courage' (*Camelot in the Nineteenth Century*, p. 6).

'Love's Splendid Lures'

lovers' deaths. This is in stark contrast to Arthurian Romances, centred as they must be on the betrayal of Arthur by Guinevere and Lancelot, and the subsequent fall of Camelot.

As this chapter has shown, O'Shaughnessy's readers were most likely unfamiliar with the stories he included in his *Lays of France*.[49] Although readers and critics complained of the obscurity of his source material, O'Shaughnessy used this obscurity to his benefit. Despite Marie's relatively unknown status, O'Shaughnessy puts her name right in the title: *The Lays of France (Founded on the Lays of Marie)*. By giving her name such prominence, he shifts some of the responsibility for the content of the volume onto the medieval poet. While the average Victorian was familiar with the Arthurian narratives, O'Shaughnessy's audience was unable to judge how little or how much O'Shaughnessy deviated from his source material. Changes made to a narrative about Arthur, Lancelot, and Guinevere could be analyzed and made suspect, but it was likely that readers would accept the more audacious elements of O'Shaughnessy's *Lays* as Marie's invention. Thus, even in his entirely original tale, 'Chaitivel', O'Shaughnessy was most likely not held accountable to the same degree as he would have been if he had labelled it an original tale.

Swinburne used the same technique throughout his career. As Freeman notes:

> The medieval world to which Swinburne gained access via Villon allowed him to challenge conventional proprieties without risking the open conflict with them generated by the first *Poems and Ballads*. In much of his finest poetry, Swinburne plays a complex game with the legitimizing authority of history, exploiting while at the same time colluding with contemporary hypocrisy in placing transgressive narratives at distant removes from the present.[50]

I suggest that O'Shaughnessy played a similar game with the authority invested in medieval literature by the popularity of the medieval revival, exploiting it to avoid the censure that had befallen him at the more audacious parts of his *An Epic of Women*. In this, O'Shaughnessy mirrors Marie herself. Each of Marie's tales is prefaced by the assertion that it is a translation of an old Breton tale – however, Joan Ferrante contends that most of the fables were probably not works of translation.[51] Ferrante suggests, 'If it is a humble female ploy to make no claim to authority, it is also a clever way to ensure freedom to say whatever she likes, since there is no source to check.'[52] O'Shaughnessy, too, very cleverly plays with the obscurity of his source material, asserting the historical authority of texts his

---

[49] A few of Marie's *lais* had been translated into English at this point, in works such as G.L. Way's 1815 *Fabliaux, or, Tales abridged from French Manuscripts of the XIIth and XIIIth centuries by M. Le Grand*. However, O'Shaughnessy did not include in *Lays of France* either of the *lais* translated by Way.

[50] Freeman, p. 139.

[51] Joan M. Ferrante, 'Way – Ellis – Weston – Mason; Do Preconceptions Influence Translations?', *Reception and Transmission*, pp. 209–24 (p. 209).

[52] Ibid., p. 210.

154 *Arthur O'Shaughnessy, A Pre-Raphaelite Poet in the British Museum*

readers were unable to access, thus granting himself freedom of expression while disallowing blame and censure.

II.

Unlike the tales of the Round Table, which all circulate around Arthur's court and feature many of the same characters moving in the background, Marie's *lais* are independent stories, set in mostly nameless kingdoms and countries. Some are dominated by the magical or supernatural, while others have no such elements. Some have a strong moral, while others are so short they barely have a plot. Some end tragically, some happily. In taking on these tales, O'Shaughnessy had the power of selection on his side; he used only five of Marie's 12 stories and thus was able to choose ones that are of a thematic type. Beyond this, however, he interweaves several elements that span the whole of the volume, making his work far more cohesive than the source material. Thematically, *Lays* is about the nature of love, and the musings on this subject that are interspersed throughout the tales help to bind the five stories together.

Like the rest of O'Shaughnessy's corpus, the *Lays* are dominated by natural settings. Nevertheless, O'Shaughnessy replicates the close-set interiority of the source material with an emphasis on the naturalistic 'bower' as a hidden place designed for love. Metonymically, nature replaces sex in O'Shaughnessy's poems, adding a Darwinian focus on the fecundity of the natural world to these medieval tales. The word 'bower', used in several of the lays, is archaic and purposefully medieval in its associations, helping to maintain both the tone of the works and the distance between the reader and the eroticism presented. This word choice is quite clever. Beyond the medieval sound of the word, it has a double meaning that plays into the sexual undertones in these naturalistic scenes. In the thirteenth and fourteenth centuries, one meaning of 'bower' was 'a lady's private apartment; a boudoir'.[53] This definition continued to be used poetically into the nineteenth century, and thus, every time the lovers retire to a bower in one of O'Shaughnessy's lays, the poem is slyly suggesting that they are, in fact, slipping away to a bedroom.[54]

A bower is primarily defined as 'a place closed in or arched over with branches of trees' and thus replicates the insularity of the domestic worlds Marie

---

[53] OED.

[54] 'Bower' appears in much of the medieval poetry of the nineteenth century, including that of Rossetti, Swinburne, and Tennyson. However, it is primarily used either to describe a garden or outdoor space, without sexual connotations, as in Swinburne's 'April' or Tennyson's *Idylls of the King* ('Balin and Balan'), or as a synonym of bedroom, without any nature imagery, as in Tennyson's *Idylls* ('The Last Tournament') or 'The Lady of Shalott'. Rossetti's use of the word is far closer to O'Shaughnessy's intermixing of nature and sexuality, as in 'Eden Bower'. However, O'Shaughnessy's use of the word in manuscripts dates as early as 1867, before the publication of Rossetti's first volume of poetry in 1870.

'Love's Splendid Lures'   155

writes about.[55] Furthermore, these settings grant a bedroom-like intimacy and privacy to the lovers. Although O'Shaughnessy never uses the word in 'Laustic', it is clearly what he is describing when he speaks of a garden that 'heavy hazel boughs shut in'.[56] Here O'Shaughnessy displaces the eroticism of the lovers onto the natural world. 'There was a garden, and a wood / Full of sweet-scented trees that stood / Shivering for pleasure in the sun'.[57] This garden is 'a pleasant place for love's sweet sin', although, as in Marie's story, the lovers never consummate their relationship.[58] Instead the garden, blooming with life and shivering with pleasure, acts out the desires that the separated lovers cannot. This displacement of desire onto the natural world is evident in one of the volume's most sensual passages. The unhappily married woman stands at her window, looking across the pleasure garden at her lover, and is caressed by the night breeze:

> Have you not stood, the summer night
> At windows; felt with soft delight
>   The air come from the balmy land
> Play in your bosom with no sin,
>   Play in your bosom like a hand?
> She stood and felt it on her brow,
>   Like a kiss straying here and there,
>   Like light lips playing in the hair;
> She felt it on her neck, and now
>   Creeping through every loosened fold
> Of the night garment, more and more
>   To slake her body with some cold
> Sweet touch of dews it thirsted for.[59]

This passage is highlighted in the story by the pleasing rhythms of the rhyming couplets, a change from the rhyme scheme of the rest of the poem, mimicking the caress of the breeze. The pleasure of the text is reinforced by the physicality of the language, dominated by touch and sensation. These lines are ostensibly a displacement of sex, deflecting the eroticism of the scene onto nature, and yet what should be a moment of frustration for the character – unable to reach her lover – becomes a moment of sexual climax instead. The passage is made all the more audacious by its implication of the reader in its opening lines, asking 'Have you not stood?' Unlike in the majority of O'Shaughnessy's corpus, the reader of the *Lays* is gendered female throughout, and thus O'Shaughnessy draws a Victorian, female readership into complicity with an adulterous sex act.

---

[55]   A bower being defined as 'A place closed in or overarched with branches of trees, shrubs, or other plants; a shady recess, leafy covert, arbour' (OED).

[56]   *Lays*, p. 11.

[57]   Ibid., p. 10.

[58]   Ibid., p. 11.

[59]   Ibid., p. 13.

156 *Arthur O'Shaughnessy, A Pre-Raphaelite Poet in the British Museum*

However, the otherwise shocking nature of this passage is mitigated by the deflection onto the natural world and the medieval setting of the story.

Whenever possible, O'Shaughnessy inserts natural settings into Marie's decidedly interior tales. In her usual economy of words, all Marie says of the moment of falling in love in 'Les Deux Amanz' is: 'They often spoke together and loved each other loyally, concealing their love as best they could so that no one would notice them.'[60] There is no indication as to *where* the lovers have their assignations. O'Shaughnessy, however, specifies a natural setting for these trysts in 'The Lay of Two Lovers':

> Many a garden place was rife
>   With tender record of fond waste
> Of hours and broken words and sighs.[61]

These gardens are then further defined as bowers, private and closed-in:

> In some close paradise of bloom,
>   Where love had made them a fair room
> With unbetraying bird and tree
> And sleek scared fawn. – O but to see
>   The warm bright chambers under leaf
> Sun-streaked and gilded morn and noon;
>   The burrow under the arched sheaf. [62]

Throughout the *Lays,* O'Shaughnessy insists on the canopy of branches in these scenes, closing these spaces in and forming interiors in the exterior world. Unlike the closely guarded rooms of their homes, it is only these bower/boudoirs that offer the lovers privacy and intimacy. Ironically it is only by moving his scenes outside that O'Shaughnessy can maintain the intimate interiority of Marie's original tales.

In 'The Lay of Two Lovers', unlike 'Laustic', the lovers do achieve intimacy, and yet the natural world is still used as a metonym for the sex act:

> O but to see, yea, once again,
>   Though but to weep, the bed they left
> Of prest and tumbled leaves with stain
>   Of fair crushed flowers, the day he reft
> The first long willing bliss from her,
> And she felt safe to touch and stir
>   The strange and gracious hair he had
> That once so lured her, as a thing
> Whereon love's blessing seemed to cling![63]

---

[60]   Marie de France, p. 83.

[61]   *Lays*, p. 51.

[62]   Ibid.

[63]   Ibid., p. 52.

'Love's Splendid Lures' 157

Again, the explicit nature of the sex act is displaced onto the natural setting. There is some violence to the imagery – the crushed flowers echo the bliss that is 'reft' from her, clearly enacting the loss of the girl's virginity.

This kind of displacement to escape censure was not always successful, of course. Robert Buchanan had so lately complained of 'females who bite, scratch, scream, bubble, munch, sweat, writhe, twist, wriggle, foam, and in a general way slaver over their lovers', referring to Rossetti's 'Willowwood', in which a well takes on the semblance of the longed-for lover and '*bubbled with brimming kisses at my mouth*' [Buchanan's emphasis].[64] In his complaint, Buchanan literalizes a metaphorical moment, inserting a physical female body where Rossetti's poem had none. In addition to the metonymic association of nature and sex, however, O'Shaughnessy's verse has the added protection of the medieval setting and its status as an alleged translation. Medieval works were known to be far more sexually explicit than what was allowed in the Victorian period; as G. Ellis states, 'in perusing the original fabliaux it is impossible to repress our astonishment at the indelicate and gross language to which our ancestors of both sexes appear to have listened without the least scruple or emotion'.[65] The known 'indelicacy' of medieval texts here serves as a protective barrier for O'Shaughnessy, since the eroticism of these passages could be attributed to Marie.

As with most of the changes O'Shaughnessy makes to Marie's original stories, Anderson finds fault with these naturalistic settings, saying, 'The idyllic setting of the love-scenes, the summer night, and the love-magic is nineteenth-century romanticism, not Marie.'[66] While Romanticism is obviously quite closely associated with nature, the kind of naturalism O'Shaughnessy employs here is more reminiscent of the French naturalism of the mid-century: a Darwinian nature that is explicitly sexualized. Coming so soon on the heels of Darwin's *Descent of Man*, the association of nature with the sexual drive to reproduce would be difficult to escape, particularly for a naturalist like O'Shaughnessy. Rather than trying to avoid that association, O'Shaughnessy exploits the connection in order to include sexually explicit passages into his verse.

I have suggested that O'Shaughnessy often neglects the moral of Marie's tales in order to highlight the thematic associations of love, fate, and death. This is readily apparent in his changes to the story 'Eliduc'. Gosse suggests, 'The best of Marie's lays is "Eliduc", and this seems to me the best of O'Shaughnessy's

---

[64]   Robert Buchanan, 'The Fleshly School of Poetry: Mr. D.G. Rossetti', *Contemporary Review* 18 (August/November 1871): 334–50 (pp. 342–3). Buchanan quotes, without attributing it, Rossetti's 'Willowwood', one of the sonnets in his sequence *The House of Life*.

[65]   Preface by G. Ellis, *Fabliaux or Tales, abridged from the French Manuscripts of the XIIth and XIIIth Centuries by M. Le Grand*, selected and translated into English verse by the late G.L. Way, Esq. (London: J. Rodwell, 1815), p. xxxv. This is among the works O'Shaughnessy records that he read in 1868, and contained two of Marie's *lais* (neither of which O'Shaughnessy chose for his volume).

[66]   Anderson, p. 543.

158   *Arthur O'Shaughnessy, A Pre-Raphaelite Poet in the British Museum*

also – tender, sad-coloured, and long-winded.'[67] Anderson counters that in 'Eliduc', 'O'Shaughnessy's narrative is derivative; and such changes as he makes do not improve the story.'[68] In this, he agrees with Elton, who complains:

> In *Eliduc* he makes the wife die broken-hearted, while her rival with the delightful name, Guilliadun, lives happy with the husband; and this is a fall indeed; for in Marie's tale the wife generously cures the rival with a magic herb and resigns her own husband to her, and becomes a nun; and so, after a time, does Guilliadun herself.[69]

One's reaction to O'Shaughnessy's twist on this tale depends on one's impression of the original ending of Marie's *lai*; however, it is true that O'Shaughnessy neglects the 'moral' of the original tale to focus on the nature of love, particularly humanity's helplessness in the face of uncontrollable desire.

In brief summary, in Marie's *lai* the knight Eliduc is exiled from his own land and travels to England, where he meets the young and beautiful girl Guilliadun. He falls in love and begins an affair with her, without revealing that he has a wife at home, to whom he has sworn to be faithful. When he is recalled to his own land, he brings Guilliadun with him. On the voyage, their ship encounters a terrible storm, and a member of the crew accuses Eliduc of bringing God's wrath upon them with his adulterous affair. Upon hearing that Eliduc has a wife, Guilliadun faints and appears dead. Arriving back in France, Eliduc places her body in an old hermitage, where he visits it daily. One day his wife follows him and discovers the girl. While she is there, a weasel enters the hermitage and is killed by a member of the lady's retinue. Another weasel follows soon after, and shows signs of distress at the dead body of the first. The creature then brings a rare herb from the forest and places it in the dead weasel's mouth, upon which it revives. Eliduc's wife, witnessing all of this, decides that her husband's happiness is more important than her own, and uses the herb to revive the girl. She then becomes a nun to allow Eliduc and Guilliadun to marry: 'Truly, I am his wife and my heart grieves for him. Because of the grief he displayed, I wanted to know where he went, and came after him and found you. I am overjoyed that you are alive and shall take you with me and return you to your beloved. I shall set him free completely and take the veil.'[70]

---

[67]   Gosse, *Silhouettes*, p. 176. One of the reasons why Gosse might consider this lay O'Shaughnessy's 'best', and the one that he compares the most to Marie, is that it is also the only poem in which O'Shaughnessy maintains the simple 'medieval' rhyming couplets. This lends a balladic feel to the work, as does its frequent use of enjambment, carrying the narrative forward in an easy, flowing fashion. In his other four lays, O'Shaughnessy at times seems to get lost or tangled in his more complex rhyme scheme, which can distract from the narrative as the reader is often left waiting for several lines for the close of a rhyme. These formal and structural distractions are not evident in 'Eliduc'.

[68]   Anderson, p. 540.

[69]   Elton, p. 112.

[70]   Marie de France, p. 125.

'Love's Splendid Lures' 159

In O'Shaughnessy's version of the story, it is Eliduc who witnesses the magic of the weasel's herb, and he is the one who revives the girl. They go off together, happy in their adulterous love, and the poem ends with the revelation (to the reader only) that the wife has died, grief-stricken at her abandonment. Despite this, the tone of the poem does not condemn the lovers; in fact, Eliduc is praised for initially attempting to overcome his love for Guilliadun. When he finally succumbs, the narrative makes it clear that he is merely accepting the inevitable. O'Shaughnessy's adaptation of this tale rejects the false morality of Marie's *lai*, in which the adulterous lovers are 'let off the hook', so to speak, by the wife's martyr-like behaviour. O'Shaughnessy's changes shift the focus of the poem away from notions of self-sacrifice to emphasize the natural selfishness of uncontrollable love, which is at the heart of the courtly love system. Throughout the *Lays* O'Shaughnessy emphasizes the inextricability of love and fate, and his changes to 'Eliduc' serve to reinforce that theme.

Although Gosse suggested that *Lays* was a turn away from the decadence that dominated O'Shaughnessy's first volume, one of the additions to 'Eliduc' betrays the continued influence of decadent literature upon O'Shaughnessy's verse.[71] Of the interlude when Guilliadun is in a coma, Marie merely says, 'He went to the chapel in the woods where the damsel lay and found her still in a swoon, for she neither recovered nor even breathed.'[72] In his usual verbosity, O'Shaughnessy devotes 10 pages to this scene, and the result is deeply strange. Eliduc visits Guilliadun, whom, it is important to note, he believes is dead. 'So Eliduc a place had found, / A place quite sweet and lone enough / To make an end of such a love'.[73] At first, he makes use of the time alone with Guilliadun's body to apologize for his indiscretions. However, he soon stops making apologies and finds:

> That joyless liberty to stir
> The fallen blossom of her face,
> To put her hand in any place ...[74]

He discovers that he has the ability to do as he pleases with her inert body. The poem continues:

> Now indeed there was none to care
> What he should do with her sweet hair;
>   But he could wind it as of old
>   Around her head, or loose its gold
> In lavish waste upon her neck
> And all the gems that used to deck
>   The fair white place above her breast.
> ...

---

[71] See my discussion of *Lays* and 'Chaitivel' in Chapter 5.

[72] Marie de France, p. 123.

[73] *Lays*, p. 223.

[74] Ibid., p. 226.

160   *Arthur O'Shaughnessy, A Pre-Raphaelite Poet in the British Museum*

> – All these were his to touch and use;
> Sad playthings now were they, alas,
> Pastimes for grief that could not pass.[75]

He treats her corpse as his to 'use': her hair, her neck, and her breasts are now his 'playthings'. Although Eliduc is only described as dressing her body and posing her as he pleases, the language calls to mind a far more lascivious kind of using/ playing. This impression is intensified as these lines suggest the influence of Swinburne's 'The Leper', in which he writes:

> Yea, though God always hated me,
> And hates me now that I can kiss
> Her eyes, plait up her hair to see
>
> How she then wore it on the brows,
> Yet I am glad to have her dead
> Here in this wretched wattled house
> Where I can kiss her eyes and head.[76]

'The Leper' is one of Swinburne's first published medieval poems, included in his *Poems and Ballads* of 1866.[77] There is no denying that O'Shaughnessy was familiar with the poem, and we cannot overlook the similar moment in which the lovers arrange the dead love's hair in the manner in which she used to wear it when alive. Swinburne's poem is, of course, much more disturbing. The body of the lover is diseased and dead – 'her keen face made of sunken bones. / Her worn-off eyelids madden me' – while his own body suffers in a similar manner, afflicted by the disease he has caught from her.[78] Beyond the influence of Swinburne's poem, both O'Shaughnessy's and Swinburne's works evoke Baudelaire's even more explicit 'A Martyr', in which the corpse of a woman – this time headless – is posed and dressed and adorned with jewels.[79] In these deliberately perverse moments, we can see the continued influence of poets like Baudelaire upon O'Shaughnessy's verse. O'Shaughnessy's verbosity, too, enacts a kind of excess suggestive of decadence, an overwrought style that mirrors the excesses depicted in decadent works. O'Shaughnessy's choice of Marie's *lais*, rather than other medieval works, also suggests the continued influence of decadence, in his emphasis on the acceptance and inevitability of forbidden or adulterous love.

---

[75]   Ibid.

[76]   Algernon Charles Swinburne, 'The Leper', *Poems and Ballads* (London: John Camden Hotten, 1866), pp. 137–43 (p. 138).

[77]   For an account of this volume's near-suppression, see Simon Eliot's 'Hotten: Rotten: Forgotten? An Apologia for a General Publisher', *Book History*, vol. 3 (University Park: Pennsylvania State University Press, 2000), pp. 61–92.

[78]   'The Leper', p. 141.

[79]   Charles Baudelaire, *The Flowers of Evil*, trans. James McGowan (Oxford: Oxford University Press, 2008), pp. 229–33.

'*Love's Splendid Lures*'   161

While O'Shaughnessy doesn't push the boundaries that Swinburne and Baudelaire do – he makes it very clear the Guilliadun's body is intact and fresh – the similarities in playing with and dressing up a presumed corpse still draw our attention. Unlike Baudelaire or Swinburne, however, O'Shaughnessy manages to present this bizarre moment of eroticized death without drawing the censure of critics or readers. In fact, this scene has never been mentioned, in review or the scant criticism that came afterwards. And yet, the salacious element cannot be overlooked:

> How sorely earned a right was this
> To know the tender mysteries
>   Of her apparel, intricate
>   In all its fragrant mazes, late
> So pure a marvel of sweet guile
> Enamouring long his heart.[80]

Again, the poem describes Eliduc arranging Guilliadun's clothing, yet the subtext is far more sexual. He explores her 'tender mysteries', her 'fragrant mazes', which are no longer 'pure', thanks to his enamoured heart. Again, O'Shaughnessy disguises the eroticism of the moment – here sex is displaced onto clothing, rather than nature, but the effect is the same.

The gilding of the apparently dead body also calls to mind one of O'Shaughnessy's unpublished poems, 'Searching about an ancient place of tombs'.[81] In this poem, an ancient tomb is opened by archaeologists, revealing great wealth adorning a desiccated skeleton. The juxtaposition of wealth and death, beauty and rot, is both horrifying and strangely alluring; the body is described as 'naked' with gold draped over her 'loins'. He writes, 'in truth it was a ghastly thing', and yet, immediately wonders 'which costliest of all the courtesans' she was. Thus, the speaker's mind is drawn to her potential sexuality, even as he shudders at the degradation of her body. Desire is interwoven with horror throughout the poem. Having wondered at her beauty when she was alive, he says, 'fancy instead the body come afresh'. In an important distinction he says 'afresh' not 'alive', which recalls again the implied necrophilia in 'Eliduc'. In the 'Ancient Tomb' he imagines a dead body, but one which is not rotting – exactly what Guilliadun appears to be in 'Eliduc'.

The *Lays*, then, are rife with moments of stark sexuality and often disturbing desire. While Swinburne's 1866 *Poems and Ballads* was harshly reviewed for its shocking content – which included 'The Leper' – O'Shaughnessy's *Lays* are never included in the complaint of his own 'over-sensuous' poetry. In a medieval setting, in a work that is supposedly not original, O'Shaughnessy is permitted far more latitude than in his other volumes.

---

[80] *Lays*, p. 227.

[81] Queen's, MS 8/6, pp. 165–74, dated 25 April 1868. This means he was working on this unpublished poem at the same time as 'Eliduc'.

III.

I have suggested that it is the permissive freedom of the courtly love system, ennobling desire and even adultery, which drew O'Shaughnessy to Marie's medieval *lais*, rather than the religious fervour of the grail quests or the nationalism of the fall of Camelot. As many critics have noted, the main preoccupation of courtly love narratives is the inextricability of love and death. The Lambdins refer to this motif as 'liebestöd' – love in death.[82] Harrison summarizes the standard courtly love plot as consisting of unrequited or unfulfilled love, the suffering of the lovers, and then a final release/consummation in death.[83] Criticism of the Victorian medieval revival typically focuses on these elements in Swinburne's poetry, with Harrison arguing that the fatalism of this view of Love appealed to the sado-masochistic side of the poet.[84] In this section, however, I will show that O'Shaughnessy was equally preoccupied with the relationships between love, death, fate, and eternity. The courtly love stories of medieval France, I suggest, provide O'Shaughnessy with a morally autonomous universe in which to grapple with these metaphysics.

During the years he was composing the *Lays*, O'Shaughnessy's own personal life was rife with many of the issues he deals with in this volume. In 1869 O'Shaughnessy began an affair with Helen Snee, a married woman – in fact, when their romance began, she was already on her second marriage (her first husband having died before she was 21). O'Shaughnessy met Helen through his friend, the illustrator of *An Epic*, J.T. Nettleship, with whom she was already having an affair. In 1869, Nettleship ended his relationship with Helen and she turned to O'Shaughnessy for comfort.[85] Thus she wrote to Arthur in August of 1869, a month after their sexual relationship had begun:

> O! Arthur, when shall I leave off grieving after [Jack]? My heart is quite broken; it is cruel to tell you this, but please give me a few more days to think of him. I am so miserable, but you are so gentle and kind, and you understand. I will really come when you tell me. I will mind you in everything, only don't let him

---

[82]   See the Lambdins' introduction to *Camelot in the Nineteenth Century* (2000), and their discussion of 'liebestöd' on page 101.

[83]   Harrison, p. 107.

[84]   Ibid., p. 20.

[85]   The affair was further complicated by the fact that O'Shaughnessy's friend John Payne – the third member of the 'Triumvirate', as they liked to style themselves, of O'Shaughnessy, Nettleship, and Payne – was also in love with Helen. In fact, the affairs with Helen destroyed the friendship of the 'Triumvirate', as she transferred her affection from Nettleship, to O'Shaughnessy, to Payne. In a letter of 1876, Payne wrote to O'Shaughnessy: 'You will doubtless be somewhat surprised at receiving a letter from me, after the long cessation of relations between us, but you will, I am sure, appreciate my motive when you know it. After all, if we are no longer friends, we are not enemies.' Eventually each man moved on from Helen and married, and by the time of O'Shaughnessy's death, Payne insisted that they were close friends again.

know just at first, until I can bear to think of him calmly. Please don't tell him, dear Arthur, will you? I have not seen him since Monday; don't tell him I sent to you then. I want to see him once more – only to look at him. I shan't ask him to make it up or kiss me, but I have his copy of Swinburne, and I must return it.[86]

The scandalous nature of the affair was compounded by the fact that O'Shaughnessy was still involved with Helen when he began his courtship of Eleanor Marston – and, in fact, he may have continued his relationship with Helen after his marriage to Eleanor. O'Shaughnessy's romance with Helen purportedly ended in 1872, at least a year after he began courting Eleanor. Clement Shorter asserts: 'In 1872 the friendship came to an abrupt end, and, as we have seen, O'Shaughnessy married in the following year.' However, the ending may not have been as complete as reported. The manuscript collection housed at Columbia University contains several drafts of O'Shaughnessy's poems copied by Helen that have been dated to 1874, a year after his marriage to Eleanor.[87] Whether this is an issue of misdating, continued friendship, or marital infidelity is impossible to say. It suggests, however, that O'Shaughnessy may have felt significant lingering guilt over the specifics of his affair with Helen.

In 1916, Clement Shorter collected remnants of the correspondence between O'Shaughnessy and Helen into a privately printed volume entitled *A Pathetic Love Episode in a Poet's Life*. This collection offers insight into the way O'Shaughnessy constructed his relationship with Helen, drawing on the language of medieval courtly love that he employed in *Lays of France* in order to depict their love as virtuous and above reproach. In an early letter, dated 4 August 1869, Helen writes, 'You have made the most perfect contrast with [Jack's] conduct it is possible to imagine. At a time too when you had every cause to be exceedingly displeased and even disgusted with mine, but you are chivalrous – a quality not often met with in the present century.'[88] This was written either before they had become intimate, or shortly thereafter, when the majority of Helen's letters are still focused on Jack. Her reference to O'Shaughnessy's 'chivalry' clearly refers to his vassal-like service; the letters paint the picture of a man at her beck and call, receiving little in return for his devoted service. By casting it in the terms of chivalry, she ennobles this behaviour, effectively sweeping under the rug the more emasculating or salacious aspects of their relationship. Vernon Lee's portrait of O'Shaughnessy as Cosmo Chough also emphasizes this pretence of chivalry. Chough is described as having 'a sort of expansive chivalry of manner, as of Sir Walter Raleigh spreading embroidered cloaks across puddles for Queen Elizabeth, which struck her as rather ridiculous, but very agreeable'.[89]

Included in Shorter's collection is what he calls 'a dissertation on Love' from O'Shaughnessy to Helen, written on their first anniversary. This offers a fascinating

---

[86] Shorter, p. 8.

[87] See the draft of 'A Song of Betrothal' in the Columbia Archive, dated 1874.

[88] Shorter, p. 9.

[89] Vernon Lee, *Miss Brown* (Edinburgh and London: William Blackwood and Sons, 1884), vol. 1, p. 282.

164   *Arthur O'Shaughnessy, A Pre-Raphaelite Poet in the British Museum*

insight into O'Shaughnessy and the way he attempted to construct his affair in the terms of medieval courtly love. Fate was central to the notion of love depicted in *Lays of France*, and in his personal life O'Shaughnessy relied on the notion of fate in order to excuse the morally dubious nature of the relationship. He writes, 'I look upon the incurring of a false love – that is, one which is not that fitted for and, so to speak, ordained to one, and which must, consequently, break off somewhere grievously and shamefully – as the worst evil that can befal [sic] a progressive and perfectible nature.'[90] There are 'false' loves which may be broken off, and then there are the true loves, which are 'ordained' and 'fitted' for one – fated, that is. This language ennobles his own relationship while denigrating matches not based on fated love (such as Helen's marriage to Frederick Snee) as truly 'shameful'. We can also see in these lines a gibe at Helen's previous relationship with Jack, which was 'broken off grievously and shamefully' and was therefore, by his definition, a 'false love'. In contrast, O'Shaughnessy says that their love 'restores to my life the right to a conscious nobleness and the glory of a visioned heaven'.[91] Here he replicates the language of courtly love in order to deny any wrongdoing in his own affairs. In one of her letters, Helen compares O'Shaughnessy to Jack, saying, 'your conduct all through the affair – it has been irreproachable – you are like Bayard'.[92] Here she is referring to Pierre Terreil, seigneur de Bayard, a medieval French soldier known as *le chevalier sans peur et sans reproche*. It is through these medieval allusions and language that O'Shaughnessy and Helen justify their scandalous relationship. As Girouard notes, 'If an affair could be embellished with talk of Art and Love, seen in terms of mediaeval romance or Pre-Raphaelite art, and sublimated as a "passion of the soul", in which sex played only a subordinate part, scruples became that much easier to overcome.'[93]

This tumultuous affair, taking place first behind the back of Helen's husband, and then O'Shaughnessy's wife, was concurrent with the composition of *Lays of France*, and can be seen as the impetus for O'Shaughnessy's specific choice of Marie de France as his source material. I suggest that it was partially an attempt to legitimize his own personal life that led O'Shaughnessy to stories in which, as Tracy Adams asserts, 'love is morally autonomous – a power unto itself, acknowledging no higher authority, a power beyond good or evil.'[94] No matter the opinion of the nineteenth-century author, sexual desire must, to an extent, be vilified in the Arthurian stories, because the affairs of Arthur and Morgause and Guinevere and Lancelot are always to some degree responsible for the fall of Camelot, just as Lancelot's sin is responsible for the failure of the grail quest. As the Lambdins assert, 'Whether one views the fall of Camelot as caused by the passion between Lancelot and Guinevere or by the incestuous coupling of Arthur

---

    [90]   Shorter, p. 13.

    [91]   Ibid., p. 14.

    [92]   Ibid., p. 9.

    [93]   Girouard, p. 204.

    [94]   Tracy Adams, *Violent Passions: Managing Love in the Old French Verse Romance* (New York: Palgrave Macmillan, 2005), p. 172.

'Love's Splendid Lures' 165

and Morgause, the destruction ultimately came about because of illicit love.'[95] Thus, the consequences of forbidden love stretch beyond the couple unit into the wider social and political sphere. In contrast, it is possible to approach the acts of adultery in Marie's stories from a morally neutral standpoint because they do not have the same overarching social consequences. In the *lais*, kingdoms do not fall when adulterous affairs are discovered, although death might come to more than one of the members of the love triangle.

I have already mentioned that O'Shaughnessy doesn't share Marie's brevity in storytelling – for which his *Lays* has been much criticized. One reason for this loquacity is that he intersperses his narratives with lengthy musings on the nature of love, fate, death, and eternity – the four major themes of this volume. He treats love and fate as the ruling deities – or deity, as they are inseparable – of this universe, much as they function in medieval literature. The moral determinism of medieval love is central to both O'Shaughnessy's construct of his own personal relationships and his interpretation of the liebestöd that dominates courtly love. Adams contends that medieval narratives 'treat amor as a sort of pathology – at least initially – that strikes the subject, unsought'.[96] In her book, Adams focuses on what she calls the 'pathology of love', refuting criticism that focuses on the idealization of love in these narratives. Rather, she examines courtly love in the light of medieval medical discourses on love and the humours, to show that love was in some ways envisaged as an illness, a spontaneous response of the body, uncontrolled by the mind.[97] Here love becomes a kind of disease, and again we can see connections between these medieval stories and the kind of decadence O'Shaughnessy invokes in his other volumes of poetry. In 'Laustic; or the Lay of the Nightingale', for instance, in which a married woman falls in love with her husband's closest friend, the wife is 'poisoned with a sweet love-wound' and 'fell / Quite weak in heart because of it'.[98] The lovers try to fight their love, yet it is a 'disease' which cannot be cured, and therefore must be accepted.[99] This pathologization of love exonerates the lovers from any wrongdoing. Thus, the poem chides the reader, 'think not any shame; / For love ye know hath longing feet, / Yea, it hath ever been the fame – / To walk in strange paths of deceit; / I pray you, therefore, think no shame'.[100]

---

[95] *Camelot in the Nineteenth Century*, p. 145.

[96] Adams, p. 20.

[97] Adams summarizes the opinion of medieval medical texts, saying, 'Lust is an unwilled movement and therefore beyond the responsibility of the lover' (p. 30). Her book focuses on the potential for violence inherent in this 'lovesickness' and the Romance as a way to neutralize that violence and bring in it line with civilized notions of love and romance. However, her conception of the 'pathology' of love fits neatly with love as O'Shaughnessy envisions it. If love is a disease, than the afflicted cannot be held responsible for either his feelings or his actions stemming from his emotions.

[98] *Lays*, p. 8, p. 12.

[99] Ibid., p. 21.

[100] Ibid., p. 9.

166   *Arthur O'Shaughnessy, A Pre-Raphaelite Poet in the British Museum*

Our understanding of *Lays of France* is shaped not only by the *lais* O'Shaughnessy selected for the volume, but also by those he did not. Marie is famous for 12 *lais*, and yet O'Shaughnessy chose to reinterpret only five of them. Of the seven that he rejected, four have happy endings and the other three, while certainly tragic, are rather judgmental of the lovers depicted. O'Shaughnessy selected the five lais that depict tragic love in an almost wholly sympathetic light. Despite being pathologized and closely associated with death, the forbidden love at the heart of each tale is celebrated in the *Lays*. Thus, in 'Yvenec' O'Shaughnessy writes,

> Ah, miracle!
> – That visitest so secretly
> The straight, the joyless inward cell
> Of many a soul that hath to dwell
>   Chained to some unknown misery
> Of thought and unattainable dream
> Of heavens: unearthly do they seem
>   Unreal and distant as a star
> Until thou, soft and sudden – light
> And glory filling day and night
>   With splendid rapture – dost unbar
> Some unimagined golden gate
>   Of love![101]

Like the 'visioned heavens' to which O'Shaughnessy compares his love of Helen, these lines raise love to a sacred level. This is truly the crux of O'Shaughnessy's conception of love. For him, the wife trapped in the tower in 'Yvenec' is symbolic of life without love, and thus love grants a kind of freedom, even though it ends in tragic death. Because, as Harrison summarizes, 'Death is, in fact, superior to love because it guarantees release from the necessary constrictions and the mutability of life, both of which prevent the perfect fulfillment of love. In obviating the further possibility of unrequited or disappointed passion, death paradoxically assures love's permanence.'[102] In the courtly love narratives, focused as they are on love and death, often the only consummation for the lovers – kept apart by earthly circumstances: family, marriage, or war – is in death, and thus the tragic ends to most of these narratives are not really seen as tragic at all.

Swinburne uses the narrative of consummation in death to great effect in *Tristram of Lyonesse*, in which the ill-fated lovers are finally brought together in the grave, and then mingled in eternity as the sea – Swinburne's unrelenting symbol of longed-for death and reintegration – washes away their tomb.[103]

---

[101]   Ibid., p. 254.

[102]   Harrison, p. 50.

[103]   Although Swinburne is most associated with the liebestöd of the courtly love narrative, *Tristram of Lyonesse* was published in 1882, a full decade after O'Shaughnessy's take on the same subject matter.

'Love's Splendid Lures'   167

As Harrison says, 'That condition was inevitably fated to end in tragedy, but tragedy redeemed by sublime participation in a cosmic and self-fulfilling generative force organically governing history, the interactions of men and women, and the relations between men and nature.'[104] *Tristram* is often considered to be one of Swinburne's best works, and certainly the best of his mature poetry. The ending of the poem is seen as the culmination of his lifelong philosophy regarding man's relation to nature, and the ultimate joy of reintegration into the universe in death.

O'Shaughnessy is not nearly as consistent in his metaphysics as Swinburne – presenting conflicting ideas of eternity even within the *Lays* – but he achieves a similar moment of transcendence in the ending to 'The Lay of Two Lovers'. In Marie's tale, the lord of Pistre is reluctant to allow his beautiful daughter to marry, so he crafts an Atalanta-esque challenge, in which any man who wishes to marry her must carry her up a neighbouring mountain. Many try and fail, but then a local youth comes forward, and the girl falls in love with him. She directs him to an elderly relative in the neighbouring town, skilled in medicine. The woman gives the youth a potion for strength, and thus he accepts the lord's challenge. However, he refuses to take the potion, even as the girl begs him to, and eventually dies of exhaustion. Seeing this, the girl dies as well, and finally her father repents of his jealousy over her and names the mountain in her honour. It is by no means the best of Marie's tales. The actions of the characters are so inexplicable as to completely undermine any drama in the story. One supposes Marie is attempting to make a point about pride, and certainly a point about the duty of fathers to relinquish their claims on their daughters and allow them to marry, but on the whole these morals are undercut by how utterly pointless the lovers' deaths are.

O'Shaughnessy follows Marie's tale fairly closely until the end, when he deviates dramatically. As they climb the mountain, the lovers gradually become aware of 'another wanderer' on the path – Death. As they ascend, life and earthliness slowly fall away from them, until they are in another world. Unlike Marie's *lai*, in which we see the aftermath of the lovers' deaths, O'Shaughnessy's poem ends here, with no return to the 'real world'. Instead, we go with the lovers into the afterlife, and thereby are granted access to the final consummation of their love that is death.

Death, as he follows them, is horrible, but patient. He does not chase, but merely waits. This is the fate of the lovers, and therefore they do not need to be hunted. They accept it and willingly move towards their own deaths.

> At length, spite of the sun,
> Nigh every day they saw him well,
> Crouched sullen, or in hideous freak
> Out on the sunny ledges sheer
> And glittering. Scarce he seemed to shun
> The sight of them; though dark and lost
> And heedless seemed he if he crost

---

[104]   Harrison, p. 82.

168   *Arthur O'Shaughnessy, A Pre-Raphaelite Poet in the British Museum*

Their path; but, now and then, would peer
    Intently at them from behind
    Some rugged hiding, with no mind
To bring to pass on them his change
    In any bitter sort.[105]

Despite the more horrific aspects of death's presence, 'in hideous freak', love increases as Death nears, because in these narratives the two are always intimately connected.

                    Their love
Was growing with them as the light
    Made in the sun's clear central mine,
    That long hath burnt a way through shred
Of vapoury veil; so they did move
And live in it, and, in the bright
    Transfiguration thereof, did shine
    Wondrously each on each, and wed
Their perfect emanating bliss
In ways of an eternal kiss.[106]

Thus, death takes the place of a marriage, binding the lovers together as effectively – or more so – as marriage vows could ever do. The 'kiss' here is not just figuratively eternal, as in a marriage ceremony, but literally, as they have entered eternity.

The final lines describe what O'Shaughnessy's refers to as 'heaven', and yet there is no mention of the Christian God. Rather, what the lovers find ruling over eternity is love. In this poem, as in most medieval romances, love equals death, but death also equals eternity, a consummation of love in death. Thus, it is something to be longed for, not dreaded. Rather than showing the consequences of the lovers' death on earth, O'Shaughnessy ends in the triumphant moment of passing.

Yet shall their fate, whate'er it be,
Come very soon on me and thee![107]

Here O'Shaughnessy achieves a moment of triumphant unity of love and death similar to that at the end of Swinburne's *Tristram*, a decade later.

The remainder of *Lays*, however, quickly complicates this poem's depiction of eternity as love unbounded. In 'Yvenec', as the hawk-knight dies the second time, he tells his lover:

---

[105]   *Lays*, p. 81. We can see in this passage that O'Shaughnessy doesn't maintain the simple rhyming couplets favoured by Swinburne or Morris in their medieval works. Rather, he counteracts the 'primitive' cadence of the iambic tetrameter and his reliance on monosyllabic words, with a more layered and complex rhyme scheme.

[106]   Ibid., p. 82.

[107]   Ibid., p. 84.

'Love's Splendid Lures'   169

> That surely he should never die
> Quite to his inmost heart; but, staying
>   Deep in his grave her sorrow too
>   Would most torment him, throbbing through
> His sleep and evermore delaying
> His peace and keeping wide the wounds ...[108]

The knight claims that his eternal peace and happiness is tied to the living woman's own emotions. This idea is developed more fully, and to a much more disturbing degree, in O'Shaughnessy's most lauded lay, 'Chaitivel'. In the 'Lay of Two Lovers', love is taken to the grave – the ultimate consummation. In 'Eliduc', love is also carried into the grave, although Eliduc remains alive. Yet, in some ways Eliduc entombs himself with Guilliadun, and enacts the consummation that the 'Two Lovers' found in death, despite his own continued life. This question of love and sex past the point of death is carried to its furthest extreme in 'Chaitivel.' Although the poem shares a title with one of Marie's lays, it is entirely an original work.[109] The only similarity in plot between O'Shaughnessy's poem and Marie's *lai* is that both are about a woman and the four men who love her. Oliver Elton calls this lay a 'sequel' to Marie's story, and George Anderson repeats this claim, but even that connection is tenuous.[110] Marie's *lai* is about a woman who is loved by four equally handsome and noble knights. She doesn't favour any of them and doesn't want to hurt their feelings, so she gives each a token of her affection. All four attend a tournament in which they compete in her name. Three are killed instantly. The fourth is mortally wounded, and she has him brought to her home, where she expresses her guilt over playing with all of their emotions. She announces her intention to write a lay about the four of them, calling it 'The Four Sorrows'. The knight tells her that instead she should call it 'The Unhappy One', as the other three are happy in their death, whereas he must suffer, knowing she doesn't love him. He says:

> But I who have escaped alive, bewildered and forlorn, constantly see the woman I love more than anything on earth, coming and going; she speaks to me morning and evening, yet I cannot experience the joy of a kiss or an embrace or of any pleasure other than conversation. You cause me to suffer a hundred such ills and death would be preferable to me.[111]

It is this central notion of happiness in death that O'Shaughnessy subverts in his lay of the same name.

---

[108]   Ibid., p. 286.

[109]   Glyn S. Burgess asserts, however, that 'Chaitivel' was found only in the Harley manuscript of Marie's *lais*, and thus O'Shaughnessy's drastic deviations could only be detected by those that had access to manuscript collection at the British Museum. *The Lais of Marie de France: Text and Context* (Athens: The University of Georgia Press, 1987), p. 50.

[110]   Elton, p. 112, and Anderson, p. 538.

[111]   Marie de France, p. 108.

170   *Arthur O'Shaughnessy, A Pre-Raphaelite Poet in the British Museum*

O'Shaughnessy's version of 'Chaitivel' contains similar elements, but is neither an adaptation nor a sequel to Marie's work. Rather than four knights competing in a single tournament for her love, the woman – here, given the name Sarrazine – has loved three men in turn, not all at once.[112] To one she gave nothing more than a smile, to one a promise and a lock of hair, and to the third, all her self.[113] At the start of the poem, all three have already died. It is then that the fourth lover – named, as in Marie, Chaitivel – enters the story. Having neatly established that death results in an eternity of love in the previous lay, O'Shaughnessy now pushes beyond the traditional ending of the courtly love narrative and his own ending of 'Two Lovers', exploring love after death.

The conception of eternity in this poem is complicated, and at times inconsistent, but interesting nonetheless. The first description of the afterlife is one of eternal slumber, filled with dreams of the beloved:

> For, verily,
> – He who had all – was not his day,
> E'en to death softened endlessly
> With love, filled to the full and more
>   With sweet of hers? And, where he lay,
> Was not the grave o'erbrimmed with store
> Of perfect memories and rich ore
>   Of a life rich in love?[114]

This is the implied state of the three dead lovers at the end of Marie's *lai*. Having died for the woman they love, they find peace in the grave. In O'Shaughnessy's lay, however, this peaceful state is tied to the living lover's emotions and affections, as the knight suggested in 'Yvenec'. The dead man's slumber is filled with memories of love, but only if Sarrazine continues to love him in life.

In 'Chaitivel', like the other lays, Love is the supreme deity. But unlike the largely benevolent god represented in the other poems, here Love functions more as a trickster – fickle and always demanding new entertainment from its subjects. Thus, we are told Sarrazine has locked herself away in a desolate tower, mourning her lost loves:[115]

---

[112]   This name, like much of the plot, is entirely original to O'Shaughnessy.

[113]   Of the three lovers only one is named in the poem – Pharamond, the second lover, to whom she gave a vow and a lock of hair, and who died in foreign 'Paynim land'. *Lays*, p. 104.

[114]   *Lays*, p. 101.

[115]   This plot device – again, not found in Marie's *lai* – seems to be a deliberate allusion to Tennyson's 'The Lady of Shalott'. In a medieval setting, a woman is locked away from the world in a tower. She falls in love with a man from the 'bright world' and is subsequently punished for leaving her tower and attempting to join the living world. There is even the suggestion of a mirror in Sarrazine's tower, as O'Shaughnessy says, 'Now she would weary out the days, / Joylessly looking on the white / Slim wonder that she was' (p. 99). While not explicit, it seems, as she then considers her grief-wasted face, that she must be looking in a mirror. These similarities are unlikely to be coincidental.

'Love's Splendid Lures' 171

Then Love, who rules the bright world, deemed
  That, all too well indeed, she bore
Such sorrow for the dead who seemed
  No longer worth one's caring for;
And, so, I ween, he sent one day
This Chaitivel.[116]

Love here is just as uncontrollable as in the other Lays; it forces Chaitivel upon Sarrazine as punishment for not dying of her grief over her dead lovers. Love's fickle nature is further described:

              Alas,
He careth not how he may hurt
  The dead, or trouble them that wait
In heaven, so he may bring to pass
  Ever some new thing passionate
And sweet upon the earth: his sun
  Hath need of you; and, if he takes
  Last year's spoiled roses and remakes
Red summer with them, shall he shun
To steal your soft hearts every one ...?[117]

Here O'Shaughnessy remakes the traditional medieval imagery of the rose, in which, as Harrison says, 'the rose is the eternal symbol of the beloved and of the perfect beauty that is fearfully transient but simultaneously immortal'.[118] To this traditional symbolism O'Shaughnessy adds a naturalistic touch, reminding the reader that nature is cyclical, not linear, and thus while the rose blooms and then fades, it will bloom again the following year. Thus, the rose is transmuted from a symbol of immortal love in death, to eternally regenerating, and therefore fickle and false, love on earth.

Having fallen in love with Chaitivel, Sarrazine tries to reason her way out of her promises to her dead lovers. She embraces this theme of regeneration and argues for an entirely naturalistic reintegration into the earth, an afterlife that could not require promises to be kept. She sings to one of her dead lovers:

Hold me no longer for a word
  I used to say or sing:
Ah, long ago you must have heard
  So many a sweeter thing:
For rich earth must have reached your heart
  And turned the faith to flowers;
And warm wind stolen, part by part,
  Your soul through faithless hours.[119]

---

[116]   *Lays*, p. 113.
[117]   Ibid., p. 110.
[118]   Harrison, p. 39.
[119]   *Lays*, p. 128.

172   *Arthur O'Shaughnessy, A Pre-Raphaelite Poet in the British Museum*

This is a fascinatingly atheistic and materialist view of the afterlife, in which not just the body, but the soul, the memories, and the loves, are reincorporated into nature. It is a startlingly earthy view of death and the afterlife; Sarrazine describes the 'odorous leaves' and the 'soft seeds', reveling in the disintegration and reintegration of the process of decomposition.

However, the poem quickly negates this cyclical view of the world and the afterlife. The lovers have not been reintegrated into the earth, nor have they forgotten Sarrazine's promises to them. As her affections are transferred to Chaitivel, each of the three 'wakes up' in the grave, realizes her falseness, and comes to claim her.[120] Of her third lover we are told: 'in mere solitude / Of death he woke, without a kiss, / And knew that fate was false ... Woman, said he ... Change; and yet / You cannot change, but earth and sky / And death will keep you mine : and I – / *Do I not live for ever?*'[121] 'Chaitivel' contains a strong element of horror not found in the rest of the volume, and certainly not in Marie's version of this story. The *Athenaeum* praised this aspect of the poem, saying, 'the supernatural element is treated with such daring but subtle art, that the spiritual terror excited is natural and unforced'.[122] Yet, as with Eliduc, there is a strange undertone of necrophilia in the poem, as the lovers rise from their graves, not intact, but obviously dead. Pharamond, clad in 'blood-stained mail' is described as 'terrible, and giving birth to wide dismay' as he leaves his grave.[123]

In one of the fastest-paced scenes of O'Shaughnessy's corpus, the three lovers visit Sarrazine in turn, interrupting the consummation of her relationship with Chaitivel. The first lover, 'He who ne'er felt upon his brow / The perfect blessing of her kiss', is content merely to watch her, haunting the bridal chamber, 'a mute, pale, / Uncertain semblance of a man'.[124] The third lover, 'he who, living, had possest / Her peerless body', comes in a far more terrible guise.[125] He is described: 'A torn grave garment seemed the last / Earth-relic on him; form and face / Were mysteries where no man could trace / A part of former man'.[126] O'Shaughnessy here leaves the reader to imagine the horrible state in which death has left him, entirely inhuman.

Breaking between Sarrazine and Chaitivel in their love-making, the third lover vows to 'have that wrecked thing I did buy / – A body for a soul!'[127] As he snatches up Sarrazine, the poem is quick to remind us that she is naked, painting a gruesome and yet suggestive picture:

---

[120]   The first lover doesn't waken until p. 133, while the third rises on p. 120, and Pharamond (her second lover), wakes on p. 129.

[121]   Ibid., p. 120–25.

[122]   'Review: *Lays of France (Founded on the 'Lays of Marie.')* by Arthur W.E. O'Shaughnessy', *Athenaeum* 2306 (6 January 1872): 8–9 (p. 9).

[123]   Ibid., p. 130.

[124]   *Lays*, p. 106, p. 134.

[125]   Ibid., p. 120.

[126]   Ibid., p. 138.

[127]   Ibid., p. 123.

'Love's Splendid Lures'   173

> Then he took her, fair
> And deathly, fainting in the clutch
> Of his grim darkness, with her hair
> Sweeping the ground, and all her bare
>   Delicious beauty free from touch.[128]

As in 'Eliduc', this scene interweaves death and sexuality, binding the two together almost as strongly as love and fate in this volume.

Chaitivel draws his sword and attempts to stab the phantom. However, given his incorporeal nature, the sword goes through the ghost and into Sarrazine, killing her. The third lover then makes off with her lifeless body, leaving her soul behind with Chaitivel. In this ending there is a strangely tentative reassertion of traditional Christian doctrine, as she is 'forgiven' her sin of polyamory:

> [T]hen, at last,
> Beheld her soul remaining white
> And whole and beautiful, no blight
>   Or ruin cleaving on it. Free
>   Of the torn frame now would she be,
> And all acquitted![129]

This, followed quickly by the sound of 'singing celestially', seems to be a reassertion of Christian ideals. However, the narrative voice throughout the poem has contradicted this, asserting that Sarrazine is wicked and false for betraying her former loves. This seemingly 'happy' ending is further complicated, as the second lover, Pharamond, enters the scene. Unlike the third lover, who came to claim her body, Pharamond is intent on Sarrazine's soul: 'Going back to take / Her soul for vows she could not break'.[130] Chaitivel attempts to fight him off, and is killed. However, in this poem, death does not end the fight, and their ghosts/souls fight on 'till doom'.[131]

Throughout the poem, then, the characters as well as the narrative voice alternate their faith in heaven, eternal slumber, and reintegration, and the poem ends still conflicted. The eternal slumber of death is sometimes described as all there is and sometimes as a kind of stasis, while one lover still lives:

> But in the separate place that death
>   Had found for him, to rest from life,
>   To dream upon it, or to wait
> Each of her lovers held the breath
>   Of his strong dauntless spirit rife
>   With memories.[132]

---

[128]   Ibid., p. 138.
[129]   Ibid., p. 140.
[130]   Ibid., p. 129.
[131]   Ibid., p. 144.
[132]   Ibid., p. 105.

174 *Arthur O'Shaughnessy, A Pre-Raphaelite Poet in the British Museum*

This is followed by a clear idea of Heaven, in which all people are reunited, and thus can only have one love:

> O women, have a care
> What if two come to claim your hair
> Of God? – what if two shall have thrown
>   Their strong arms round your body, quite
>   Belonging with an equal right
> To each for ever?[133]

Neither seems to be the truth of the poem. We are told that Sarrazine is forgiven, which implies the judgment of a higher power, yet if God sanctions her love with Chaitivel, why does the poem end in eternal misery and strife? There is no heaven here for true love – presumably that of Sarrazine and Chaitivel – or even eternal sleep. Thus, the 'acquittal' of Sarrazine means almost nothing, as none of the characters end happily. Furthermore, the revelation that Sarrazine was true in her love to Chaitivel undermines much of the judgment that has been cast on her throughout the poem, not just by the dead lover, but also by the narrator. This vilification of Sarrazine is made explicit in O'Shaughnessy's references to some of his other poetry in connection with her character, particularly 'Creation'. Additionally, 'Chaitivel' is paired with the short lyric 'Fair yellow murderess' (reprinted as 'To a Young Murderess' in *Music and Moonlight*), implicitly accusing Sarrazine of causing the death of the three lovers by not returning their love. That lyric begins, 'Fair yellow murderess, whose gilded head / Gleaming with deaths'.[134] This theme of the gilded head belying the death mask underneath is continued in the narrative of 'Chaitivel', which asks, 'will ye see / How gold hair hath its perjury?'[135] The poem's depictions of love and the afterlife are complicated and inconsistent, yet nevertheless compelling portraits of the ideas of fate, love, death, and eternity that are the central preoccupations of *Lays of France*.

Much of the criticism surrounding the revival of medievalism in the nineteenth century has touted it as a conservative movement that attempted to craft an ideal of an 'old-fashioned' gentleman that would uphold Victorian moral values and gender roles in the face of the modern, industrial world.[136] In the only existing criticism on O'Shaughnessy's *Lays*, Anderson supports this conservative reading, insisting that O'Shaughnessy forces his Victorian sensibilities on the medieval

---

[133] Ibid., p. 111.

[134] Ibid., 88.

[135] Ibid., 91.

[136] Cf. Chandler, Girouard. In Inga Bryden's *Reinventing King Arthur*, she insists that stories of knights and heroes reinforced Victorian ideas of masculinity and that 'Malory's Arthurian society also acted as a model for nineteenth-century attitudes towards women and offered an exploration of loyalty and its implications. It provided models of moral social behaviour well-suited to an industrial, imperialistic society and the potential leaders or heroes of that society.' Bryden, p. 74.

texts he reinterprets, bowdlerizing the tales. In contrast, I argue that O'Shaughnessy specifically turns to the French stories of courtly love in order to subvert Victorian sexual mores. He attempts to negate modern morality – so apparent in Tennyson's interpretation of the Arthurian stories, in which adulterous love is roundly condemned – by turning to a social system that made it possible to be a chivalrous gentleman *and* an adulterer.[137] Courtly love, in fact, elevated love, sexual desire, and even adultery to the level of a virtue. O'Shaughnessy chooses the stories of Marie de France, rather than the more popular Arthurian tales, because in them he is able to depict forbidden love freed from social consequences. Here he is able both to enact a kind of justification for his own personal relationship with Helen Snee, and to evade the censure he faced in reviews of *An Epic of Women*. He adopts the popular 'language' of medievalism, familiar to a reading public and often interpreted as conservative, and presents his lays in the guise of translation, allowing him the freedom to publish some of the most erotic poetry of his career. In *Lays of France*, rather than merely imitating poets who had come before him, O'Shaughnessy attempts to define his personal conception of the metaphysics of love and death, through a combination of the ennobling power of the medieval courtly love system, the excesses and fatalism of decadence, and his own unique strain of melancholy lassitude.

---

[137] See Rebecca Cochran's 'Tennyson's Hierarchy of Women in *Idylls of the King*' in *History and Community*, in which she notes that, unlike the women in Malory's *Morte D'Arthur*, '[a]s guardians of the public good, Tennyson's Arthurian women should inspire their partners to perform noble deeds in accordance with the king's dictates. In order to do so, the female figures must comply with the Victorian prototype of the perfect woman, who is sexually pure and is both a submissive wife and a selfless mother' (p. 81). Thus, she summarizes, 'The creation of a hierarchy of women who are assessed according to the values of Tennyson's audience reveals the extent to which the poet transformed the medieval legend to suit Victorian sensibilities' (p. 105).

Conclusion

When T.S. Eliot wrote 'What is Minor Poetry?' he claimed that he was attempting to dispel 'any derogatory association connected with the term "minor poetry"'.[1] And yet, by writing about 'majority' and 'minority' in the terms that he did, Eliot upholds these categories as important or useful to a study of poetry. His estimation of Arthur O'Shaughnessy as a minor poet who has 'written just one, or only a very few, good poems', has condemned studies of O'Shaughnessy to engage with ideas of majority and minority in Eliot's terms, forever branding O'Shaughnessy a 'minor Pre-Raphaelite'.[2] In this work I have attempted to show that the category of 'minority' is neither important nor useful to the study of O'Shaughnessy's body of work. I have refuted the claim that minor writers are not innovators and have no lasting literary value by demonstrating that O'Shaughnessy wrote on the cutting edge of several literary movements, operating as an innovator in both formalism and aestheticism.

As a poetic category, distinct from the artistic movement of the same name, Pre-Raphaelitism is often defined by the major figures of the movement – thus, to be a Pre-Raphaelite is to write poetry like Rossetti, Morris, or Swinburne. This definition encourages the categories of major and minor, as well as the perception that a minor poet is an imitative poet. However, a consideration of O'Shaughnessy's entire corpus, and not merely the few poems that are reprinted in anthologies and collections, challenges traditional definitions of Pre-Raphaelitism, revealing it to be less of an insular, Rossetti-centred movement than it is customarily perceived to be. As this study has shown, O'Shaughnessy was embedded in a broad cultural arena, with significant scientific and literary networks, which demonstrates Pre-Raphaelitism's wider engagement with modern culture. O'Shaughnessy's cultural significance lies in the many networks he forged outside the Pre-Raphaelite movement, drawing ties between Pre-Raphaelitism and labour theory, modern scientific thought, and literary movements in France.

Work as a concept is key to an understanding of O'Shaughnessy's poetry. Broadly speaking, his corpus reveals the perceived differences and overlaps between work and art during this period, as well as the relationship between middle-class work culture and elitist aestheticism. More specifically, his poetry is intimately shaped by his relationship to his position at the British Museum as a lowly clerk within a nineteenth-century bureaucracy. From both his life and poetry we can see the frustrations inherent to a man in this position, belonging neither to the ruling elite, nor to the burgeoning political body of the

---

[1] T.S. Eliot, 'What is Minor Poetry?', *On Poetry and Poets* (London: Faber, 1957), p. 39.

[2] Ibid., p. 44.

working class. O'Shaughnessy represents the middle class, not as the new captains of industry, but as the petty-bourgeois, those who worked low-level jobs within the industrial and capitalist system – the moved, not the movers. These categories were being created and defined during the mid-century, and thus O'Shaughnessy offers a sometimes-overlooked perspective on the changing face of work and class during this period.

Furthermore, O'Shaughnessy's relationship to work provides a new way to think about the intersections between science and literature during this period. The study of literature and science is often considered from the perspective of literature about science, or the influence of literature on great scientific minds like Darwin's. The work of the low-level scientific practitioner – the lab assistant, the transcriber, the clerk – is rarely considered. O'Shaughnessy's role at the Museum allows great insight into science as a profession, a new category at the time, because he truly practised science as nothing more than a job. He wrote reports, he filed papers, he transcribed letters, and he bottled specimens. Despite the apparent mundanity of his job, the influence of science on O'Shaughnessy in practice and theory is evident. His verse reveals what a technician of natural science thought about the theoretical work being done in his field, offering a bottom-up perspective from the ranks of natural history. His poetry illuminates the many ways in which the practices of art and science overlap and intersect, as studies of the physical world.

O'Shaughnessy's ties to scientific practice, as well as the mere fact of needing a 'day job', set him apart within the Pre-Raphaelite movement. Beyond that, however, he maintained wide literary networks that give the lie to the notion of Pre-Raphaelitism as a fleeting and insular poetic movement. A study of O'Shaughnessy provides greater context for the literary shift towards aestheticism and decadence that came at the end of the nineteenth century. Major and controversial literary figures such as Swinburne and Wilde are credited with leading this movement towards a French-influenced aesthetic in England. However, a study of O'Shaughnessy reveals the wider conduit for French literary works into England. He was among the first of a number of writers of the 1870s who embraced French literature, translating, reviewing, and imitating the work of the French decadents and Parnassians. These men – Edmund Gosse, John Payne, Austin Dobson, Andrew Lang, and George Saintsbury, among others – are now largely absent from the literary canon, yet, along with O'Shaughnessy at their fore, they reveal a bigger picture of the interactions between France and England at the time. O'Shaughnessy's poetry shows English decadence to be in bloom as early as 1870, and illustrates the path that brought English literature to the works of the 1890s and fin de siècle.

Despite what Eliot asserted, we have seen that O'Shaughnessy's literary legacy extends far beyond the single 'Ode'. It lies not just in his poetic corpus, but in the connections he forged between medievalism, aestheticism, Pre-Raphaelitism, French decadence, and scientific practice and theory, revealed through his biography, his scientific papers, his letters, and his unpublished works.

Conclusion 179

The import of the collective whole of O'Shaughnessy's life and works defies Eliot's use of 'major' and 'minor' as well as his definitions of these categories.[3] What is then revealed are O'Shaughnessy's far-reaching contributions to the culture and literature of the nineteenth century.

---

[3]   Thus Eliot writes, 'We seem, so far, to have arrived at the tentative conclusion that, whatever a minor poet may be, a major poet is one the whole of whose work we ought to read, in order fully to appreciate any part of it' (47).

Bibliography

Archives

Belfast, UK, Queen's University, O'Shaughnessy Manuscript Collection, MS 8/1–26.

Durham, NC, Duke University Manuscript Collection, 6th 11:A Box 1, c.1.

London, UK, Natural History Museum Archives, records DF ZOO.

London, UK, Central Archive, British Museum, Standing Committee Minutes, 1861–1874.

New York, NY, Columbia University, Rare Book & Manuscript Library, MS #0956.

Primary Texts

O'Shaughnessy, Arthur W.E. 'Notes on Lizards of the Group Anolis'. *Annals and Magazine of Natural History* 4, no. 3 (1869): 183–92.

———. *An Epic of Women and Other Poems*. London: John Camden Hotten, 1870.

———. 'Description of a new species of lizard of the genus Celestus'. *Annals and Magazine of Natural History* 4, no. 14 (1874): 257–8.

———. 'Descriptions of a new species of Scincidae in the Collection of the British Museum'. *Annals and Magazine of Natural History* 4, no. 13 (1874): 298–301.

———. 'Descriptions of a new species of Skink'. *Annals and Magazine of Natural History* 4, no. 14 (1874): 35.

———. *Lays of France (Founded on the Lays of Marie)*, 2nd ed. London: Chatto & Windus, 1874.

———. *Music and Moonlight: Poems and Songs*. London: Chatto & Windus, 1874.

———. 'Descriptions of new species of Gekkotidae in the British Museum Collection'. *Annals and Magazine of Natural History* 4, no. 16 (October 1875): 262–6.

———. 'Descriptions of new species of Gobiidae in the collection of the British Museum'. *Annals and Magazine of Natural History* 4, no. 15 (1875): 144–8.

———. 'List and Revision of the species of Anolidae in the British Museum Collection'. *Annals and Magazine of Natural History* 4, no. 15 (1875): 270–81.

———. 'Review: *L'Exile: Poésies*, par François Coppée'. *Athenaeum*, no. 2589 (1877): 734–5.

———. 'In Memoriam; Elegy'. *Athenaeum*, no. 2678 (1879): 248.

———. *Songs of a Worker*. London: Chatto & Windus, 1881.

O'Shaughnessy, Arthur W.E. and Eleanor O'Shaughnessy. *Toyland*. London: Daldy, Isbister, & Co., 1875.

Secondary and Comparative Texts

Adams, James Eli. *Dandies and Desert Saints: Styles of Victorian Masculinity.* Ithaca and London: Cornell University Press, 1995.

Adams, Tracy. *Violent Passions: Managing Love in the Old French Verse Romance.* New York: Palgrave Macmillan, 2005.

Adorno, Theodor. *Aesthetic Theory.* Translated by C. Lenhardt and edited by Gretel Adorno and Rolf Tiedemann. London and New York: Routledge & Kegan Paul, 1986.

Aldington, Richard, ed. *The Religion of Beauty: Selections from the Aesthetes.* London: William Heinemann, 1950.

Allaire, Gloria, ed. *Modern Retellings of Chivalric Texts.* Aldershot: Ashgate, 1999.

Allen, Harrison. 'Poetry and Science'. *Poet Lore* 3, no. 5 (1891): 233–49.

Altieri, Charles. *Canons and Consequences: Reflections on the Ethical Force of Imaginative Ideals.* Evanston, IL: Northwestern University Press, 1990.

Anderson, George K. 'Marie de France and Arthur O'Shaughnessy: A Study in Victorian Adaptation'. *Studies in Philology* 36 (1939): 529–49.

Arac, Jonathan and Harriet Ritvo, eds. *Macropolitics of Nineteenth-Century Literature: Nationalism, Exoticism, Imperialism.* Philadelphia: University of Pennsylvania Press, 1991.

Armstrong, Isobel, ed. *Victorian Scrutinies: Reviews of Poetry 1830–1870.* London: The Athlone Press, 1972.

———. *Language as Living Form in Nineteenth-Century Poetry.* Brighton: Harvester, 1982.

———. *Victorian Poetry: Poetry, Poetics, and Politics.* London and New York: Routledge, 1993.

Arnold, Matthew. *Culture and Anarchy.* Cambridge: Cambridge University Press, 1955.

Auden, W.H. *Nineteenth Century Minor Poets.* London: Faber & Faber, 1966.

Auerbach, Nina. *Woman and the Demon: The Life of a Victorian Myth.* Cambridge, MA: Harvard University Press, 1982.

Barber, Lynn. *The Heyday of Natural History, 1820–1870.* London: Jonathan Cape, 1980.

Barczewski, Stephanie L. *Myth and National Identity in Nineteenth Century Britain: The Legends of King Arthur and Robin Hood.* Oxford: Oxford University Press, 2000.

Barlow, George. 'The Fall of Woman'. *Contemporary Review* 90 (1906): 95–106.

Barringer, Tim. *Men at Work: Art and Labour in Victorian Britain.* New Haven and London: Yale University Press, 2005.

Bates, Henry Walter. *The Naturalist on the River Amazons: A Record of Adventures, Habits of Animals, Sketches of Brazilian and Indian Life, and Aspects of Nature Under the Equator During Eleven Years of Travel,* 2 vols. London: John Murray, 1863.

Baudelaire, Charles. *Selected Writings on Art and Artists.* Translated by P.E. Charvet. Cambridge: Cambridge University Press, 1972.

Bibliography 183

————. *The Flowers of Evil*. Translated by James McGowan. Oxford: Oxford University Press, 2008.

Beach, Joseph Warren. *The Concept of Nature in Nineteenth-Century English Poetry*. New York: The Macmillan Co., 1936.

Beer, Gillian. *Darwin's Plots: Evolutionary Narrative in Darwin, George Eliot and Nineteenth-Century Fiction*. Cambridge: Cambridge University Press, 2000.

Behrisch, Erika. "'Far as the eye can reach"; Scientific Exploration and Explorers' Poetry in the Arctic, 1832–53'. *Victorian Poetry* 41, no. 1 (2003): 73–91.

Bernheimer, Charles, T. Jefferson Kline, and Naomi Schor, eds. *Decadent Subjects: The Idea of Decadence in Art, Literature, Philosophy and Culture of the Fin de Siècle in Europe*. Baltimore and London: The Johns Hopkins University Press, 2002.

Bevir, Mark. *The Making of British Socialism*. Princeton: Princeton University Press, 2011.

Birkett, Jennifer. *The Sins of the Fathers: Decadence in France, 1870–1914*. London and New York: Quartet Books, 1986.

Bloch, R. Howard. *The Anonymous Marie de France*. Chicago: The University of Chicago Press, 2003.

Boos, Florence Saunders, ed. *History and Community: Essays in Victorian Medievalism*. New York and London: Garland Publishing, Inc., 1992.

————. 'The Pre-Raphaelites'. *Victorian Poetry* 45, no. 3 (2007): 321–30.

Bourdieu, Pierre. *The Field of Cultural Production: Essays on Art and Literature*. Edited and introduced by Randal Johnson. Cambridge: Polity Press, 1993.

Bowler, Peter J. *Evolution: the History of an Idea*. Berkeley: University of California Press, 1984.

————. *Monkey Trials and Gorilla Sermons: Evolution and Christianity from Darwin to Intelligent Design*. Cambridge, MA: Harvard University Press, 2007.

Bristow, Joseph, ed. *The Victorian Poet: Poetics and Persona*. London and New York: Croom Helm, 1987.

Brody, Saul Nathanial. *Disease of the Soul: Leprosy in Medieval Literature*. Ithaca: Cornell University Press, 1974.

Bromwich, David, ed. *Romantic Critical Essays*. Cambridge: Cambridge University Press, 1987.

Brönner, Oskar. *Das Leben Arthur O'Shaughnessy's*. Würzburger Beiträge zur englischen Literaturgeschichte, no. 5. Heidelberg, 1933.

Bryden, Inga, ed. *The Pre-Raphaelites: Writings and Sources*, vol. 1. New York: Routledge/Thoemmes Press, 1998.

————. *Reinventing King Arthur: The Arthurian Legends in Victorian Culture*. Aldershot: Ashgate, 2005.

Buchanan, Robert (as Thomas Maitland). 'The Fleshly School of Poetry: Mr. D.G. Rossetti'. *Contemporary Review* 18 (1871): 334–50.

Buckley, Jerome Hamilton. *The Triumph of Time*. Cambridge, MA: Harvard University Press, 1967.

Burgess, Glyn S. *The Lais of Marie de France: Text and Context*. Athens: The University of Georgia Press, 1987.

Carley, James P., ed. *Arthurian Poets: A.C. Swinburne*. Suffolk: The Boydell Press, 1990.

Carlyle, Thomas. *Chartism*. London: James Fraser, 1840.

Carter, A.E. *The Idea of Decadence in French Literature, 1830–1900*. Toronto: University of Toronto Press, 1958.

Chamberlain, David. '*Marie de France's Arthurian Lai*: Subtle and Political'. *Culture and the King: The Social Implications of the Arthurian Legend*. Edited by Martin B. Shichtman and James P. Carley. Albany: State University of New York Press, 1994.

Chandler, Alice. *A Dream of Order: The Medieval Ideal in Nineteenth-Century English Literature*. London: Routledge & Kegan Paul, 1971.

Chapman, Raymond. *The Sense of the Past in Victorian Literature*. London and Sydney: Croom Helm, 1986.

Cochran, Rebecca. 'Tennyson's Hierarchy of Women in *Idylls of the King*'. In Boos, *History and Community*, pp. 81–108.

Colvin, Sidney. 'Review: An Epic of Women and Other Poems'. *The Academy* (15 November 1870): 32–3.

Cosslett, Tess. *The 'Scientific Movement' and Victorian Literature*. Sussex/New York: The Harvester Press/St. Martin's Press, 1982.

Court, Franklin E. *Institutionalizing English Literature: The Culture and Politics of Literary Study, 1750–1900*. Stanford, CA: Stanford University Press, 1992.

Cristie, John and Sally Shuttleworth. *Nature Transfigured: Science and Literature, 1700–1900*. Manchester and New York: Manchester University Press, 1989.

Cunningham, Valentine, ed. *The Victorians: An Anthology of Poetry and Poetics*. Oxford: Blackwell, 2000.

Curran, Stuart. *Poetic Form and British Romanticism*. Oxford: Oxford University Press, 1986.

Damon, S. Foster. 'Marie de France: Psychologist of Courtly Love'. *PMLA* 44, no. 4 (1929): 968–96.

Danahay, Martin A. *Gender at Work in Victorian Culture: Literature, Art and Masculinity*. Aldershot: Ashgate, 2005.

Darwin, Charles. *On the Origin of Species by Means of Natural Selection: or the Preservation of Favoured Races in the Struggle for Life*, 6th ed. London: John Murray, 1872.

———. *The Descent of Man, and Selection in Relation to Sex*, 2 vols. Princeton: Princeton University Press, 1981.

Davidoff, Lenore. *Worlds Between: Historical Perspectives on Gender and Class*. New York: Routledge, 1995.

Davidoff, Lenore and Catherine Hall. *Family Fortunes: Men and Women of the English Middle Class, 1780–1850*. London: Hutchinson, 1987.

Davis, Whitney. 'Decadence and the Organic Metaphor'. *Representations* 89 (2005): 131–49.

Dawson, Gowan. 'Intrinsic Earthliness: Science, Materialism, and the Fleshly School of Poetry'. *Victorian Poetry* 41, no. 1 (2003): 113–29.

Bibliography 185

————. *Darwin, Literature and Victorian Respectability*. Cambridge: Cambridge University Press, 2007.

Dawson, Gowan and Sally Shuttleworth. 'Introduction: Science and Victorian Poetry'. *Victorian Poetry* 41, no. 1 (2003): 1–10.

de Certeau, Michel. *The Practice of Everyday Life*. Translated by Steven Rendell. Berkeley: University of California Press, 1984.

Deleuze, Gilles and Félix Guattari. *Kafka: Toward a Minor Literature*. Translated by Dana Polan. Minneapolis: University of Minnesota Press, 1986.

Delheim, Charles. 'Interpreting Victorian Medievalism'. In Boos, *History and Community*, pp. 39–58.

Dijkstra, Bram. *Idols of Perversity: Fantasies of Feminine Evil in Fin-de-Siècle Culture*. New York and Oxford: Oxford University Press, 1986.

Donoghue, Denis. *Speaking of Beauty*. New Haven and London: Yale University Press, 2003.

Dowling, Linda. *The Vulgarization of Art: The Victorians and Aesthetic Democracy*. Charlottesville and London: University Press of Virginia, 1996.

Eliot, Simon. 'Hotten: Rotten: Forgotten? An Apologia for a General Publisher'. *Book History*, vol. 3. University Park: Pennsylvania State University Press, 2000.

Eliot, T.S. *On Poetry and Poets*. London: Faber, 1957.

Ellis, G. 'Preface'. *Fabliaux or Tales, abridged from the French Manuscripts of the XIIth and XIIIth Centuries by M. Le Grand*. Selected and translated into English verse by G.L. Way, Esq. London: J. Rodwell, 1815.

Elton, Oliver, ed. *A Survey of English Literature, 1830–1880*. Vol. 4. New York: The Macmillan Co., 1920.

Evangelista, Stefano. *British Aestheticism and Ancient Greece: Hellenism, Reception, Gods in Exile*. Basingstoke, UK: Palgrave Macmillan, 2009.

Fairchild, Hoxie N. 'Rima's Mother'. *PMLA* 68, no. 3 (1953): 357–70.

Ferguson, Christine. 'Decadence as Scientific Fulfillment'. *PMLA* 117, no. 3 (2002): 465–78.

Fishman, Solomon. *The Interpretation of Art: Essays on the Art Criticism of John Ruskin, Walter Pater, Clive Bell, Roger Fry and Herbert Read*. Berkeley and Los Angeles: University of California Press, 1963.

Flaubert, Gustave. *Salammbô*. Translated by J.C. Chartres. London: Dent Everyman's Library, 1969.

Fletcher, Ian, ed. *Decadence and the 1890s*. London: Edward Arnold, 1979.

Flint, Kate. *The Victorians and the Visual Imagination*. Cambridge: Cambridge University Press, 2001.

Foucault, Michel. *The History of Sexuality*, Vol. 1: An Introduction. Translated by Robert Hurley. New York: Vintage Books, 1990.

Fredeman, William E. 'A Shadow of Dante: Rossetti in the Final Years (Extracts from W.M. Rossetti's Unpublished Diaries, 1876–1882)'. *Victorian Poetry* 20, no. 3/4 (1982): 217–45.

————, ed. *The Correspondence of Dante Gabriel Rossetti*. 9 vols. Cambridge and Rochester: D.S. Brewer, 2002–2010.

Gagnier, Regenia. *Idylls of the Marketplace: Oscar Wilde and the Victorian Public.* Aldershot: Scolar, 1987.

Gallagher, Catherine and Stephen Greenblatt. *Practicing New Historicism.* Chicago and London: University of Chicago Press, 2000.

Gatty, Margaret. *Parables from Nature.* London: Bell and Daldy, 1864.

Gautier, Théophile. *Charles Baudelaire: His Life.* Translated by Guy Thorne. London: Greening and Co., 1915.

———. 'Clarimonde'. *Tales from Gautier.* Translated by Lafcadio Hearn. London: Eveleigh Nash & Grayson, 1927.

———. *Mademoiselle de Maupin.* Translated by Joanna Richardson. Middlesex and New York: Penguin Books, 1981.

———. *Théophile Gautier: Selected Lyrics.* Edited and translated by Norman R. Shapiro. New Haven and London: Yale University Press, 2011.

Girouard, Mark. *The Return to Camelot: Chivalry and the English Gentleman.* New Haven and London: Yale University Press, 1981.

Gosse, Edmund. 'Review: *Music and Moonlight: Poems and Songs* by Arthur O'Shaughnessy'. *The Academy* (1874): 359–60.

———. 'Obituary: Arthur O'Shaughnessy'. *The Academy* 457 (1881): 98–9.

———. *Silhouettes.* Essay Index Reprint Series. Freeport, NY: Books for Libraries Press, 1971.

Gosse, Philip Henry. *Evenings at the Microscope: or, Researches Among the Minuter Organs and Forms of Animal Life.* London: Society for Promoting Christian Knowledge, 1884.

Guillory, John. *Cultural Capital: the Problem of Literary Canon Formation.* Chicago and London: University of Chicago Press, 1993.

Günther, Albert C.L.G. *The History of the Collections Contained in the Natural History Department of the British Museum.* London: Printed by Order of the Trustees of the British Museum, 1904–12.

Guyer, Paul. *Values of Beauty: Historical Essays in Aesthetics.* Cambridge: Cambridge University Press, 2005.

Haass, Sabine. 'Victorian Poetry Anthologies: Their Role and Success in the Nineteenth-Century Market'. *Publishing History* 17 (1985): 51–64.

Hadfield, John, ed. *Everyman's Book of English Love Poems.* London: J.M. Dent & Sons, 1980.

Hamilton, Walter. *The Aesthetic Movement in England.* London: Reeves & Turner, 1882.

Harrison, Antony H. *Swinburne's Medievalism: A Study in Victorian Love Poetry.* Baton Rouge and London: Louisiana State University Press, 1988.

Harrison, Fraser. *The Dark Angel: Aspects of Victorian Sexuality.* London: Sheldon Press, 1977.

Hawkins, Mike. *Social Darwinism in European and American Thought, 1860–1945: Nature as Model and Nature as Threat.* Cambridge: Cambridge University Press, 1997.

Bibliography 187

Helsinger, Elizabeth K. *Poetry and the Pre-Raphaelites*. New Haven and London: Yale University Press, 2008.

Henderson, Philip. *Swinburne: The Portrait of a Poet*. London: Routledge & Kegan Paul, 1974.

Herrnstein Smith, Barbara. *Contingencies of Value: Alternative Perspectives for Critical Theory*. Cambridge, MA, and London: Harvard University Press, 1988.

Hoch, Adrian S. 'The Art of Alessandro Botticelli through the Eyes of Victorian Aesthetes'. *Victorian and Edwardian Responses to the Italian Renaissance*. Edited by John Easton Law and Lene Østermark-Johansen. Aldershot: Ashgate, 2005.

Hollinghead, John. *Ragged London in 1861*. London: Smith, Elder and Co., 1861.

Holloway, Loretta M. and Jennifer A. Palmgren. *Beyond Arthurian Romances: The Reach of Victorian Medievalism*. New York: Palgrave Macmillan, 2005.

Holmes, John. *Darwin's Bards: British and American Poetry in the Age of Evolution*. Edinburgh: Edinburgh University Press, 2009.

Holmes, S.C.A. 'Arthur O'Shaughnessy: a poet among the Lacertidae'. *Journal of the Society for the Bibliography of Natural History* 8 (1976): 28–30.

Hueffer, F. 'Troubadours, Ancient and Modern'. *Macmillan's Magazine* 43 (1880/1881): 45–52.

Huxley, Thomas Henry. *Evidence as to Man's Place in Nature*. New York: D. Appleton and Co., 1873.

Huysmans, Joris-Karl. *A rebours*. Translated by Margaret Mauldon. Oxford: Oxford University Press, 1998.

Inwood, Stephen. *A History of London*. London: Papermac, 2000.

Jauss, Robert. *Toward an Aesthetic of Reception*. Translated by Timothy Bahti. Minneapolis: University of Minnesota Press, 1982.

Jefferies, Richard. *After London, or Wild England*. Oxford: Oxford University Press, 1980.

Kant, Immanuel. *Critique of Judgment*. New York: Cosimo Press, 2007.

Keats, John. *The Poetical Works of John Keats*, a new edition. London: Edward Moxon, 1847.

Kingston, Charles. *Society Sensations*. London: Stanley Paul & Co., 1922.

Knoepflmacher, U.C. and G.B. Tennyson, eds. *Nature and the Victorian Imagination*. Berkeley and Los Angeles: University of California Press, 1977.

Lambdin, Laura C. and Robert T. Lambdin. *Camelot in the Nineteenth Century: Arthurian Characters in the Poems of Tennyson, Arnold, Morris and Swinburne*. Westport, CT: Greenwood Press, 2000.

Lang, Cecil Y., ed. *The Swinburne Letters*. 5 vols. New Haven: Yale University Press, 1959–1962.

———, ed. *The Pre-Raphaelites and Their Circle*. 2nd ed. Chicago and London: University of Chicago Press, 1975.

Lankester, E. Ray. *Degeneration: A Chapter in Darwinism*. London: Macmillan and Co., 1880.

Larkin, P.A. 'Palgrave's Last Anthology: A.E. Housman's Copy'. *The Review of English Studies* New Series 22, no. 87 (1971): 312–16.

Leavis, F.R. *New Bearings in English Poetry: A Study of the Contemporary Situation.* London: Chatto & Windus, 1950.

Lee, Vernon. *Miss Brown*, 3 vols. Edinburgh and London: William Blackwood and Sons, 1884.

Lefebvre, Henri. *Critique of Everyday Life.* Vol. 1. Translated by John Moore. London: Verso, 1991.

———. *Critique of Everyday Life: Foundations for a Sociology of the Everyday.* Vol. 2. Translated by John Moore. London: Verso, 2002.

Leighton, Angela. *On Form: Poetry, Aestheticism, and the Legacy of a Word.* Oxford: Oxford University Press, 2007.

Letsios, Vassilios. 'The Life and Afterlife of Political Verse'. *Journal of Modern Greek Studies* 23, no. 2 (2005): 281–312.

Levine, George, ed. *One Culture: Essays in Science and Literature.* Madison: The University of Wisconsin Press, 1987.

———. *Aesthetics and Ideology.* New Brunswick, NJ: Rutgers University Press, 1994.

———. 'Two Ways Not To Be a Solipsist: Art and Science, Pater and Pearson'. *Victorian Studies* 43, no. 1 (2000): 7–41.

———. 'Reflections on Darwin and Darwinizing'. *Special Issue: Darwin and the Evolution of Victorian Studies* 51, no. 2 (2009): 223–45.

Lindenberger, Herbert. *The History in Literature: On Value, Genre, Institutions.* New York: Columbia University Press, 1990.

Lombroso, Cesare and William Ferrero. *The Female Offender.* New York: D. Appleton and Co., 1895.

———. *Criminal Man.* Translated by Mary Gibson and Nicole Hahn Rafter. Durham, NC: Duke University Press, 2006.

Machen, Arthur. *The Autobiography of Arthur Machen.* London: The Richards Press, 1947.

———. *The Great God Pan.* London: Creation Classics, 1993.

Mackridge, Peter. 'The Metrical Structure of the Oral Decapentasyllable'. *Byzantine and Modern Greek Studies* 14 (1990): 200–212.

Maréchal, Chantal, ed. *The Reception and Transmission of the Works of Marie de France, 1774–1974.* Medieval Studies, vol. 23. Lewiston: The Edwin Mellen Press, 2003.

Marie de France. *The Lais of Marie de France.* Translated by Glyn S. Burgess and Keith Busby, second ed. London: Penguin Books, 2003.

Marx, Karl. 'Estranged Labour'. *Economic and Philosophical Manuscripts of 1844.* Marxists Internet Archive. http://www.marxists.org/archive/marx/works/1844/manuscripts/labour.htm.

———. *Capital: A critical analysis of capitalist production.* Vol. 1. Translated from the 3rd German edition by Samuel Moore and Edward Aveling, and edited by Frederick Engels. London: Swan Sonnenschein, Lowrey, & Co., 1887.

Bibliography 189

————. *Manifesto of the Communist Party*. From the English edition of 1888, ed. Friedrich Engels. Chicago: Charles H. Kerr, 1910.

Maxwell, Catherine. *The Female Sublime from Milton to Swinburne: Bearing Blindness*. Manchester and New York: Manchester University Press, 2001.

————. *Second Sight*. Manchester and New York: Manchester University Press, 2008.

McSweeney, Kerry. *Tennyson and Swinburne as Romantic Naturalists*. Toronto, Buffalo, and London: University of Toronto Press, 1981.

Mendès, Catulle. 'Recent French Poets'. Translated by Arthur O'Shaughnessy. *Gentleman's Magazine* 245, no. 1786 (October 1879): 478–504.

Merrill, Lynn L. *The Romance of Victorian Natural History*. New York and Oxford: Oxford University Press, 1989.

Midgley, Mary. *Beast and Man: The Roots of Human Nature*. Hassocks, UK: The Harvester Press, 1978.

————. *Science and Poetry*. London and New York: Routledge, 2001.

Miles, Alfred H., ed. *The Poets and the Poetry of the Century*. 10 vols. Vol. 1. London: Hutchinson & Co., 1891. Vol. 8. London: Routledge & Sons, 1906.

Morris, William. *Signs of Change*. Bristol, UK: Thoemmes Press, 1994.

Moulton, Louise Chandler. *Arthur O'Shaughnessy: His Life and Work with Selections from His Poems*. Cambridge and Chicago: Stone & Kimball, 1894.

Murphy, Peter T. *Poetry as an Occupation and an Art in Britain, 1760–1830*. Cambridge: Cambridge University Press, 1993.

Najarian, James. 'Canonicity, Marginality, and the Celebration of the Minor'. *Victorian Poetry* 41, no. 4 (2003): 570–74.

Nash, Andrew, ed. *The Culture of Collected Editions*. New York: Palgrave Macmillan, 2003.

Neads, Lynda. *Victorian Babylon*. New Haven and London: Yale University Press, 2000.

North, Julian. *De Quincey Reviewed: Thomas De Quincey's Critical Reception, 1821–1994*. Columbia, SC: Camden House, Inc., 1997.

O'Donnell, William H. and Douglas N. Archibald, eds. *The Collected Works of W.B. Yeats*. Vol. 3: *Autobiographies*. New York: Scribner, 1999.

Olsen, Donald J. *The Growth of Victorian London*. London: B.T. Batsford, 1976.

Ormond, Leonee. 'Vernon Lee as a Critic of Aestheticism in Miss Brown'. *Colby Library Quarterly* 9, no. 3 (1970): 131–54.

Ovid. *Metamorphoses*. Translated by A.D. Melville. Oxford: Oxford World Classics, 1998.

Paden, W.D. 'Arthur O'Shaughnessy in the British Museum: or, the case of the misplaced fusees and the reluctant zoologist'. *Victorian Studies* 8, no. 1 (1964): 7–30.

————. 'Arthur O'Shaughnessy: the Ancestry of a Victorian Poet'. *Bulletin of the John Rylands Library* 46 (1964): 429–47.

Palgrave, Francis T., ed. *The Golden Treasury; Of the Best Songs and Lyrical Poems in the English Language*. London: Macmillan, 1861.

Pater, Walter. *The Renaissance: Studies in Art and Poetry*. Edited by Adam Phillips, 2nd ed. Oxford: Oxford World Classics, 1998.

Percy, William Alexander, ed. *Poems of Arthur O'Shaughnessy*. New Haven: Yale University Press, 1923.

Porter, Lawrence M. 'The Evolution of Mallarmé's Social Consciousness'. *Nineteenth-Century French Studies* 41, no. 3/4 (2013): 272–91.

Porter, Roy. *London: A Social History*. London: Penguin Books, 2000.

Praz, Mario. *The Romantic Agony*. Translated by Angus Davidson. London: Oxford University Press, 1933.

Prettejohn, Elizabeth, ed. *After the Pre-Raphaelites*. Manchester: Manchester University Press, 1999.

Price, Leah. *The Anthology and the Rise of the Novel*. Cambridge: Cambridge University Press, 2000.

Proudhon, Pierre-Joseph. *La Pornocratie, ou les Femmes dans le temps Modernes*. Paris: A. Lacroix et Co., Éditeurs, 1875.

Quiller-Couch, Arthur, ed. *The Oxford Book of English Verse, 1250–1918*. 2nd ed. Oxford: Clarendon Press, 1939.

Reed, John R. 'Mixing Memory and Desire in Late Victorian Literature'. *English Literature in Transition, 1880–1920* 14, no. 1 (1971): 1–15.

Renza, Louis A. *'A White Heron' and the Question of Minor Literature*. Madison: University of Wisconsin Press, 1984.

Ricks, Christopher, ed. *The Poems of Tennyson*. Longman Annotated English Poets. London: Longman, 1969.

Ricoeur, Paul. 'The Power of Speech: Science and Poetry'. *Philosophy Today* 29, no. 1 (1985): 59–70.

Roberts, Phil. *How Poetry Works*. 2nd ed. London: Penguin Books, 2000.

Robinson, James K. 'A Neglected Phase of the Aesthetic Movement: English Parnassianism'. *PMLA* 68, no. 4 (1953): 733–54.

Rose, Marilyn Gaddis. 'The Daughters of Herodias in "Hérodiade", "Salomé" and "A Full Moon in March"'. *Comparative Drama* 1, no. 3 (1967): 172–81.

Rosenberg, John D. *Elegy for An Age: The Presence of the Past in Victorian Literature*. London: Anthem Press, 2004.

Rossetti, Dante Gabriel. 'The Stealthy School of Criticism'. *Athenaeum* 2303 (1871): 792–4.

Rossetti, William Michael. *Dante Gabriel Rossetti: His Family Letters, with a Memoir*. Vol. 1. London: Ellis and Elvey, 1895.

Rupke, Nicolaas A. *Richard Owen: Victorian Naturalist*. New Haven and London: Yale University Press, 1994.

Ruskin, John. *Lectures on Art: Delivered Before the University of Oxford in Hilary Term, 1870*. New York: John Wiley & Son, 1870.

Russett, Margaret. *De Quincey's Romanticism: Canonical Minority and the Forms of Transmission*. Cambridge: Cambridge University Press, 1997.

Said, Edward W. *Orientalism*. London: Penguin Books, 2003.

Saintsbury, George. 'Review: Songs of a Worker, by Arthur O'Shaughnessy'. *The Academy* 483 (1881): 100–101.

Bibliography

Sanyal, Debarati. *The Violence of Modernity: Baudelaire, Irony, and the Politics of Form.* Baltimore: The Johns Hopkins University Press, 2006.

Schiller, Friedrich. *On the Aesthetic Education of Man, in a Series of Letters.* Edited and translated by Elizabeth M. Wilkinson and L.A. Willoughby. Oxford: Clarendon Press, 1967.

Sharp, E.A. and J. Matthay, eds. *Lyra Celtica: An Anthology of Representative Celtic Poetry.* 2nd ed. Edinburgh: John Grant, 1924.

Shorter, Clement King, ed. *A Pathetic Love Episode in a Poet's Life, being letters from Helen Snee to Arthur W.E. O'Shaughnessy. Also a letter from him containing a dissertation on Love.* London: printed for private circulation, 1916.

Showalter, Elaine. *Sexual Anarchy: Gender and Culture at the Fin de Siècle.* New York and London: Viking Penguin, 1990.

Simons, John, ed. *From Medieval to Medievalism.* London: Macmillan, 1992.

Slinn, E. Warwick. *Victorian Poetry as Cultural Critique: The Politics of Performative Language.* Charlottesville and London: University of Virginia Press, 2003.

Smith, Jonathan. 'Une Fleur du Mal? Swinburne's "The Sundew" and Darwin's Insectivorous Plants'. *Victorian Poetry* 41, no. 1 (2003): 131–50.

———. 'Domestic Hybrids: Ruskin, Victorian Fiction, and Darwin's Botany'. *SEL Studies in English Literature 1500–1900* 48, no. 4 (2008): 861–70.

Souffrin, E. 'Coup d'oeil sur la bibliothèque anglaise de Mallarmé'. *Revue de littérature comparée* 32 (1958): 390–97.

Spencer, Herbert. *Principles of Biology.* Vol. 1. London: Williams and Norgate, 1864.

Stableford, Brian. *Glorious Perversity: The Decline and Fall of Literary Decadence.* San Bernardino, CA: The Borgo Press, 1998.

Stearn, William T. *The Natural History Museum at South Kensington: A History of the British Museum (Natural History) 1753–1980.* London: Heinemann, 1981.

Stedman, Edmund C. 'Some London Poets'. *Harper's New Monthly Magazine* 64, no. 384 (1882): 874–92.

Stein, Richard L. 'Dante Gabriel Rossetti: Painting and the Problem of Poetic Form'. *Studies in English Literature, 1500–1900* 10, no. 4 (1970): 775–92.

Stern, Karl. *The Flight From Women.* London: George Allen Unwin, 1966.

Stevenson, Lionel. *Darwin Among the Poets.* New York: Russell & Russell, 1963.

———. *The Pre-Raphaelite Poets.* Chapel Hill: University of North Carolina Press, 1972.

Stuart, Mel. Dir. *Willy Wonka & the Chocolate Factory.* Screenplay by Roald Dahl. Perf. Gene Wilder, Jack Albertson, and Peter Ostrum. Paramount Pictures, 1971. DVD.

Swinburne, Algernon Charles. 'Charles Baudelaire: Les fleurs du mal'. *The Spectator*, no. 1784 (6 September 1862): 998–1000.

———. *Notes on Poems and Reviews.* London: John Camden Hotten, 1866.

———. *Poems and Ballads.* London: John Camden Hotten, 1866.

———. 'Mr. George Meredith's Modern Love'. *The Spectator* (1872): 632–3.

————. *Tristram of Lyonesse and other poems*. 5th ed. London: Chatto & Windus, 1896.

Symons, Arthur. *Silhouettes*. 2nd ed. London: Leonard Smithers, 1896.

————. *The Symbolist Movement in Literature*. New York: E.P. Dutton & Co., 1919.

Thomas, David Wayne. *Cultivating Victorians: Liberal Culture and the Aesthetic*. Philadelphia: University of Pennsylvania Press, 2004.

Thornton, R.K.R. *The Decadent Dilemma*. London: Edward Arnold, 1983.

Trudgill, Eric. *Madonnas and Magdalens: The Origins and Development of Victorian Sexual Attitudes*. London: Heinemann, 1976.

Turquet-Milnes, G. *The Influence of Baudelaire in France and England*. London: Constable and Co., 1913.

Untermeyer, Louis. *Modern British Poetry*. New York: Harcourt, Brace, & Co., 1920.

Ward, T.H., ed. *English Poets*. Vol. 4. New York: Macmillan, 1902.

Warner, Eric and Graham Hough, eds. *Strangeness and Beauty: An Anthology of Aesthetic Criticism, 1840–1910. Vol. 1, Ruskin to Swinburne*. Cambridge: Cambridge University Press, 1983.

Warner, Marina. *Fantastic Metamorphoses, Other Worlds: Ways of Telling the Self*. Oxford: Oxford University Press, 2002.

Warner, Oliver. *Chatto & Windus: A Brief Account of the Firm's Origin, History and Development*. London: Chatto & Windus, 1973.

Waters, Chris. 'Marxism, Medievalism, and Popular Culture'. In Boos, *History and Community*, pp. 137–68.

Weineck, Silke-Maria. 'Loss of Outline: Decadence as the Crisis of Negation'. *Pacific Coast Philology* 29, no. 1 (1994): 37–50.

Wilde, Oscar. 'The Decay of Lying: a Dialogue'. *The Nineteenth Century: A Monthly Review* 25 (January–June 1889): 35–56.

————. 'The Critic as Artist'. *Intentions*, 13th ed. London: Methuen & Co., 1919.

Williams, Raymond. *Culture and Society 1780–1950*. London: Chatto & Windus, 1958.

————. *Keywords: A Vocabulary of Culture and Society*. London: Fontana Press, 1988.

Wright, Thomas. 'John Payne and his Work; An Intimate Appreciation'. *Academy and Literature* 83 (1912): 351–2.

————. *The Life of John Payne*. London: T. Fisher Unwin, 1919.

Zagona, Helen Grace. *The Legend of Salome and the Principle of Art for Art's Sake*. Genève: Libraire e Droz, 1960.

Zola, Émile. *Abbé Mouret's Transgression*. Translated by Ernest Alfred Vizetelly. New York: The Marion Co., 1915.

Unknown Author

'Anecdote of Mr. O'Shaughnessy the Poet'. *The Dundee Courier* (Dundee, Scotland). 26 May 1882.

Bibliography

'Births, Deaths, Marriages, and Obituaries'. *The Standard* (London, UK). Monday, 7 February 1881; p. [1]; Issue 17645.

'The Bookman's Table'. *The Bookman* (1874): 57.

The Lancaster Gazette and General Advertiser for Lancashire, Westmorland, and Yorkshire (Lancaster, UK). Friday, 31 December 1881; Issue 5201.

'Minor Poetry'. *The Saturday Review* (1871): 282–3.

'Mr. Arthur O'Shaughnessy'. *Athenaeum* 2780 (1881): 196–7.

'Mr. O'Shaughnessy's Lays of France'. *The Examiner* (1872): 211–2.

'Mr. O'Shaughnessy's New Poems'. *Athenaeum* 2421 (1874): 382–3.

'Recent Verses'. *The Saturday Review* (1881): 492–3.

'Review: An Epic of Women and Other Poems'. *The Examiner and London Review* (1870): 694.

'Review: Lays of France'. *Athenaeum* 2306 (1872): 8–9.

'Review: Music and Moonlight'. *The Examiner* (1874): 320–21.

'Review: Poems of Arthur O'Shaughnessy, edited by William Alexander Percy'. *Contemporary Review* 126 (1924): 125–8.

'Two Young Poets'. *Athenaeum* 2245 (1870): 585–6.

Index

1870s, poets of 9–10, 20, 178

aestheticism 15, 65, 67, 71, 76, 94–113
alienated labour 3–7, 16, 33–4, 36–7, 60,
    64, 66–72, 81, 83, 125–6
'An Epic of Women' (O'Shaughnessy,
    poem sequence) 17, 76, 95–104,
    107–9, 122–4, 126–30, 133–4,
    137–40, 141
An Epic of Women and Other Poems
    (O'Shaughnessy, collection) 8–11,
    17, 32, 67, 89–90, 118, 120–21,
    124–6, 142, 153, 162, 175
Annals and Magazine of Natural History
    12, 37, 41–3
Arnold, Matthew 78–80, 83, 111–12
'art for art's sake' 61–2, 95, 105
'art for humanity' 20, 61, 77–9, 83–6, 109
Arthur (king) and the Arthurian legends
    112, 141–2, 147, 152–3, 164–5,
    174–5
artificial world of art 5, 66–71, 84
atavism, *see* degeneration
'Azure Islands' (O'Shaughnessy) 39–42

ballad form 47–8, 86, 92–4, 142, 158
Balzac, Honoré de 69, 119–20, 127
Bates, Walter Henry 26–7, 32, 37–9
Baudelaire, Charles 33, 89–90, 95–6,
    115–20, 121, 125–6, 130
    on 'art for art' 61
    works
        'Les Bijoux' 123
        Les fleurs du mal 128
        'A Martyr' 128, 160–61
        'The Painter of Modern Life' 64–6,
            67–72, 77, 132
Beer, Gillian 34–5, 41, 43, 48, 54, 56–7
'Bisclavaret' (O'Shaughnessy) 45–53, 55,
    56, 58, 131–2, 142, 146–8
Botticelli, Sandro 98–9

bourgeois/middle-class morality (and
    rejection of) 62–3, 88–9, 91–2, 94,
    103–4, 108–9, 111–13, 115–16
British Museum
    Board of Trustees 29–31
    Department of Printed Books 1, 8, 25,
        27
    Departments of Natural History 1, 3, 8,
        23, 25–33, 82, 124–5, 153
        Department of Zoology 2, 28
            catalogue of fish 2, 28, 82
            spirit room 2, 4, 27, 29–30,
                35, 38
        Entomology Department 28
    Library 3, 119, 142–3
    new museum in South Kensington 12,
        14, 26, 136
    nomination to employment 25–9
Brönner, Oskar 18, 151
Brown, Ford Madox 9–10, 17, 73–4
Browning, Robert 19, 102
Buchanan, Robert 88–9, 92, 95, 115–16,
    136, 157
Bulwer-Lytton, Edward (Lord)
    and the British Museum 8, 29, 31–2
    in correspondence with O'Shaughnessy
        1, 3
    rumoured to be O'Shaughnessy's father
        23–5

Carlyle, Thomas 74, 143–4
'Carrara' (O'Shaughnessy) 106–9, 113
'Chaitivel; or, the Lay of Love's
    Unfortunate' (O'Shaughnessy)
    11, 17, 126–30, 148–9, 151, 153,
    169–75
Chopin, Frédéric 8, 71
Christianity 52–9, 69, 96, 98–9, 110–13,
    144, 168, 173–4
'Cleopatra' I & II (O'Shaughnessy) 97,
    100, 103, 122, 127

'Colibri' (O'Shaughnessy) 59–60, 134–5, 138–9
consumerism in art 62–4, 67, 70, 87, 94, 104, 108–9
Coppée, François 90, 117, 120
courtly love 152, 159, 162–7, 170, 175
'Creation' (O'Shaughnessy) 96–100, 127, 174

dandy, the 73–4, 76
Darwin, Charles 26–7
   Darwinian theory 20, 23, 46–9, 53, 56–60
      decadence, linked to 130–33, 136
   Descent of Man 49, 53, 133, 136, 157
   fictive qualities of *On the Origin of Species* 41, 43
   hybridity suggested by the theory of natural selection 45
   On the Origin of Species 41, 44, 45, 48–9, 133
   progressive misreading of 54–5, 59
   sexual selection 133
   Social Darwinism 48–53
   'survival of the fittest', *see* Spencer, Herbert
'Daughter of Herodias' (O'Shaughnessy) 17, 97, 118–19, 123, 127, 134
de Certeau, Michel 5–6
Deacon, Alfred W.N. 12–14, 24–5, 61, 81
Deacon, Laura (a.k.a. 'Mrs. Grant') 24
decadence 2, 20, 120–30, 159–61
decadent naturalism 20, 53–9, 130–40, 154–7
degeneration 45–55, 130, 132
'Dialogue between Two Venuses' (O'Shaughnessy) 112–13
'A Discord' (O'Shaughnessy) 70–71, 77
Doyle, May 36, 120, 138

'Eden' (O'Shaughnessy) 53–9
Elgar, Edward 19
Eliot, T.S. 18–19, 177–9
entomology 27–9, 72, 85
'Europe' (O'Shaughnessy) 79–80, 105
'Exile' (O'Shaughnessy) 67–8, 70–72, 125

femme fatale, the 107–8, 121–2, 127, 135
   misogyny of 76–7

as symbol of aestheticism 95–104
fixed form poetry 90, 92–4, 113
'The Fleshly School of Poetry', *see* Buchanan, Robert
form vs. content 90–92, 104–5, 113, 117
'Fountain of Tears' (O'Shaughnessy) 17, 93, 124
France
   comparison of English and French writers 115–16
France, Marie de 46–7, 92, 93, 127, 129, 141–75

Gagnier, Regenia 62–6, 73, 88
Gautier, Théophile 62–5, 80, 89–90, 95–6, 99, 101–2, 105, 117, 119–21, 123, 129, 140
   works
      'L'Art' 105–6, 110
      'Cærulei Oculi' 121–2
      'Le château du souvenir' 101–2, 128–9
      'Lied' 138
      'La morte amoureuse' 128, 132
      'Le Poème de la femme' 101
      'Preface' to *Mademoiselle de Maupin* 62, 109
gender division (separate spheres) 72–5, 82–5, 174
Gosse, Edmund
   in correspondence with Alfred W.N. Deacon 24, 81
   defending O'Shaughnessy's 'Creation' 96, 99
   as 'English Parnassian' 178
   on *Lays of France* 130, 148–9, 157–9
   on Lord Lytton and O'Shaughnessy's relationship 24
   on the 'Ode' (O'Shaughnessy) 19
   on O'Shaughnessy as naturalist 1–4, 29
   on O'Shaughnessy's death 14–15
   on O'Shaughnessy's ties to France 116–18
   review of *Music and Moonlight* 11, 40, 124, 126
   on *Songs of a Worker* 81
Gosse, Philip Henry 136–7
Gray, J. Edward 26–7, 30–33
Günther, Albert 2, 37–43, 45, 92

'Helen' (O'Shaughnessy) 97, 99
herpetology 2–3, 28–9, 33, 37, 42–3
Hotten, John Camden 8, 10, 20, 160
Hugo, Victor 14, 61, 66, 68, 80, 115–17, 120
Huxley, T.H. 45
Huysmans, Joris-Karl 98

'I mused upon the universe of things' (O'Shaughnessy) 43–5
ichthyology 1–3

Jones, John Winter (Principal Librarian of the British Museum) 26–8, 30–31

Kant, Immanuel 63, 87–8
Keats, John
  'The Eve of St. Agnes' 52
  'Ode on a Grecian Urn' 36–7, 94–5, 97
Knight, Joseph 9, 20, 147

laissez-faire economics 48–52, 88
Lankester, E. Ray 39, 45–6, 59
'Laustic; or the Lay of the Nightingale' (O'Shaughnessy) 148, 151–2, 155–6, 165
'The Lay of Eliduc' (O'Shaughnessy) 148, 157–61, 169, 172–3
'The Lay of Two Lovers' (O'Shaughnessy) 148, 156–7, 167–70
'The Lay of Yvenec' (O'Shaughnessy) 148, 150–51, 166, 168–70
Lays of France (O'Shaughnessy) 10–11, 17, 93, 112, 126–7, 129–30, 151–75
Lee, Vernon (*Miss Brown*) 15–16, 18, 25, 119, 124, 163
Lefebvre, Henri 4–7, 33–4, 64–7, 81–2, 98, 125–6
Levine, George 41, 43
liebestöd (love in death) 162, 165–6
'The Line of Beauty' (O'Shaughnessy) 110
'Lynmouth' (O'Shaughnessy) 42–3

Maitland, Thomas, *see* Buchanan, Robert
Mallarmé, Stéphane 56, 90, 98, 117–18, 120
Marston, P.B. 10
Marston, Westland 9–11, 20, 53, 75

Marx, Karl 4–7, 21, 36–8, 65, 87–8, 144–5
masculinity, construction of 67, 72–7, 82–4, 144
medieval revival 50, 92, 141–6, 148
Mendès, Catulle 56, 90–91, 98, 116–17, 120
'The Miner: A Ballad' (O'Shaughnessy) 93
minor poetry 4, 10, 18–20, 74, 177–9
Miss Brown, see Vernon Lee
Moreau, Gustave 98
Morris, William 9–10, 15, 18, 20, 65–6, 74, 88, 140, 187
  Defence of Guenevere 141–2, 168
  medievalism as radical socialism 144–7, 152
  Red House 106
  social engagement 78–85
  'Useful Work versus Useless Toil' in *Signs of Change* 7, 65, 78, 81–5
Moulton, Louise Chandler 2, 8–9, 12, 17, 46, 75, 96, 100, 107, 119, 129
Music and Moonlight: Poems and Songs (O'Shaughnessy) 11, 14, 17, 77–80, 124, 174

necessity of 'earning a living' 3–4, 8, 11, 14–15, 20–21, 64, 66, 88, 124–5, 178
'A Neglected Harp' (O'Shaughnessy) 35–8, 40
Nettleship, J.T. (Jack) 3, 8, 30, 50, 96–7, 162–4
New Historicism 19–20
'Nostalgie des Cieux' (O'Shaughnessy) 35, 37, 41–3, 60, 67–72, 110

'Ode' (O'Shaughnessy) 18–19, 77–80, 85, 88, 178
On the Aesthetic Education of Man, see Schiller, Friedrich
O'Shaughnessy, Eleanor (née Marston) 10–14, 76, 116, 120, 163
O'Shaughnessy, Louisa (mother) 7–8, 23–5, 116
O'Shaughnessy, Oscar (brother) 7–8
Owen, Richard 12, 26–33, 37–9, 136

Paden, W.D. 1, 3–4, 7, 12–13, 18, 27, 32, 136

'Pagan' (O'Shaughnessy) 76–7, 97
'Palm Flowers' (O'Shaughnessy) 39–40
Parnassian movement, the 14, 20, 90–92, 98, 105, 116–20, 140, 178
'Paros' (O'Shaughnessy) 106–7
Pater, Walter 22, 91–2, 99, 105, 110–13
Payne, John 8–9, 88, 90, 119, 142, 162, 178
'Pentelicos' (O'Shaughnessy) 105–6
Percy, W.A. (*Poems of Arthur O'Shaughnessy*) 17–18, 40, 46–8, 51
professionalization of science 11–12, 23, 37–8, 178
'Prophetic Spring' (O'Shaughnessy) 138
Prudhomme, Sully 18, 90, 120
Pygmalionism 100, 106–10

Renza, Louis A. 4
romantic ideal of the isolated artist 67–70
Romantiques (France) 20, 90–91, 103, 120–22, 139
'Rondel' (O'Shaughnessy) 92–3
Rossetti, D.G. 6, 9–10, 15, 18, 53, 65–6, 74–5, 99, 140, 177
    Buchanan's attack upon 88–9, 95, 115–16, 136, 157
    medievalism of 141
    on O'Shaughnessy 46, 123, 89–90, 123, 147–8
Ruskin, John 43, 62, 87–8, 113

Salome (character) 98, 118–19
Schiller, Friedrich 91–2, 105, 113
'scientific poetry' 59
sculpture
    craft of art, metaphor for 83–4, 87, 104–13
    nudity in 108
    Walter Pater on 91
'Searching about an ancient place of tombs' (O'Shaughnessy) 161
separate spheres, *see* gender division
'Seraphitus' (O'Shaughnessy) 69, 76, 84, 110
'She has gone wandering away' (O'Shaughnessy), *see* 'Rondel'
Showalter, Elaine 73, 130–31
Snee, Helen 3, 18, 36, 74–5, 119–20, 141, 162–4, 175

socialism 20, 77–80, 144–6
'Song of a Fellow-Worker' (O'Shaughnessy) 81–6
Songs of a Worker (O'Shaughnessy) 7, 14, 17–18, 21, 59, 61, 81–6, 104–6, 115, 117, 138, 141
Spencer, Herbert 48–53, 59
    'survival of the fittest' 48–53, 59–60, 132
Stedman, Edmund 2, 16–17, 56
Stevenson, Lionel 10, 34
Swinburne, Algernon Charles 9, 15, 17, 18, 20, 24–5, 65–6, 70, 120, 163, 177–8
    on Baudelaire's *Les fleurs du mal* 128
    as a 'fleshly' poet 88
    medievalism of 112, 141–2, 148, 162
    non-visual descriptions of 100–102
    objecting to the false morality of the age 62–3, 89, 92, 96
    translations of Villon 152–3
    works
        'Anactoria' 52, 100
        'Faustine' 52, 100
        'Hermaphroditus' 101
        'The Leper' 160–61
        Poems and Ballads (1866) 8, 10, 51–2, 118, 119, 161
        Tristram of Lyonesse 166–8
Symons, Arthur 109, 118, 133
synaesthesia (artistic) 94–5, 97, 104, 113, 139

taxonomy 23, 28–9, 35, 37–9, 41–3, 85
    collector vs. cataloguer (natural history) 37–9
Tennyson, Lord Alfred 19, 34, 120, 141–2, 147, 152, 170, 175
'Thoughts in Marble' (O'Shaughnessy, poem sequence) 17, 104–13, 140
Toyland (O'Shaughnessy and Eleanor O'Shaughnessy) 12–13
translations, O'Shaughnessy's 18, 90, 117, 140
    O'Shaughnessy's *Lays of France*, *see* *Lays of France*
'A Troth for Eternity' (O'Shaughnessy) 97, 102–4

utility in art, *see* 'art for humanity'; work

Index

Venus (character) 97–9, 101, 103, 106, 108, 112–13
vision (O'Shaughnessy's poor eyesight) 28, 31, 38, 69–70, 124

Wallace, Alfred Russell 26
'What is Minor Poetry?', *see* T.S. Eliot
'The Wife of Hephaestus' (O'Shaughnessy) 97, 133–4
Wilde, Oscar 63, 73, 98, 112–13, 118, 178
Willy Wonka & the Chocolate Factory 19

work
    art as 'revolution of non-work' 61–2, 63–71, 73
    art as work 77–86, 89–90, 94, 108
    'brain labour' vs. manual labour 73–4, 82–3
    manual labour, idealization of 73–4, 82–3

Zola, Émile 56–8, 135–6

# Taylor & Francis eBooks

Helping you to choose the right eBooks for your Library

Add Routledge titles to your library's digital collection today. Taylor and Francis ebooks contains over 50,000 titles in the Humanities, Social Sciences, Behavioural Sciences, Built Environment and Law.

Choose from a range of subject packages or create your own!

Benefits for you
- Free MARC records
- COUNTER-compliant usage statistics
- Flexible purchase and pricing options
- All titles DRM-free.

Benefits for your user
- Off-site, anytime access via Athens or referring URL
- Print or copy pages or chapters
- Full content search
- Bookmark, highlight and annotate text
- Access to thousands of pages of quality research at the click of a button.

REQUEST YOUR FREE INSTITUTIONAL TRIAL TODAY

Free Trials Available
We offer free trials to qualifying academic, corporate and government customers.

eCollections – Choose from over 30 subject eCollections, including:

Archaeology	Language Learning
Architecture	Law
Asian Studies	Literature
Business & Management	Media & Communication
Classical Studies	Middle East Studies
Construction	Music
Creative & Media Arts	Philosophy
Criminology & Criminal Justice	Planning
Economics	Politics
Education	Psychology & Mental Health
Energy	Religion
Engineering	Security
English Language & Linguistics	Social Work
Environment & Sustainability	Sociology
Geography	Sport
Health Studies	Theatre & Performance
History	Tourism, Hospitality & Events

For more information, pricing enquiries or to order a free trial, please contact your local sales team:
www.tandfebooks.com/page/sales

 Routledge | The home of
Taylor & Francis Group | Routledge books

www.tandfebooks.com